Madame Alexander

Linda Crowsey

2005
Collector's
Dolls
Price Guide
#30

COLLECTOR BOOKS
A Division of Schroeder Publishing Co., Inc.

On the Front Cover

Left: Cissy Ebony and Ivory, 1996, $650.00.
Center: 14", Wendy (Peter Pan), 1969, $275.00.
Right: 8" Maggie Mixup Angel, 1961, $900.00.

On the Back Cover

16½" Elise Bride, 1963, $750.00.

Cover design: Beth Summers
Book design: Kelly Dowdy

Collector Books
P.O. Box 3009
Paducah, KY 42002-3009

www.collectorbooks.com

The current values in this book should be used only as a guide. They are not intended to set prices, which vary from one section of the country to another. Auction prices as well as dealer prices vary greatly and are affected by condition and demand. Neither the author nor the publisher assumes responsibility for any losses which might be incurred as a result of consulting this guide.

Searching For A Publisher?

We are always looking for people knowledgeable within their fields. If you feel that there is a real need for a book on your collectible subject and have a large comprehensive collection, contact Collector Books.

Dedication

The 2005 *Madame Alexander Collector's Dolls Price Guide* is dedicated to the memory of Patricia R. Smith who died in 2003. Pat authored dozens of books and price guides on all types of dolls from bisque to Barbie®. I knew Pat primarily in the Alexander world. Her books laid the foundation of knowledge of what we know about Madame Alexander dolls. Pat was a friend and pen pal to Madame Alexander. She received the Madame Alexander Doll Club's highest award, The Service Award, for her years of work writing articles, researching, and giving lectures.

I will always be indebted to Patricia Smith for the honor of asking me to author this price guide in 1997. Pat will be missed in the doll world because of the many lives she touched.

Madame Alexander Doll Club

For membership information write to:
Madame Alexander Doll Club (M.A.D.C.)
P.O. Box 2739
New York, NY 10027-9998

Photo credits

Gary Green, Louise Henderson, Susan Huey, Ann McCurdy, Christene McWilliams, Mary Lou Pendergrass, Terri Queen, Ben and Helen Thomas, Mike Way.

The Madame Alexander Doll Company

The Madame Alexander Doll Company was started by Madame Beatrice Alexander and her husband, Phillip Behrman, and began manufacturing dolls in New York City in 1923. Madame Alexander's father, Maurice Alexander, owned the first doll hospital in New York City. He repaired dolls and sold new ones and fine porcelain pieces. Madame grew up seeing how much joy dolls brought to children. Madame and her sisters made the first dolls out of cloth. The Alexander Company made beautiful composition dolls through the 1940s, such as the Dionne Quints, Jane Withers, and Princess Elizabeth, that are highly prized by collectors today. Madame received numerous awards for her dolls, her philanthropy, and achievements in the doll world. Madame died in 1990 but the dolls she made insure that she will never be forgotten.

The Alexander Company received the Lifetime Achievement Award that was given by Jones Publishing at the 2004 Banquet and Expo. Wooden Wendy won the Award of Excellence from *Dolls Magazine* for the Alexander Company. Olivia Saves the Circus won the Platinum Seal Award from the Oppenhiem Toy Portfolio. The Alexander Company continues to be an award-winning company for its designs and newly created dolls. In 2004 the Alexander Company introduced Coquette Cissy, a totally new 10" fashion doll.

The Alexander Company is very interested in collectors and all aspects of collecting. Tours of the factory, showroom, factory store, and birthday parties are some of the events hosted by the Alexander Company at their New York building on 131st Street. A statement in a 1952 Alexander catalog is as true today as it was then that the Alexander Company is the manufacturer of the largest collection of the most beautiful dolls in the world.

Cindy DiCaro (left) and Linda Crowsey at the Madame Alexander Club Office in New York City.

Linda Crowsey (left), Johnnie Benson (center), and Laura Colpus (right) having a good time in the Alexander Factory Store in New York City.

What Is a Price Guide?

Price guides must be based upon values for a perfect doll since all collectors need accurate prices for insurance purposes. Insurance companies and postal services must have a way to determine the value of a damaged or stolen doll. Collectors must also have a way to appraise and insure their collections. A price guide, while not the final word, is a starting point to determine the value of a doll. The prices listed are for perfect dolls. Imperfect dolls will bring considerably less than exceptional dolls, which collectors call "tissue mint." Original boxes are important because the information on the box helps determine the age and manufacturer of the doll. The prices quoted are for dolls without their boxes prior to 1972. Prices for dolls from 1973 to present are for dolls with their original boxes. Prices of these dolls would be adjusted lower if they are missing their boxes. Boxes can be a fire hazard. It is possible to fold most boxes and store them inside a larger box and place the boxes in an airy, dry room. Collectors will pay a higher price for a doll in its original box. Beware of storing dolls for a long time in their boxes — clothing, wigs, and vinyl can fade or change colors. Also, vinyl dolls tend to become greasy or sticky when stored in their boxes.

Jo of Little Women (left) is a mint, all original doll with pretty face coloring. Jo (right) has hair out of the original set and poor face coloring. Her apron is made by Alexander but not for this doll. Her value would only be 20% of the mint doll.

Perfect Dolls
✶ Complete outfit on correct doll
✶ Beautiful face color
✶ Clothes and doll in excellent condition
✶ Has all accessories, such as hats, etc.
✶ Clothes not laundered or ironed
✶ Hair in original set

Less Than Perfect Dolls
✶ Re-dressed or has part of original clothes
✶ Washed, cleaned, ironed clothes
✶ Stains, soil, faded, shelf dust, holes in fabric
✶ Faded face color
✶ Tag cut or missing
✶ Hair mussed or dirty

Exceptional Dolls
✶ Extremely rare doll
✶ Has wrist tag or original box
✶ Autographed by Madame Alexander
✶ Unique outfit or doll
✶ "Tissue mint" condition
✶ Has wardrobe or trunk
✶ Matched set of same year
(such as "Little Women")

There is no guarantee that any doll, antique or modern, will appreciate year after year. Prices remain high on exceptional dolls and always will.

Mold Marks

Mold marks can be the same for an extended period of time. For example, 14" Mary Ann dolls will be marked "1965" which is the first year the doll was made. From then to now, all Mary Ann dolls will be marked "1965." Another example is the 21" Jacqueline first introduced in 1961. This doll has been used for the Portraits since 1965 and up to now still bears the 1961 date mark on the head. Determining the exact year can be difficult for that reason.

Doll Names

The dolls named after real people are listed with last name first (example: Bliss, Betty Taylor). Make-believe doll names will be listed with first name first (example: Tommy Snooks).

Abbreviations

h.p. – hard plastic
comp. – composition
FAD – factory altered dress
SLNW – straight leg, non-walker
SLW – straight leg walker
BKW – bend knee walker
BK – bend knee
U.F.D.C. – United Federation of Doll Clubs
M.A.D.C. – Madame Alexander Doll Club
C.U. – Collectors United

Box Numbers

Order/box numbers for the 8" dolls with "0" prefix (example: 0742) were used in 1973 only. It must be noted the box numbers found with doll's name are from the Madame Alexander catalogs, but many dolls were placed in wrong boxes by the stores from which they were sold.

Auction Prices

Auction prices have little or no effect on general pricing for Madame Alexander dolls. Dolls often sell at auction for exorbitant prices. It is as simple as two or more people wanting the same item — the bidders just get carried away! Another reason is the rarity or the pristine condition of a doll. This type of doll is extremely difficult to find and warrants the high auction price.

The final word is Madame Alexander dolls have always been collectible and should continue to be. They should endure in time and value. Wise collectors purchase dolls that they really like rather than purchasing dolls that are rumored to go up in value. Then, even if the doll's value doesn't go up, the collector has a beautiful doll that he or she loves. We hope you will continue to build the collections you desire, be they of older dolls or the wonderful current dolls that become available each year.

8" Alexander-Kins, Wendy Ann, Wendy, or Wendy-Kin

1953 – 1976:
Has "Alex" on back of doll.

1953:
First year of production, straight leg, non-walker. Only year Quiz-Kins were produced with two buttons on their back for the head to nod yes or no.

1954:
Straight leg walker.

1955:
Straight leg walker with no painted lashes under the eye.

1956 – 1965:
Bend knee walker.

1965 – 1972:
Bend knee, does not walk.

1973 – 1976:
Straight leg, non-walker with "Alex" on back of doll.

1977 – Present:
Has "Alexander" on back.

The Many Faces of
Madame Alexander Dolls

Wendy Ann (composition)

Tiny & Little Betty

Princess Elizabeth

Maggie

Margaret (O' Brien)

Cissy

The Many Faces of Madame Alexander Dolls

Elise (1950s – 1960s)

Lissy (1950s)

Cissette

Mary-Bel

Jacqueline

Mary Ann

The Many Faces of Madame Alexander Dolls

Elise (1960s – 1980s)

Polly & Leslie

Nancy Drew

Wendy Ann – new 1988 face

Maggie Mixup (1960 – 1961)

Wendy Ann (1953 – 1965)

Active Miss

Active Miss — 18" h.p., 1954 only (Violet/Cissy) $850.00

Adams, Abigail — 1976 – 1978, Presidents' Ladies/First Ladies Series, First Set (Mary Ann) $150.00

Adams, Louisa — 1976 – 1978, Presidents' Ladies/First Ladies Series, First Set (Louisa) $125.00

Addams Family — #31130, 1997 – 1998, set of four dolls (8", 10") and Thing $250.00

    #31110, 1997 – 1998, 10" Gomez and Morticia $150.00

    #31120, 1997 – 1998, 8" Wednesday and Pugsley $125.00

Adorable Silk Victorian — 8", #26875, 2001, white dress $90.00

Africa — 8" h.p., #766, 1966 – 1971, BK (Wendy Ann) $275.00

    8" h.p., straight leg, re-issued, #523 – 583, 1988 – 1992 (Wendy Ann) $55.00

African Bride — 10", #28600, 2001, includes broom $100.00

African Safari — 8", #33501, Caucasian, 2002, tan costume with lion $80.00

    8", #33500, African-American, 2002 ....$80.00

Agatha — 18" h.p. (Cissy)

    1954 only, Me and My Shadow Series, rose taffeta dress, excellent face color ....$1,900.00 up

    8" h.p. (Wendy Ann), #00308, 1953 – 1954, black top and floral gown ....$1,400.00 up

    21" Portrait, #2171, 1967, red gown (Jacqueline) $650.00

        #2297, 1974, rose gown with full length cape (Jacqueline) $475.00

        #2291, 1975, blue with white sequin trim (Jacqueline) $375.00

        #2294, 1976, blue with white rick-rack trim (Jacqueline) $275.00

        #2230, 1979, 1980, lavender; #2230, 1981, turquoise blue (Jacqueline) $275.00

        #2230, 1981, turquoise blue (Jacqueline) $275.00

    10" Portrette, #1171, 1968 only, red velvet (Cissette) $425.00

Age of Innocence — 10", #28400, 2001, dark blue vintage gown $120.00

Agnes — cloth/felt, 1930s $750.00

Aladdin — 8" h.p., #482, 1993; #140482, 1994 only, Storybook Series $55.00

Alaska — 8", #302, 1990 – 1992, Americana Series (Maggie smile face) $50.00

Albania — 8", straight leg, #526, 1987 only (Wendy Ann) $60.00

Alcott, Louisa May — 14", #1529, 1989 – 1990, Classic Series (Mary Ann) $80.00

    8" h.p., #409, 1992 only, Storyland Series (Wendy Ann) $90.00

    8" h.p., #36760, 2003, long brown dress with black trim, book $90.00

Alegria — 10" h.p., #20118, 1996 Cirque du Soleil, silver outfit $80.00

Alex — 16" plastic/vinyl, 2000, Fashion Doll Editor-in-Chief, 2000, #25570,

    brown skirt, white sweater, camel coat $95.00

    Millennium Ball, 2000, #25580, ball gown with beading $125.00

    Museum Gala, 2000, #27280, gray sweater, beaded taffeta skirt $120.00

    Runway Review, 2000 – 2002, #27275, black evening dress $90.00

    Magazine Launch, 2000, #27285, beaded jet black suit $85.00

    Alexandra Fairchild Ford, 2000, #26930, pink chiffon and taffeta dress $85.00

    Lunch at 2, 2000, #27290, gray crepe dress $75.00

    Woman of the Year, 2001 – 2002, #30640, stunning gold gown $125.00

    Tides, #30630, 2001 – 2002 BK, redhead $70.00

    Tides, #30620, 2001 – 2002 BK, blonde $70.00

    Tides, #30625, 2001 – 2002 BK, brunette $70.00

    Book Tour, #31625, 2001 ....$150.00

    Mardi Gras, #31155, 2001 – 2002 ....$250.00

    Cyber Launch, #31215, 2001 ....$80.00

    Sunset Grille, #31165, 2001 – 2002 ....$100.00

    Milano, #31221, 2001 ....$100.00

    New Year's Eve, #28455, 2001 – 2002 ....$150.00

    Music Video Awards, #31220, 2001 ....$85.00

    Santa Baby, #30635, 2001, red dress, coat with Christmas room $250.00

    Paris, 16", 2001 African-American Fashion Doll Grand Entrance, #31170, 2001 – 2002,

        stunning orange gown with lavender accents $200.00

    La Concorde, #31175, 2001 ....$100.00

    Crocus, 16", long gown, #33260, 2002 ....$110.00

    Newport, 16", #33255, 2002 ....$100.00

Breakfast at the Breakers, 16", brunette, #33246, blonde, #33245, honey blonde, #33247,
    striped p.j's, white robe, 2002 . . . . $80.00
Graphic Impact, 16", #33605, 2002, two-piece black check dress (Jadde) $90.00
VIP, 16", #33265, 2002 (Paris), limited to 1,000 . . . . $90.00
Backstage Pass, 16", #33270, 2002 (Paris) $90.00
Cherry Blossom, 16", #33275, 2002 (Jadde) $80.00
Sedona, 16", #33205, 2002 (Alex) $80.00
Houston Blues, 16", #32181, 2002 (Alex) $90.00
Denver Days, 16", #33210, 2002 (Alex) $90.00
Arabesque, 16", #33215, 2002 (Alex), black silk and velvet gown $150.00
Twilight, 16", #33225, 2002 (Alex), blue formal silk ballgown $150.00
Blue Maxe Jadde Lee, 16", 2003, #36530, blue dress, limited to 750 . . . . $120.00
Sold Out Show Paris Williams, 16", 2003, #36535, long lacy dress, limited to 750 . . . . $180.00
Back to the Basic Alexandra Fairchild Ford, 16", #36250, black dress, hat, limited to 750 . . . . $120.00
Cheongsam Jadde Lee, 16", 2003, #36520, pink short kimono, limited to 500 . . . . $120.00
Spotlight Paris Williams, 16", #36235, black and white ballgown, limited to 500 . . . . $160.00
Dancing Til Dawn Alexandra Fairchild Ford, 16", 2003, #37995, long ballgown $170.00
Bordeaux Alex, 16", 2003, #36190, long wine gown, limited to 750 . . . . $115.00
Breathtaking Jadde, 16", 2003, #36525, tan gown trimmed in faux fur, limited to 750 . . . . $150.00
Dots Alex, 16", #36225, 2003, black dress with big dots at hem, limited to 750 . . . . $110.00
Bouquet Alex, 16" 2003, #36210, pink sequin gown, limited to 750 . . . . $180.00
Dinner for Two Paris, 16", 2003, #36545, black pants, cream suede jacket, limited to 750 . . . . $130.00
Firecracker Alex, 16", 2003, #36195, red skirt, black top, limited to 750 . . . . $160.00
Red Label Alex, 16", 2003, #36200, two outfits with red coat, limited to 750 . . . . $200.00
Fuchsia Jadde, 16", 2003, #36740, fuchsia and black gown, limited to 750 . . . . $160.00
Camellia Paris, 16", 2003, #36730, pink ballgown, limited to 750 . . . . $130.00
Betrayal Alex, 16", 2003, #36755, long black gown and cape, limited to 750 . . . . $125.00
Greed Paris, 16", 2003, #36715, ballgown, tiara, and candlestick, limited to 750 . . . . $130.00
Desire Jadde, 16", 2003, #36720, red ballgown, dagger, limited to 750 . . . . $130.00
Red Carpet Alex, 16", 2003, #36390, black sequin gown, limited to 750 . . . . $140.00
Amanda Fairchild, 16", 2003, #36220, ballgown, limited to 500 . . . . $150.00
Strike A Pose, 2004, six hair colors, body suits $70.00
Alexandra Fairchild Ford, 16", denim bathing suit, 2004,` $60.00

Alexander-Kin, 8", crepe gown (Wendy),
1960.

Alexander-Kin, 8", 1955, #403
(Wendy), SLW.

Alexander-Kins

Alexander-Kins — 7½" – 8" h.p., must have excellent face color (also referred to as Wendy, Wendy Ann, or Wendy-Kin). If doll is not listed here, see regular listing for name. (Add more for mint or mint in box dolls. Special hairdos are higher priced.)

Straight leg non-walker, 1953. (Add more for Quiz-Kins.)

Coat/hat (dress)	$650.00
Cotton dress/organdy or cotton pinafore/hat	$550.00
Dresser/doll/wardrobe, mint	$3,200.00 up
Easter doll	$950.00 up
Felt jackets/pleated skirt dresses	$550.00 up
Garden Party long gown	$1,400.00 up
Jumper/one-piece bodysuit	$395.00
Nightgown	$275.00
Nude/perfect doll (excellent face color)	$325.00
Organdy dress/cotton or organdy pinafore/hat	$575.00
Satin dress/organdy or cotton pinafore/hat	$650.00
Sleeveless satin dress/organdy or cotton pinafore	$475.00
Taffeta dress/cotton pinafore/hat	$650.00
Robe/nightgown or p.j.'s	$300.00

Straight leg walker, 1954 – 1955, must have good face color. (Add more for mint or mint in box dolls.)

Basic doll in box/panties/shoes/socks	$525.00
Coat/hat (dress)	$475.00
Cotton dress/pinafore/hat	$475.00 up
Cotton school dress	$375.00
Day in Country	$950.00
Garden Party, long gown	$1,400.00 up
Maypole Dance	$600.00
Nightgown, robe, or p.j.'s	$300.00
Jumper dress with blouse effect, any material	$425.00
Organdy party dress/hat	$500.00 up
Riding Habit	$375.00 up
Sailor dress	$950.00 up
Sleeveless organdy dress	$375.00
Swimsuits (mint)	$350.00 up
Taffeta/satin party dress/hat	$575.00 up

Bend knee walker, 1956 – 1965, must have good face color. (Add more for mint or mint in box dolls.) "Alexander-Kin" dropped in 1963 and "Wendy Ann" used through 1965.

Nude (excellent face color)	$175.00
Basic doll in box/panties/shoes/socks (mint in box)	$475.00
Carcoat set	$1,600.00
Cherry Twin	$1,500.00 up
Coat/hat/dress	$450.00
Cotton dress/cotton pinafore/hat	$450.00
Cotton or satin dress/organdy pinafore/hat	$475.00 up
Easter Egg/doll, 1965, 1966 only	$1,500.00 up
Felt jacket/pleated skirt/dress/cap or hat	$425.00 up
First Dancing Dress (gown)	$800.00
Flowergirl	$875.00
French braid/cotton dress, 1965	$600.00
June Wedding	$750.00
Long party dress	$800.00 up
Nightgown/robe	$275.00

Neiman-Marcus (clothes must be on correct doll with correct hairdo)

Doll in case with all clothes	$1,400.00 up
Name of store printed on dress material	$750.00
Two-piece playsuit, navy with red trim	$600.00
Robe, navy	$325.00

Nude, perfect doll with excellent face color, bend knee/non-walker $80.00
Organdy dress/hat, 1965 . . . .$475.00
Organdy dress/organdy pinafore/hat $500.00
Riding habit, boy or girl $400.00
   Devon Horse Show $850.00
Riding habit, check pants, girl, 1965, boy, 1965 . . . .$375.00
Sewing Kit/doll, 1965, 1966 only . . . .$950.00 up
Skater . . . .$750.00 up
Sundress $375.00
Swimsuits, beach outfits $325.00
Taffeta party dress/hat $475.00
Tennis $425.00

Alexander Rag Time Dolls — cloth, 1938 – 1939 only . . . .$850.00 up
Algeria — 8" straight leg, #528, 1987 – 1988 only (Maggie) $60.00
Alice — 18" h.p., 1951 only, saran wig to waist (Maggie) $750.00
Alice and Her Party Kit — 1965 only, included case, wardrobe, and wigs, mint (Mary Ann) $750.00
Alice (in Wonderland) — 16" cloth, 1930 flat face, eyes painted to side $875.00
   1933 formed mask face $675.00
7" compo., 1930s (Tiny Betty) $425.00
9" compo., 1930s (Little Betty) $425.00
11" – 14" compo., 1936 – 1940 (Wendy Ann) . . . .$425.00 – 525.00
13" compo., 1930s, has swivel waist (Wendy Ann) $425.00
14½" – 18" compo., 1948 – 1949 (Margaret) . . . .$450.00 – 800.00
21" compo., 1948 – 1949 (Margaret, Wendy Ann) $950.00
14" h.p., 1950 (Maggie) $700.00
17" – 23" h.p., 1949 – 1950 (Maggie & Margaret) . . . .$600.00 – 950.00
15", 18", 23" h.p., 1951 – 1952 (Maggie & Margaret) . . . .$450.00 – 950.00
14" h.p. with trousseau, 1951 – 1952 (Maggie) . . . .$1,600.00 up
15" h.p., 1951 – 1952 (Maggie & Margaret) $575.00
17" h.p., 1949 – 1950 (Maggie & Margaret) $700.00
23" h.p., 1942 – 1952 (Maggie & Margaret) . . . .$850.00 up
29" cloth/vinyl, 1952 (Barbara Jane) . . . .$700.00 up
8" h.p., #465 – #590, 1955 – 1956 (Wendy Ann) . . . .$800.00 up
8", #494, Storyland Series, blue/white eyelet pinafore, 1990 – 1992 . . . .$65.00
   #492, 1993, #140492, 1994 blue/white with red trim $70.00
8" h.p., 1972 – 1976, Disney crest colors (Disneyland, Disney World) $450.00
8" h.p., blue with lace trim, organdy pinafore, 1995 . . . .$65.00
8" h.p., #13000, 1997 – 1998, Alice with calendar, blue party dress, gold crown, #13001, 1999 – 2000 . . . .$75.00
12", Prom Party set, 1963 (Lissy) . . . .$950.00 up
14" plastic/vinyl, #1452 to 1974, #1552, 1966 – 1992, Literature & Classic Series (Mary Ann) $75.00
14" plastic/vinyl, #87001, 1996 Storyland Friends $85.00
14" h.p., #25905 (Margaret), 2000 – 2001, blue with white dot dress, organdy pinafore $130.00
10", 1991, with white rabbit (see Disney under Special Events/Exclusives)
18", #16001, 1996 Rag Doll Series (cloth doll) . . . . .not available for sale
8", #30665, 2001 – 2004, includes plush rabbit, eyelet pinafore, blue dress $50.00
5", #36295, 2004, vinyl, with rabbit $25.00
All-American Wendy — 8", #35600, 2003, patriotic outfit, bear $80.00
Allison — 18" cloth/vinyl, 1990 – 1991 . . . .$110.00
All Star — 8" h.p., #346 – 346-1, Americana Series, 1993 white or black, 1994 white only $55.00
Aloha — 8", #38870, 2004, Latin doll, grass skirt, surfboard $85.00
Alpine Boy and Girl — 1992 (see Christmas Shoppe under Special Events/Exclusives)
Altar Boy — 8" h.p., #311, 1991 only, Americana Series $60.00
Amanda — 8" h.p., #489, 1961 only, Americana Series, burnt orange/lace trim (Wendy Ann) . . . .$2,000.00 up
American Babies — 16" – 18" cloth, 1930s . . . .$175.00 – 375.00
American Beauty — 10" Portrette, #1142, 1991 – 1992, all pink $75.00
American Farm Couple — 8", 1997, #22160, 1930s rural America $125.00

American Flag Wendy

American Flag Wendy — 8", 2001, Caucasian, African-American $70.00
American Girl — 7 – 8" compo., 1938 (Tiny Betty) $385.00
    9" – 11" compo., 1937 (Little Betty, Wendy Ann) ....$325.00 – 550.00
    8" h.p., #388, #788, 1962 – 1963, became "McGuffey Ana" in 1964 – 1965 (Wendy Ann) $350.00
American Indian — 9" compo., 1938 – 1939 (Little Betty) $350.00
American Legend, An — 10", #12510, 1999, with hardcover book with doll (Cissette) $225.00
    #17330, 1999 – 2002, hardcover book, no slipcase $50.00
    #12520, 1999 – 2002, deluxe book, slipcase $75.00
American Parade — 8", #36465, 2003, black and red check dress, with bear on tricycle $90.00
American Sweetheart — 8", #39110, 2004, red skirt $50.00
American Tots — 16" – 21" cloth, dressed in child's fashions ....$275.00 – 500.00
American Women's Volunteer Service (A.W.V.S.) — 14" compo., 1942 (Wendy Ann) ....$850.00 up
Amish Boy — 8" h.p., BK, #727, 1966 – 1969, Americana Series (Wendy Ann) $375.00
Amish Girl — 8" h.p., BK, #726, 1966 – 1969, Americana Series (Wendy Ann) $375.00
Amy — (see Little Women)
Amy Goes to Paris Trunk Set — 8", #14635, 1996 ....$200.00
Amy the Bride — 10", #14622, 1996, ivory lace dress $95.00
Anastasia — 10" Portrette, #1125, 1988 – 1989 (Cissette) $75.00
    14" (see M.A.D.C. under Special Events/Exclusives)
    8" h.p., 2003 – 2004, #35695, white dress, blue bodice, gold locket $85.00
Anatolia — 8" straight leg, #524, 1987 only $60.00
Angel — 8", in pink, blue, off-white gowns (Wendy & Maggie) ....$950.00 up
    Baby Angel — 8" h.p., #480, 1955, multi-layered chiffon wings (Wendy Ann) ....$975.00 up
    Guardian Angel — 8", #480, 1954 only (Wendy Ann) ....$800.00 up
    Guardian Angel — 8", #618, 1961 (Maggie smile face) ....$800.00 up
    Guardian Angel — 10", #10602, 1995, first in series, all pink with white wings $100.00
    Pristine Angel — 10", #10604, 1995, second in series, white with gold trim $100.00
    Angel of Bliss — 10", #32155, 2000, long pink dress, white wings $100.00
Angel and 8" Music Box Creche — 8", #19530, 1997 – 2000, Nativity set $250.00
Angel Face — (see Shirley's Doll House under Special Events/Exclusives)
Angelique Innocence Angel — 10", #35855, 2003, white gown, wings $150.00
Angel Tree Topper — (see Tree Topper)
Anglund, Joan Walsh — Joy, 10", #28805 ....$40.00
Anna and the King of Siam — 8", 1996, #14656, sold as set $150.00
Anna Ballerina — 18" compo., 1940, Pavlova (Wendy Ann) ....$950.00 up

American Girl, 7", composition, mohair wig (Tiny Betty). Mint with original box.

Annabelle — 14" – 15" h.p., 1951 – 1952 only, Kate Smith's stories of Annabelle (Maggie) $650.00
    14" – 15" trousseau/trunk, 1952 only, FAO Schwarz (Maggie) ....$1,500.00 up
    18" h.p., 1951 – 1952 (Maggie) ....$650.00 up
    20" – 23" h.p., 1951 – 1952 (Maggie) ....$675.00 – 1,000.00
Annabelle at Christmas — (see Belks & Leggett under Special Events/Exclusives)
Anna Karenina — 21" Portrait, #2265, 1991 (Jacqueline) $325.00
    10", #21900 (Cissette) bustle dress, 1998 – 1999 ....$100.00
    10", #21910 (Cissette) Trunk set, doll, 3 outfits, 1998 – 1999 ....$250.00
Ann Estelle — 8", #17600, 1999 – 2001, Mary Engelbreit sailor outfit $75.00
Anne of Green Gables — 14", #1530, 1989 – 1990 only (Mary Ann) $100.00
    14", #1579, 1992 – 1994, Goes to School, with trunk/wardrobe (Louisa/Jennifer) $165.00
    14", #1570 in 1993 only, #261501 in 1995, Arrives at Station $95.00
    14", 1993, Becomes the Teacher $95.00
    8" h.p., 1994 – 1995, #260417, At the Station (Wendy Ann) $90.00
    8" h.p., #260418, 1994, puff sleeve dress $100.00

8" h.p., #26423, 1995, concert dress $100.00
8" h.p., #26421, 1995, trunk playset $225.00
8" h.p., #13830, 1998 – 1999, floral dress, drawstring bag, straw hat $75.00
8" h.p., #36115, 2003 – 2004, brown print dress, straw hat $85.00
Annette — 1993 (see Disney under Special Events/Exclusives)
Annie Laurie — 14" compo., 1937 (Wendy Ann) $650.00
   17" compo., 1937 (Wendy Ann) $925.00
Annie the Artist — 20", #35001, 1996, artist outfit, crayons . . . . .not available for sale
Antique Chaos the Bear and Wendy — 8", #36420, 2003 – 2004, 5" bear $95.00
Antoinette — 21" compo., 1946, extra make-up, must be mint (Wendy Ann) . . . .$2,300.00 up
Antoinette, Marie — 21", 1987 – 1988 only, multi-floral with pink front insert $350.00
Antony, Mark — 12", #1310, 1980 – 1985, Portraits of History (Nancy Drew) $65.00
Apple A Day, An — 8", #38530, 2004, doctor outfit with chart, etc $85.00
Apple Annie of Broadway — 8" h.p., 1953 – 1954 (Wendy Ann) . . . .$1,100.00 up
Apple Picking — 8", #33025, 2002 (Maggie), denim dress, basket of apples $60.00
Apple Pie — 14", #1542, 1991 only, Doll Classics (Mary Ann) $65.00
Apple Tree — 8", #13290, 2000 – 2001, dressed as a tree trunk with leaves and apples $80.00
April — 14", #1533, 1990 – 1991, Doll Classics (Mary Ann & Jennifer) $75.00
April Showers Bring May Flowers — 8", #13480, 1998 – 1999, pink taffeta and lace, parasol $90.00
Aquarius — 8", #21310, 1998, orange and gold mermaid costume $85.00
Argentine Boy — 8" h.p., BKW & BK, #772, 1965 only (Wendy Ann) $450.00
Argentine Girl — 8" h.p., BK, #0771-571, 1965 – 1972 (Wendy Ann) $135.00
   BKW, #771 (Wendy Ann) $175.00
   8" h.p., straight legs, #571, 1973 – 1976, marked "Alex" $60.00
   8" h.p., straight legs, #571, 1976 – 1986 (1985 – 1986 white face) $50.00
Argyle Twist Total Moves Wendy — 8", 2004, #38800 . . . .$95.00
Aries — 8", #21330, 1998, gray furry ram outfit $90.00
Armenia — 8", #507, 1989 – 1990 (Wendy Ann) $60.00
Arriving in America — 8" h.p., #326, 1992 – 1993 only, Americana Series (Wendy Ann) $65.00
Artie — 12" plastic/vinyl, 1962, sold through FAO Schwarz (Smarty) $275.00
Artiste Wendy — 8", #31250, 1998 – 1999, pink smock and black beret $70.00
Ashley — 8", #628, 1990 only, Scarlett Series, tan jacket/hat $125.00
   8" h.p., #633, 1991 – 1992 only, Scarlett Series, as Confederate officer $150.00
Ashley Rose — 14", #34335, 2002 – 2003, African-American, print dress $90.00
Astor — 9" early vinyl toddler, 1953 only, gold organdy dress and bonnet $150.00
Astrological Month Dolls — 14" – 17" compo., 1938 (Wendy) $525.00
A-Tisket-A-Tasket — 8", #34315, 2002 – 2003, pink dress, white pinafore, basket $80.00
Aunt Agatha — 8" h.p., #434, 1957 (Wendy Ann), checked taffeta gown . . . .$1,400.00 up
Aunt Betsy — cloth/felt, 1930s $900.00
Auntie Em — 8" h.p., #14515, 1995 only, Wizard of Oz Series $85.00
Aunt March — 8", #14621, 1996. . . . . $70.00
Aunt Pitty Pat — 14" – 17" compo., 1939 (Wendy Ann),
   from *Gone with the Wind* . . . .$1,500.00 up
   8" h.p., #435, 1957 (Wendy Ann), from *Gone with
   the Wind* . . . .$1,600.00 up
   8" h.p., straight leg, #636, 1991 – 1992, Scarlett
   Series $85.00
   8" h.p., #33465, 2002, blue dress, black lace
   trim $100.00
Australia — 8" only (Wendy Ann) $60.00
   8" h.p., #35965, 2003 – 2004, kangaroo skirt,
   binoculars, plush kangaroo $90.00
Austria Boy* — 8" h.p., 1974 – 1989 (Wendy Ann), straight
   legs, #599 – #533, 1973 – 1975, marked "Alex". . .$70.00

Argentine Girl, 8", 1981 (left), BK doll made between 1966 and 1972 (right).

*Formerly Tyrolean Boy.

Austria Boy

#599, 1976 – 1989, marked "Alexander" $55.00

Austria Girl* — 8" h.p., 1974 – 1993 (Wendy Ann) straight legs, #598, 1973 – 1975, marked "Alex" $70.00

    #598 – #532, 1976 – 1990, marked "Alexander" $55.00

    Reintroduced, #110539 (Maggie), 1994 only $60.00

Autumn — 14", 1993, Changing Seasons doll with four outfits $125.00

    5" porcelain, #25860, 2000, brown dress and jacket, black hat $60.00

Autumn in N.Y. — (see First Modern Doll Club under Special Events/Exclusives)

Autumn Leaves — 14", 1994, Classic Dolls $90.00

Avril, Jane — 10" (see Marshall Fields under Special Events/Exclusives)

Baa Baa Black Sheep — 8", #34020, 2002 – 2003, black polka dot outfit, white hat $75.00

Babbie — cloth with long thin legs, inspired by Katharine Hepburn . . . .$1,000.00 up

    16" cloth child doll, 1934 – 1936 . . . .$795.00 up

    14" h.p. (Maggie) . . . .$800.00 up

Babette — 10" Portrette, #1117, 1988 – 1989, black short dress (Cissette) $65.00

Babs — 20" h.p., 1949 (Maggie) $850.00

Babsie Baby — compo./cloth, moving tongue $550.00

Babsie Skater (roller) — 15", 1941 (Princess Elizabeth) $850.00

Babs Skater — 18" compo. (Margaret) . . . .$1,250.00 up

    15" h.p., 1948 – 1950 (Margaret) . . . .$1,200.00 up

    17" – 18" h.p. . . . .$1,300.00 up

    21" h.p. . . . .$1,500.00 up

Baby Betty — 10" – 12" compo., 1935 – 1936 . . . .$300.00

Baby Brother and Sister — 20" cloth/vinyl, 1977 – 1979 (Mary Mine) . . . .$125.00 ea.

    14", 1979 – 1982 . . . .$75.00 ea.

    14", re-introduced 1989 only . . . .$65.00 ea.

Baby Clown — See Clowns

Baby Ellen — 14", 1965 – 1972 (black Sweet Tears) $135.00

Baby Genius — 11" all cloth, 1930s $425.00

    11" – 12" compo./cloth, 1930s – 1940s . . . .$250.00 up

    16" compo./cloth, 1930s – 1940s $250.00

    22" compo./cloth, 1940s $525.00

    15", 18" h.p. head, vinyl limbs, 1949 – 1950 (some get sticky or turn dark) . . . .$100.00 – 175.00

    21" h.p. head, vinyl limbs, 1952 – 1955 . . . .$350.00

    8" h.p./vinyl, 1956 – 1962 (see Little Genius)

Baby in Louis Vuitton trunk/wardrobe or wicker basket with legs —

    Any year . . . .$900.00 up

Baby Jane — 16" compo., 1935 . . . .$950.00 up

Baby Lynn — 20" cloth/vinyl, 1973 – 1976 . . . .$125.00

    14" cloth/vinyl, 1973 – 1976 . . . .$100.00

Baby Madison — 14", #29750, 1999, vinyl, with layette $80.00

Baby McGuffey — 22" – 24" compo., 1937 . . . .$350.00

    20" cloth/vinyl, 1971 – 1976 . . . .$150.00

    14" cloth/vinyl, 1972 – 1978 . . . .$125.00

Baby Precious — 14" cloth/vinyl, 1975 only $125.00

    21" cloth/vinyl, 1974 – 1976 . . . .$150.00

Baby Shaver — 12" cloth h.p., 1941 – 1943, yellow floss wig, round painted eyes (Little Shaver) . . . .$650.00 up

Baby Sister — 18", #30300, cloth, 2001 –2002, pink check dress $45.00

Baby Snoopy Huggums — 8", #26440, 2002, Snoopy booties $60.00

Bad Little Girl — 16" cloth, 1966 only, blue dress, eyes and mouth turned down, looking sad $250.00

Bali — 8" h.p., #533, 1993 only $60.00

Ballerina — (Also see individual dolls – Leslie, Margaret, etc.)

    9" compo., 1935 – 1941 (Little Betty) $375.00

    11" – 13", 1930s (Betty) $400.00

    11" – 14" compo., 1936 – 1938 (Wendy Ann) $425.00

*Formerly Tyrolean Girl.

17" compo., 1938 – 1941 (Wendy Ann) . . . .$700.00 up

21" compo., 1947, "Debra" ("Deborah") Portrait ballerina in mint condition (Wendy Ann) . . . .$8,500.00 up

(Also see Enchanted Doll House under Special Events/Exclusives)

(Also see M.A.D.C. under Special Events/Exclusives)

SLNW, #354, 1953 – 1954, lavender, yellow, pink, or blue, 8" h.p. (Wendy Ann) . . . .$750.00 up

SLW, #454, 1955, lavender, yellow, pink, or white . . . .$675.00 up

BKW, #564, 1954 – 1960, golden yellow $575.00

#454, 1955, white $475.00

#564, 1956, rose $650.00

#564 – 631, 1956, yellow $700.00

#364, 1957, blue $375.00

#544, 1958, pink $375.00

#420, 1959, gold $750.00

#420, 1961, lavender $700.00

#640, 1964, pink $375.00

BK, #620 – 730, 1965 – 1972, yellow $375.00

#440 – 730, 1962 – 1972, blue $275.00

#440 – 730, 1962 – 1972, pink $250.00

8" straight leg, #0730, #530, #430, 1973 – 1992 (1985 – 1987 white face) $65.00

SLNW, #330, 1990 – 1991 (black or white dolls, 1991), Americana Series, white/gold outfit (Wendy Ann) $65.00

#331 – 331-1, 1992, black or white doll in pink/silver outfit (Wendy Ann) $65.00

#331, 1993, white doll only pink/silver outfit $65.00

#100331, 1994 – 1995, white doll, pink tutu $60.00

#13900, 1998, lace tutu over pink tulle $65.00

#17640, 1999 – 2000, blue Ballet Recital, wears silver crown $65.00

#17660, 2000 – 2001, pink Ballet Class $60.00

#17650, 1999 – 2000, lilac Ballet Recital, lilac and silver $65.00

#17690, 1999 – 2000, pink Ballet Recital, pink knit outfit $65.00

#25030, 2000, Irish Dream, green bodice, white tutu with shamrocks $75.00

#26810, 2000, pink petal, light pink costume $70.00

#35075, Twirling Confetti Ballerina, 2004, 8", lavender tutu $50.00

#35635, The Red Shoes, 2004, 8", white tutu, red shoes $75.00

#38560, 8", Plie Total Moves Wendy, pink tutu $95.00

#38620, Land of Sweets Ballerina, 2004, 8", gold tutu $85.00

#38855, 2004, 8", Caucasian, with dog, bear, and cat $90.00

#38856, 2004, 8", African-American, with dog, bear, and cat . . .$90.00

#39100, Tutu Cute, 2004, 8", white tutu, pastel top $75.00

#38857, 2004, 8", Asian, with dog, bear, and cat $90.00

Autumn Ballerina, #30445, 2002, 5" porcelain, white tutu $75.00

Spring Ballerina, #30435, 2002, 5" porcelain, pink tutu $75.00

Summer Ballerina, #30440, 5" porcelain, green ballet costume, 2002 ..$75.00

Winter Ballerina, #30450, 5" porcelain, white ballet costume, 2002 . .$75.00

10 – 11" h.p., #813, 1957 – 1960, must have excellent face color

    (Cissette) $385.00

12", 1964 only (Janie) $275.00

12", 1989 – 1990, "Muffin" (Janie) $75.00

12", 1990 – 1992 only, Romance Collection (Nancy Drew) $65.00

12", 1993 only, in lavender (Lissy) $150.00

14", 1963 only (Melinda) $325.00

15" – 18" h.p., 1950 – 1952, must have good face color

    (Margaret) . . . .$625.00 – 900.00

16½" h.p., 1957 – 1964, jointed ankles, knees and elbows, must have

    good face color (Elise) $475.00

1957, yellow, rare $900.00

Elise Ballerina, 17", #1640, 1982.

Ballerina

        1958, white $425.00
        1959, gold $450.00
        1960, pink $400.00
        1961, upswept hairdo, pink $475.00
        1962, blue $400.00
        1963 – 1964 only, small flowers in 1963; large flowers in 1964 (Mary-Bel) (18" also Elise) $400.00
     16" plastic/vinyl, #38350, Principal Ballerina, 2004, white/gold tutu $220.00
     16" plastic/vinyl, #38355, Dance Under the Star, 2004, blue tutu $220.00
     17" plastic/vinyl, 1967 – 1989, discontinued costume (Elise) $100.00
     17" plastic/vinyl, 1990 – 1991, "Firebird" and "Swan Lake" (Elise) $125.00
     17", 1966 – 1971 only (Leslie – black doll) $450.00
     16", Classic Ballerina, #22700, 2000 only $150.00
Bandstand Swing Set — 8", girl, boy, #39610, 2004, poodle skirt $135.00
Barbara Jane — 29" cloth/vinyl, 1952 only, mint $500.00
Barbara Lee — 8", 1955, name given by FAO Schwarz $650.00
Barton, Clara — 10", #1130, 1989 only, Portrette, wears nurse's outfit (Cissette) $125.00
Baseball Boy — 8", #16313, 1997, red, white baseball outfit $55.00
Baseball Girl — 8", #16300, baseball outfit with ball glove $55.00
Bathing Beauty — (see U.F.D.C. under Special Events/Exclusives)
Bathing Beauty Coca-Cola — 10", red vintage bathing suit, life preserver $125.00
Beary Best Friends — 8" with 2½" bear, #32160, 2000, white dress $70.00
    8", #32161, 2002, with 3½" bear, 100th Anniversary Edition $85.00
Beast — 12", #1317, 1992 only, Romance Series (Nancy Drew) $100.00
    8", #140487 Storyland Series – 1994, Fairy Tales Series – 1995 . . . .$70.00
Beau Brummel — cloth, 1930s $800.00
Beauty — 12", #1316, 1992 only, Romance Series (Nancy Drew) $100.00
    8", #140486 Storyland Series – 1994, Fairy Tales Series – 1995 . . . .$75.00
Beauty Queen — 10" h.p., 1961 only (Cissette) $375.00
Beaux Arts Dolls — 18" h.p., 1953 only (Margaret, Maggie) . . . .$2,500.00 up
Beddy-Bye Brenda — (Brooke's sister) (see FAO Schwarz under Special Events/Exclusives)
Beddy-Bye Brooke — (see FAO Schwarz under Special Events/Exclusives)
Bee My Friend — 8", #38125, 2004, dress with bees on it $85.00
Being a Prom Queen — (see Wendy Loves)
Being Just Like Mommy — (see Wendy Loves)
Belgium — 8" h.p., BK, #762, 1972 only (Wendy Ann) $110.00

Closeup of Belle Brummel's gorgeous Muslim face.

Beau Brummel, 13", cloth, 1935. Rare, all original doll.

Belle Brummel, 13", cloth, 1935. Muslim face, yarn hair, felt jacket. All original.

8" straight legs, #0762, #562, 1973 – 1975, marked "Alex" $65.00

8" straight legs, #562, 1976 – 1988, marked "Alexander" $60.00

7" compo., 1935 – 1938 (Tiny Betty) $275.00

9" compo., 1936 only (Little Betty) $300.00

Belle — 14", #18402, 1996 Dickens, red jacket, long skirt $100.00

10", #36375, 2004, vinyl, yellow dress $35.00

Belle Brummel — cloth, 1930s $800.00

Belle of the Ball — 10", #1120, 1989 only, Portrette, deep rose gown (Cissette) $125.00

Belle's Enchanted Christmas — 10", #34945, 2002, red satin ballgown with plastic Angelique $130.00

Belle Watling — 10", 1992 only, Scarlett Series (Cissette) $125.00

21", #16277, 1995 only, red outfit with fur trim (Jacqueline) $325.00

10", #30820, 2001, gold satin dress, brown trim $125.00

Bellows' Anne — 14" plastic/vinyl, #1568, 1987 only, Fine Arts Series $75.00

Belk & Leggett Department Stores — (see Special Events/Exclusives)

Bernhardt, Sarah — 21", #2249, 1987 only, dressed in all burgundy $300.00

Berries and Cream — 8", #28475, 2001 – 2002, pink stripe dress, hat $90.00

Bessy Bell — 14" plastic/vinyl, #1565, 1988 only, Classic Series (Mary Ann) $75.00

Bessy Brooks — 8", #487, 1988 – 1991, Storybook Series (Wendy Ann) $65.00

8", 1990 (see Collectors United/Bride under Special Events/Exclusives)

Best Friend — 8", #26090, 2000, blue silk dress with smocking $100.00

8", #26085, 2000 – 2001, pink silk dress with smocking $100.00

Best Friends — 8", #36895, 2003 – 2004, doll, 18" Chaos Bear, toy box $160.00

Best Man — 8" h.p., #461, 1955 only (Wendy Ann) $875.00

Beth — (see Little Women) 10" (see Spiegel's under Special Events/Exclusives)

Betty — 14" compo., 1935 – 1942 ....$425.00

12" compo., 1936 – 1937 only $350.00

16" – 18" compo., 1935 – 1942 ....$425.00

19" – 21" compo., 1938 – 1941 ....$550.00

14½" – 17½" h.p., 1951 only, made for Sears (Maggie) $575.00

30" plastic/vinyl, 1960 only $400.00

Betty Bag — 23" all cloth, holds clothes back of head $225.00

Betty Blue — 8" straight leg, #420, 1987 – 1988 only, Storybook Series (Maggie) $55.00

Betty Boop — 10", #17500 (Cissette), red dress, 1999 – 2001 ....$130.00

21", #25125, 2000, doll with two outfits $225.00

10", #26450, 2000 – 2001, Razzle Dazzle, long white dress, hat $125.00

Betty, Little — 9" compo., 1935 – 1943 ....$350.00 up

Betty, Tiny — 7" compo., 1934 – 1943 ....$350.00 up

Bible Character Dolls — 8" h.p., 1954 only (Wendy Ann)

(Mary of Bethany, David, Martha, Ruth, Timothy, Rhoda,
Queen Esther, and Joseph) ....$7,500.00 up

1995 (see Delilah, Joseph, Queen Esther, and Samson)

Big Sister Wendy — 8", #36550, 2003 – 2004, blue dress,
stuffed doll, book $100.00

Bill/Billy — 8" h.p., #320, #567, #420, 1955 – 1963, has boy's clothes
and hairstyle (Wendy Ann) ....$450.00 up

#577, #464, #466, #421, #442, #488, #388, 1953 – 1957, as groom ..$450.00 up

Billie Holiday — 10", #22070, 1997, long silver gown $100.00

Billy-in-the-Box — 8" jester, 1996, Alexander signature box $125.00

Binah — 8", #39450, 2004 (Wendy), with mouse $85.00

5", #39440, 2004, petite, red skirt $25.00

9", #39435, 2004, vinyl, with mouse $35.00

6", #39445, 2004, cloth, red skirt $10.00

Binnie — 18" plastic/vinyl toddler, 1964 only $350.00

Binnie Walker — 15" – 18" h.p., 1954 – 1955 only (Cissy) ....$200.00 – 425.00

15", 1955 only, in trunk with wardrobe $750.00

15", 1955 only, h.p. skater ....$700.00 up

Bessy Brooks, 8", #487, 1988 – 1991,
(Wendy).

Binnie Walker

18", toddler, plastic/vinyl, 1964 only . . . . $350.00 up

25", 1955 only, in formals . . . . $550.00 up

25", h.p., 1954 – 1955 only, dresses $400.00

Birds, The — 10", #14800, green dress, fur coat, pictured 1998 catalog . . . . not available for sale

Birthday Dolls — 7" compo., 1937 – 1939 (Tiny Betty) . . . . $375.00 up

Birthday, Happy — 1985 (see M.A.D.C. under Special Events/Exclusives)

Bitsey — 11" – 12" compo., 1942 – 1946 . . . . $250.00

11" – 16", with h.p. head, 1949 – 1951 . . . . $250.00

19" – 26", 1949 – 1951 . . . . $150.00 – 375.00

12" cloth/vinyl, 1965 – 1966 only $150.00

Bitsey, Little — 9" all vinyl, 1967 – 1968 only $125.00

11" – 16" . . . . $75.00 – 250.00

Black Forest — 8", #512, 1989 – 1990 (Wendy Ann) $60.00

Black and White Ball — 10", #38735, 2004, white gown, black flowers $150.00

Blast Off 2000 — 8", #17830, 2000 only (Maggie), silver and gold costume $85.00

Bless The Night Treetopper — 8", #38710, 2004, wine and beige angel costume $100.00

Bliss, Betty Taylor — 1979 – 1981, second set Presidents' Ladies/First Ladies Series (Mary Ann) $100.00

Blooming Rose — 8", #28470, 2001 – 2002, pink stripe dress, hat $85.00

Blue Bird Shadow Wendy — 8", #37135, African-American or Caucasian, 2004, white dress, straw hat $95.00

Blue Boy — 16" cloth, 1930s $650.00

7" compo., 1936 – 1938 (Tiny Betty) $350.00

9" compo., 1938 – 1941 (Little Betty) $375.00

12" plastic/vinyl, #1340, 1972 – 1983, Portrait Children (Nancy Drew) $60.00

1985 – 1987, dressed in blue velvet $75.00

8", #22130, 1997 – 1998, blue satin outfit $65.00

Blue Danube — 18" h.p., 1953 only, pink floral gown (#2001B – blue floral gown) (Maggie) . . . . $1,800.00 up

18" h.p., 1954 only, Me and My Shadow Series, blue taffeta dress (Margaret) . . . . $1,700.00 up

Blue Edwardian Lady — 5" porcelain, #27025, long blue gown, 2000 . . . . $75.00

Blue Fairie — 10", #1166, 1993; #201166, 1994, Portrette, character from Pinocchio (Cissette) $125.00

Blue Fairy — 8", #32135, 2000, blue gown, wings $80.00

10", #31760, 2003 – 2004 and 10" wooden Pinocchio, long blue ballgown $200.00

Blue Gingham Chloe — 14" vinyl, #25350, 2001 . . . . $70.00

Blue Hat Doll — 8", #25310, 2000, Maud Humphrey design $70.00

Blue Mist Angel — 10", #25290, 2000 – 2001, Caucasian doll, blue costume $125.00

10", #25291, 2000 – 2001, African-American doll, blue costume $125.00

Blue Moon — 14", #1560, 1991 – 1992 only, Classic Series (Louisa) $90.00

Blue Skies Angel — 8", #37900, 2003 – 2004, blue and white dress $90.00

Blue Zircon — 10", #1153, 1992 only, Birthday Collection, gold/blue flapper $125.00

Blynkin — (see Dutch Lullaby)

Bobby — 8" h.p., #347, 1957 only (Wendy Ann) $575.00

8" h.p., #361, #320, 1960 only (Maggie Mixup) $625.00

Bobby Q. — cloth, 1940 – 1942 . . . . $750.00

Bobby (Bobbie) Soxer — 8" h.p., 1990 – 1991 (see Disney under Special Events/Exclusives)

Bobo Clown — 8", #320, 1991 – 1992, Americana Series (Wendy Ann) $80.00

Bohemia — 8", #508, 1989 – 1991 (Wendy Ann) $50.00

Bolivia — 8" h.p., BK & BKW, #786, 1963 – 1966 (Wendy Ann) $375.00

Bonnet Top Wendy — 8", #14487, 1995, Toy Shelf Series, yarn braids and large bonnet $65.00

Bonnie (Baby) — 16" – 19" vinyl, 1954 – 1955 . . . . $125.00 – 250.00

24" – 30", 1954 – 1955 . . . . $125.00 – 350.00

Bonnie Blue — 14", #1305, 1989 only, Jubilee II (Mary Ann) $150.00

8" h.p., #629, #630, 1990 – 1992 (Wendy Ann) $135.00

8", #16649, 1995, side-saddle riding outfit $100.00

Bonnie Goes to London — 8", #640, 1993, Scarlett Series #160640 – 1994 . . . . $125.00

Bonnie Toddler — 18" cloth/h.p. head/vinyl limbs, 1950 – 1951 . . . . $175.00

19" all vinyl, 1954 – 1955 . . . . $200.00

23" – 24" $275.00

Bon Voyage — 8" and 10" (see I. Magnum under Special Events/Exclusives)

Boone, Daniel — 8" h.p., #315, 1991 only, Americana Series, has no knife (Wendy Ann) $60.00

Bo Peep, Little — 7" compo., 1937 – 1941, Storybook Series (Tiny Betty) $375.00

    9" – 11" compo., 1936 – 1940 (Little Betty, Wendy Ann) $350.00

    7½" h.p., SLW, #489, 1955 only (Wendy Ann) $675.00

    8" h.p., BKW, #383, 1962 – 1964 (Wendy Ann) $325.00

    8" h.p., BK, #783, 1965 – 1972 (Wendy Ann) $150.00

    8" h.p., straight leg, #0783 – 483, 1973 – 1975, marked "Alex" (Wendy Ann) $75.00

    8" h.p., 1976 – 1986, #483 – #486, marked "Alexander" (Wendy Ann) $65.00

    14", #1563, 1988 – 1989, Classic Series (Mary Ann) $100.00

    14", #1567, 1992 – 1993 only, candy stripe pink dress (Mary Ann) $90.00

    12" porcelain, #009, 1990 – 1992 . . . .$150.00

    10" Portrette Series, 1994 . . . .$100.00

    8" (see Dolly Dears under Special Events/Exclusives)

    8", #25960, 2000 – 2003, long blue dress and hat with staff $85.00

Boys Choir of Harlem — 8", #20170, 1997 – 1998, maroon blazer,

    Kufi hat $75.00

Brazil — 7" compo., 1937 – 1943 (Tiny Betty) $350.00

    9" compo., 1938 – 1940 (Little Betty) $375.00

    8" h.p., BKW, #773, 1965 – 1972 (Wendy Ann) $125.00

     BK, #773 . . . .$100.00

    8" h.p., straight leg, #0773, #573, 1973 – 1975, marked "Alex" (Wendy Ann) $65.00

    8" h.p., straight leg, #573, #547, #530, 1976 – 1988, marked "Alexander" $60.00

     #573, #547, #530, 1985 – 1987 . . . .$55.00

    8" straight leg, #11564, 1996 International, carnival costume $55.00

Breakfast in Bed — 8", #34040, 2003, white dress, tray with coffee, glasses $70.00

Brenda Starr — 12" h.p., 1964 only (became "Yolanda" in 1965) $350.00

  Bride $375.00

  Street dresses $375.00

  Ballgown $450.00

  Beach outfit $250.00

  Raincoat/hat/dress $325.00

Briar Rose — (see M.A.D.C. under Special Events/Exclusives)

  10", #14101, 1995, Brothers Grimm Series, blue floral with apron (Cissette) $90.00

Brick Piggy — 12", #10010, 1997, denim overalls, maize felt cap $90.00

Bride — Tiny Betty: 7" compo., 1935 – 1939 . . . .$325.00

    9" – 11" compo., 1936 – 1941 (Little Betty) $350.00

  Wendy Ann: 13", 14", 15" compo., 1935 – 1941 (Wendy Ann) . . . .$300.00 – 550.00

    17" – 18" compo., 1935 – 1943 (Wendy Ann) $475.00

    21" – 22" compo., 1942 – 1943 (Wendy Ann) . . . .$650.00 up

     In trunk/trousseau (Wendy Ann) . . . .$1,650.00 up

    21" compo., 1945 – 1947, Royal Wedding/Portrait

     (Wendy Ann) . . . .$2,400.00 up

  Margaret, Maggie: Hard plastic

    15" h.p., 1951 – 1955 (Margaret) . . . .$675.00 up

    17" h.p., 1950, in pink (Margaret) . . . .$850.00 up

    18" h.p., tagged "Prin. Elizabeth" (Margaret) $700.00

    18" h.p., 1949 – 1955 (Maggie, Margaret) $700.00

    21" h.p., 1949 – 1953 (Margaret, Maggie) . . . .$1,200.00 up

    18" – 21", pink bride, 1953 (Margaret) . . . .$1,200.00 up

    23" h.p. 1949, 1952 – 1955 (Margaret) . . . .$850.00 up

    25" h.p., 1955 only (Margaret) . . . .$875.00 up

  Elise: 16½" h.p., 1957 – 1964, jointed ankles, elbows and

    knees, must have good face color, 1957, nylon tulle,

    chapel length veil $475.00

Bride, 8", #435, 1985 (Wendy). All original.

Bride

1958, wreath pattern on hem of skirt $550.00
1959, tulle puffed sleeves, long veil (pink) $800.00
1960, satin gown, lace bodice with sequins and beads $450.00
1961, short bouffant hair, tulle with puff sleeves $475.00
1962, lace pattern bodice and trim on tulle skirt $425.00
1963, tulle, rows of lace on bodice $450.00
1964, lace bodice and sleeves, lace on skirt, chapel length veil $400.00
2000, 16", Classic Bride, white lace and tulle gown $175.00

Cissy: 20" h.p., 1955 – 1958
1955 only, Dreams Come True Series, brocade gown with floor length veil . . . . $1,500.00 up
1956 only, tulle gown, tulle cap and chapel length veil, Fashion Parade Series . . . . $1,200.00 up
1957 only, Models Formal Gowns Series, nylon tulle with double train of satin . . . . $950.00 up
1958 only, Dolls to Remember Series, lace circles near hem (wreath pattern), #2280 . . . . $1,200.00 up
1959 only, tulle over white satin $850.00

Cissette: 10" h.p., 1957 – 1963, must have good face color
1957, tulle gown, short veil or lace and tulle cap veil $375.00
1958, lace wreath pattern, matches Elise and Cissy $525.00
1959 – 1960, tulle gown, puff sleeves $425.00
1961, tulle, rhinestones on collar and veil $425.00
1962, lace bodice and trim on skirt, long veil $375.00
1963, tulle, rows of lace on bodice and at hem (matches Elise the same year) $475.00
In trunk/trousseau, various years . . . . $900.00 up
#1136, 1990 – 1991, Portrette $90.00
#14103, 1995, 1920s style $100.00
#22470, 10" Empire Bride, 1998, lace gown, straw bonnet $110.00
#22460, 10" Rococo Bride, 1998, peach gown, lace train $125.00
#22480, 10" Victorian Bride, 1998, blue satin gown $100.00
#26880, 10", Contemporary Bride (blonde) $120.00
#26881 (brunette), 2000 . . . . $120.00
#32990 (blonde), 2002, white gown, pink trim, limited to 1,000 . . . . $100.00
#33325 (blonde), #33326 (brunette), Down the Aisle, 2002 – 2003 . . . . $100.00
#33327, African-American, 2002 – 2003, Down the Aisle $100.00
#38750, 10", 2004, My Special Day, blonde, white dress, lace trim $140.00
#38751, 10", 2004, My Special Day, brunette, white dress, lace trim $140.00

Bride, 21", #2192, 1969 (Jacqueline). One of the 1969 Portrait dolls on cover of catalog.

#38752, 10", 2004, My Special Day, African-American, white dress, lace trim $140.00
Lissy: 12" h.p., 1956 – 1959
1956, jointed knees and elbows, tulle, tulle cap veil $650.00
1957, same as 1956 except long veil $550.00
1958 – 1959, dotted net, tulle veil $675.00
Porcelain, 1991 – 1992 only (version of 14" head) $150.00
Jacqueline: 21" Portrait
#2151, 1965, full lace, wide lace edge on veil (Jacqueline) $950.00
#2192, 1969, full lace overskirt and plain veil $750.00
Alexander-Kin (Wendy Ann): 8" h.p. or plastic/vinyl
8" h.p., #315, 1953 only, Quiz-Kin . . . . $700.00 up
8" h.p., 1954 . . . . $650.00 up
SLW, BKW, #735 in 1955, #615 in 1956, #410 in 1957;
#582 in 1958 . . . . $375.00 – 575.00
BKW, #482, 1959, pink . . . . $1,100.00 up
BKW, #735, 1960 . . . . $400.00
BKW, #480, 1961 . . . . $375.00
BKW, #760 (#630 in 1965), 1963 – 1965 . . . . $350.00
BK, #470 in 1966; #735 in 1967 – 1972 . . . . $175.00
Straight leg, #0735-435, 1973 – 1975, marked "Alex" $100.00
Straight leg, #435, 1976 – 1994, marked "Alexander" $70.00

#337, white doll; #336-1, black doll, 1991 – 1992 . . . .$65.00

#337, 1993, white only $60.00

#435, 1985 – 1987 . . . .$55.00

Collectors United (see under Special Events/Exclusives)

#10395, 1995, Special Occasion Series – African-American $70.00

#10392, 1995, Special Occasion Series, three hair colors $60.00

#17016, 1996 white lace and satin gown $60.00

#21030, 1997 – 1998, white gown, comes with cake top, #21033 – African-American $100.00

#21171, 1999, blonde or brunette, satin ribbon at hem $65.00

#25015 (blonde), #25016 (brunette), 2000 . . . .$70.00

#25017, 2000, African-American $70.00

#30650 (blonde), #30652 (brunette), 2001 – 2002, white dress, sequin trim $70.00

#30651, African-American, 2001 – 2002, Memories of a Lifetime $70.00

#36275 (blonde), 2003 – 2004, Rosette Dreams, white dress, pink roses $85.00

#36276 (brunette), 2003 – 2004, Rosette Dreams $85.00

#36277 (African-American), 2003 – 2004, Rosette Dreams $85.00

Mary Ann, Jennifer, Louisa: 14" plastic/vinyl

#1465 (#1565 in 1974, #1565 in 1977, #1570 in 1976), 1973 – 1977 (Mary Ann) $100.00

#1589 in 1987 – 1988; #1534 in 1990, Classic Series (Mary Ann, Jennifer) $90.00

#1566, reintroduced 1992 only, ecru gown (Louisa, Jennifer) $100.00

Elise, Leslie, Polly: 17" plastic/vinyl or 21" porcelain

1966 – 1988 (Elise) $175.00

1966 – 1971 (Leslie) $250.00

1965 – 1970 (Polly) $250.00

Porcelain, 1989 – 1990, satin and lace look like bustle $250.00

Porcelain, Portrait Series, 1993 – 1994 . . . .$250.00

Bridesmaid — 9" compo., 1937 – 1939 (Little Betty) $350.00

11 – 14" compo., 1938 – 1942 (Wendy Ann) . . . .$325.00 – 475.00

15 – 18" compo., 1939 – 1944 (Wendy Ann) . . . .$375.00 – 600.00

20 – 22" compo., 1941 – 1947, Portrait (Wendy Ann) . . . .$1,800.00 up

21½" compo., 1938 – 1941 (Princess Elizabeth) . . . .$950.00 up

15 – 17" h.p., 1950 – 1952 (Margaret, Maggie) . . . .$425.00 – 550.00

15" h.p., 1952 (Maggie) $650.00

18" h.p., 1952 (Maggie) . . . .$700.00 up

Bridesmaid, 12", #1248, 1956 (Lissy).
Pleated nylon tulle dress with ribbon
sash.

Lissy Bridesmaid, 12", #1161, 1957.
Nylon dress, wide Val lace. Hat has a
tulle sash.

Bridesmaid

21" h.p., 1950 – 1953, side part mohair wig, deep pink or lavender gown (Margaret) ....$800.00 up

19" rigid vinyl, in pink, 1952 – 1953 (Margaret) ....$550.00 up

15" h.p., 1955 only (Cissy, Binnie) $425.00

18" h.p., 1955 only (Cissy, Binnie) $475.00

25" h.p., 1955 only (Cissy, Binnie) ....$475.00 up

20" h.p., 1956 only, Fashion Parade Series, blue nylon tulle & net (Cissy) ....$1,500.00 up

10" h.p., 1957 – 1963 (Cissette) $475.00

12" h.p., 1956 – 1959 (Lissy) ....$750.00 up

16½" h.p., 1957 – 1959 (Elise) ....$475.00 up

8", h.p. SLNW, 1953, pink, blue, or yellow ....$900.00 up

8" h.p., SLW, #478, 1955 (Wendy Ann) ....$800.00 up

    BKW, #621, 1956 ....$750.00 up

    BKW, #408, #583, #445, 1957 – 1959 ....$700.00 up

8", 2000, Little Gardenia, #26855 (Wendy), white tulle and satin $75.00

8", 2000, Little Pearl, #26800 (Wendy), lace bodice $80.00

17" plastic/vinyl (Elise) 1966 – 1987 ....$125.00

17" plastic/vinyl, 1966 – 1971 (Leslie) $325.00

Brigitta — 11" and 14" (see Sound of Music)

Brooke — (see FAO Schwarz under Special Events/Exclusives)

Bubbles the Clown — 8" h.p., #342, 1993 – 1994, Americana Series $100.00

Buck Rabbit — cloth/felt, 1930s ....$700.00 up

Bud — 16" – 19" cloth/vinyl, 1952 only (Rosebud head) $175.00

    19" and 25", 1952 – 1953 only ....$125.00 – 350.00

Bulgaria — 8", #557, 1986 – 1987, white face (Wendy Ann) $60.00

Bumble Bee — 8" h.p., #323, 1992 – 1993, only Americana Series $65.00

Bunny — 18" plastic/vinyl, 1962 only, mint $275.00

Bunny Tails — 8", #28200, 2000 – 2003, yellow dress, bunny pinafore, basket of eggs $80.00

Burma — 7" compo., 1939 – 1943 (Tiny Betty) $350.00

Butch — 11" – 12" compo./cloth, 1942 – 1946 ....$175.00

    14" – 16" compo./cloth, 1949 – 1951 ....$185.00

    14" cloth, vinyl head and limbs, 1950 only $175.00

    12" cloth/vinyl, 1965 – 1966 only $125.00

Butch, Little — 9" all vinyl, 1967 – 1968 only $125.00

Butch McGuffey — 22" compo./cloth, 1940 – 1941 ....$275.00

Bridesmaid, 17", 1940s (Wendy Ann). Came in several colors.

Bridesmaid, 7", composition (Tiny Betty). All original.

Butterfly Queen — 8", #25670, 2000 – 2001 (Wendy), lavender costume $75.00
C.U. — (see Collectors United under Special Events/Exclusives)
Cafe Rose and Ivory Cocktail Dress — 10", #22200 – white, #22203 – black, 1997 – 1998 ....$100.00
Caitlin — 5", #27405, 2003, Petite, check sundress $20.00
Cake Topper — 6", Caucasian, 2002, bride and groom, #33570 ....$80.00
    6", #33571, 2002, African-American bride and groom $80.00
Calamity Jane — 8" h.p., Americana Series, 1994 only (Wendy Ann) $70.00
Calendar Girls — 5", #33070 – 33130, Jan. – Dec., 2002 – 2004, set of 12, $320.00 ....$20.00 each
Calendar Girls Prepack — 5", #33065, 2002, 12 dolls, Jan. – Dec. ....$20.00 each
Calla Lilly — 10", #22390, 1998 (Cissette), white gown, hand beaded jewels $200.00
Cameo Lady — (see Collectors United under Special Events/Exclusives)
Camelot — (see Collectors United under Special Events/Exclusives)
Camille — 21" compo., 1938 – 1939 (Wendy Ann) ....$3,500.00 up
Canada — 8" h.p., BK, #760, 1968 – 1972 (Wendy Ann) $90.00
    Straight legs, #0706, 1973 – 1975, marked "Alex" $65.00
    Straight legs, #560 (#534 in 1986), 1976 – 1988 (white face 1985 – 1987), marked "Alexander" $55.00
    Straight legs, #24130, 1999, hockey skater $65.00
Cancer — 8", #21360, 1998, red crab costume $80.00
Candy Kid — 11" – 15" compo., 1938 – 1941 (Wendy Ann), red/white striped dress ....$275.00 – 450.00
    8", #27060, 2000, h.p., Peter Pan series, red coat, black pants $80.00
Candy Land Game — Princess Lolly, 8", #25250, 2000, yellow costume $80.00
Capricorn — 8", #21300, 1998 (Maggie), fuchsia snakeskin body $75.00
Captain Hook — 8" h.p., #478, 1992 – 1993 only, Storyland Series (Peter Pan) (Wendy Ann) $100.00
    8", #27060, 2000 – 2001, h.p., Peter Pan series, red coat, black pants $95.00
Careen — (see Carreen)
Carhop Takes Your Order — 8", #17710, 2000, black check dress $80.00
Carmen — Dressed like Carmen Miranda, but not marked or meant as such.
    7" compo., 1938 – 1943 (Tiny Betty) $350.00
    9" – 11" compo., 1938 – 1943, boy and girl (see also "Rumbera/Rumbero") (Little Betty) .....$325.00 ea.
    11" compo., 1937 – 1939, has sleep eyes (Little Betty) $350.00
    14" compo., 1937 – 1940 (Wendy Ann) $450.00
    17" compo., 1939 – 1942 (Wendy Ann) $650.00
    21" compo., 1939 – 1942, extra make-up, mint (Wendy Ann) ....$1,400.00 up
    21" compo., 1939 – 1942, Portrait with extra make-up ....$1,900.00 up
    14" plastic/vinyl, #1410, 1983 – 1986, Opera Series (Mary Ann) $75.00
    10" h.p., #1154, 1993 only, Portrette Series (Miranda), yellow/red $85.00
    16", #28395, 2001, red Spanish dress, black lace $200.00
Carmen Miranda Lucy — 10", #25760, 2000, white dress with ruffles $150.00
Carnavale Doll — (see FAO Schwarz under Special Events/Exclusives)
Carnival in Rio — 21" porcelain, 1989 – 1990 ....$400.00
Carnival in Venice — 21" porcelain, 1990 – 1991 ....$400.00
Caroline — 15" vinyl, 1961 – 1962 only, in dresses, pants/jacket $400.00
    In riding habit $400.00
    In case/wardrobe ....$900.00 up
    8", 1993 (see Belk & Leggett under Special Events/Exclusives)
    8", 1994 (see Neiman-Marcus under Special Events/Exclusives)
Carreen/Careen — 14" – 17" compo., #1593, 1937 – 1938 (Wendy Ann) ....$750.00 up
    14" plastic/vinyl, 1992 – 1993 only (Louisa/Jennifer) $125.00
    8" plaid, two large ruffles at hem, #160646, 1994 only $90.00
    8", #15190, 1999 (Wendy), blue dress, straw hat $85.00
Carrot Kate — 14", #25506, 1995, Ribbons & Bows Series, vegetable print dress (Mary Ann) $125.00
Carrot Top — 21" cloth, 1967 only $125.00
Casey Jones — 8" h.p., 1991 – 1992 only, Americana Series $60.00
Casper's Friend Wendy — 8" (Maggie), #15210, 1999, red costume, broom $80.00
Catch a Falling Star — 8", #33060, 2002, white dress $70.00
Caterpillar — 8" h.p., #14594, 1995 – 1996, has eight legs, Alice in Wonderland Series $100.00

Cat on a Hot Tin Roof

Cat on a Hot Tin Roof — 10", #20011, "Maggie," white chiffon dress $125.00

Cats — 16" plush, dressed, glass eyes, long lashes, felt nose $350.00

Celebrating America — 8", #38515, 2004, patch quilt dress, vintage $85.00

Celia's Dolls — (see Special Events/Exclusives)

Celtic Bride — 10", #28595, 2001, white gown, gold trim, red rose headpiece and bouquet $100.00

Celtic Dancer — 8", #34145, 2002 – 2003 (Maggie), lavender dress, blue bodice $90.00

Century of Fashion — 14" and 18" h.p., 1954 (Margaret, Maggie and Cissy) . . . .$2,000.00 up

Changing Seasons — (Spring, Summer, Autumn, Winter) 14", 1993 – 1994 . . . .$125.00 ea.

Chanukah Celebration — 8", #27330, 2001 – 2002, blue dress, brunette $90.00

Charity — 8" h.p., #485, 1961 only, Americana Series, blue cotton dress (Wendy Ann) . . . .$1,900.00 up

Charlie Brown — 10", #26425, 2001 – 2003, Peanuts Gang, includes Snoopy and ball glove $40.00

    10", #33710, 2002 – 2004 Charlie Brown Christmas, tree, Snoopy, blanket $50.00

    10", #36055, 2003 – 2004 Trick or Treat, with Snoopy and doghouse $60.00

    10", #38805, Happy Birthday, 2004, with cake and Snoopy $70.00

Champs-Elysées — 21" h.p., black lace over pink, rhinestone on cheek . . . .$6,000.00 up

Charlene — 18" cloth/vinyl, 1991 – 1992 only $100.00

Chatterbox — 24" plastic/vinyl talker, 1961 only $250.00

Cheerleader — 8", #324, 1990 – 1991 only, Americana Series (Wendy Ann) $65.00

    8", 1990 (see I. Magnin under Special Events/Exclusives)

    8" h.p., #324, #324-1, 1992 – 1993 only, Americana Series, black or white doll, royal blue/gold outfit $60.00

Chef Alex — 8", #31260, 1998 (Maggie), chef attire $80.00

Cheri — 18" h.p., 1954 only, Me and My Shadow Series, white satin gown, pink opera coat (Margaret) . . . . .$1,800.00 up

Cherry Blossom — 14", #25504, 1995, Ribbons & Bows Series, cherry print dress (Mary Ann) $125.00

Cherry Girl — 8", #17590, 1999 – 2001, Mary Engelbreit, comes with basket and card $90.00

Cherry Twins — 8" h.p., #388E, 1957 only (Wendy Ann) . . . .$1,500.00 up ea.

    8", BK, #17700, 1999, pair, remake of 1957 set $130.00

Cherub — 12" vinyl, 1960 – 1961 . . . .$250.00

    18" h.p. head/cloth and vinyl, 1950s $350.00

    26", 1950s $375.00

Cherub Babies — cloth, 1930s . . . .$450.00 up

Cheshire Cat — 8", #13070, 1997 – 1999 Storyland Series, pink velvet cat suit $65.00

Child at Heart Shop — (see Special Events/Exclusives)

Children's Prayer — 8", #28385, 2001 – 2002, pink gown, bonnet $85.00

Christening Baby, 13", vinyl body,
1954. Long organdy dress and bonnet.

Closeup of 1954 Christening Baby.

Child's Angel — 8", #14701, 1996, gold wings, harp, halo $70.00

Chile — 8" h.p., #528, 1992 only (Maggie) $65.00

China — 7" compo., 1936 – 1940 (Tiny Betty) $325.00

    9" compo., 1935 – 1938 (Little Betty) $300.00

    8" h.p., BK, #772, 1972 (Wendy Ann) $100.00

    8" (Maggie) $125.00

        Straight leg, #0772 – #572, 1973 – 1975, marked "Alex" $65.00

        Straight leg, #572, 1976 – 1986, marked "Alexander" (Wendy Ann) $60.00

        #572, 1987 – 1989 (Maggie) $60.00

    8", #11550, 1995 only, three painted lashes at edges of eyes (Wendy Ann) $60.00

    8", #11561, 1996 International, Little Empress costume $70.00

    8", #26280, 2000 – 2001 (Wendy), red silk costume with panda bear $70.00

Chinese New Year — 8", 2 dolls, #21040, 1997 – 1998 . . . .$130.00

    8", three dolls, dragon, #21050, 1997 – 1998 . . . .$200.00

Chloe — Blue gingham, 14", #25350, 2000, dress and hat $60.00

    Pink gingham, 14", #25345, 2000, white dress with pink check $60.00

Christening Baby — 11" – 13" cloth/vinyl, 1951 – 1954 . . . .$150.00

    16" – 19" $175.00

Christmas Angels — (see Tree Toppers)

Christmas at Grandma's — 8", #27445, 2000 – 2002, red coat and hat, black trim $90.00

Christmas Ballerina — 8", white tulle, red bodice, green leaves, 2003 – 2004 . . . .$80.00

Christmas Bear with Lenox Ornament — 8", Wendy, Lenox bear, #38535, 2004 . . . .$95.00

Christmas Candy — 14", #1544, 1993 only, Classic Series $90.00

Christmas Cardinals — 8", #38850, 2004, cardinals on pinafore $80.00

Christmas Carol — 8" (see Saks Fifth Avenue under Special Events/Exclusives)

Christmas Caroler — 8", #19650, 1997, red velvet cape, print skirt $80.00

Christmas Caroling — 10", #1149, 1992 – 1993 only, Portrette, burnt orange/gold dress $100.00

Christmas Cookie — 14", #1565, 1992 (also see 'Lil Christmas Cookie, 8") (Louisa/Jennifer) $125.00

Christmas Eve — 14" plastic/vinyl, #241594, 1994 only (Mary Ann) $100.00

    8", #10364, 1995, Christmas Series $70.00

Christmas Holly — 8", #19680, 1998 – 1999, print dress, red coat $80.00

Christmas Shoppe — (see Special Events/Exclusives)

Christmas Song — 10", #33455, 2002, long red dress, limited to 1,000 . . . .$140.00

Christmas Stocking — Dancing Wendy, 20" stocking, #28530, 2001 . . . .$50.00

    Skating Maggie, 20" stocking, #31255, 2001 . . . .$50.00

Christmas Stocking Stuffers — 8", #38890, 2004, stocking with toys $90.00

Christmas Tea with Ornament — 8", #38540, 2004, with teapot ornament $96.00

Christmas Tree Topper — 8" (see Spiegel's under Special

    Events/Exclusives; also Tree Topper)

Christopher Robin — 8", #31890, 2003 – 2004, yellow top,

    blue pants, 4½" Pooh bear $85.00

Chrysanthemum Garden Ball — 10", #31245, 2001,

    green and pink ballgown $125.00

Churchill, Lady — 18" h.p., #2020C, 1953 only, Beaux Arts Series,

    pink gown with full opera coat (Margaret) . . . .$2,300.00 up

Churchill, Sir Winston — 18" h.p., 1953 only, has hat

    (Margaret) . . . .$1,250.00 up

Cinderella — (see also Topsy Turvy for two-headed version)

    7" – 8" compo., 1935 – 1944 (Tiny Betty) $325.00

    9" compo., 1936 – 1941 (Little Betty) $350.00

    13" compo., 1935 – 1937 (Wendy Ann) $375.00

    14" compo., 1939 only, Sears exclusive (Princess Elizabeth) $500.00

    15" compo., 1935 – 1937 (Betty) $450.00

    16" – 18" compo., 1935 – 1939 (Princess Elizabeth) . . . .$550.00 up

    8" h.p., #402, 1955 only (Wendy Ann) $900.00

    8" h.p., #498, 1990 – 1991, Storyland Series (Wendy Ann) $60.00

Cinderella, 14" (Mary Ann), #1548, 1984 – 1986.

Cinderella

8", #476, 1992 – 1993, blue ballgown, #140476, 1994 Storyland Series $70.00

8", #475, 1992 only, "Poor" outfit in blue with black stripes $70.00

8" h.p., #14540, 1995 – 1996, pink net gown with roses, Brothers Grimm Series, #13400, 1997 – 2000 ....$75.00

8" h.p., #13410, 1997 – 1999, calico skirt with broom and pumpkin $70.00

8" h.p., #13490, 1999 – 2001, Cinderella's wedding, white gown $100.00

8", At the Ball, #30670, 2002 – 2003, white dress, long blue cape $80.00

8", #35625, 2004, Stroke of Midnight, blue ballgown $80.00

5", #36320, vinyl, petite, 2004, pink gown $25.00

12" h.p., 1966 only, Literature Series (Classic Lissy) ....$950.00 up

12" h.p., 1966, "Poor" outfit $675.00

1966, in window box with both outfits ....$1,700.00 up

14" h.p., 1950 – 1951, ballgown (Margaret) ....$900.00 up

14" h.p., 1950 – 1951, "Poor" outfit (Margaret) ....$700.00 up

14" h.p., #25940, 2000, pink, lace trimmed long gown $100.00

18" h.p., 1950 – 1951 (Margaret) ....$800.00 up

21", #45501, 1995, pink and blue, Madame's Portfolio Series $300.00

14" plastic/vinyl (#1440 to 1974; #1504 to 1991; #1541 in 1992) 1967 – 1992, "Poor" outfit
(can be green, blue, gray, or brown) (Mary Ann) $75.00

14", #140 on box, 1969 only, FAO Schwarz, all blue satin/gold trim, mint (Mary Ann) $425.00

14" plastic/vinyl, #1445, #1446, #1546, #1548, 1970 – 1983, Classic Series, dressed in pink (Mary Ann) $100.00

#1548, #1549, 1984 – 1986, blue ballgown, two styles (Mary Ann) $100.00

14", #1546, #1547, 1987 – 1991, Classic Series, white or blue ballgown (Mary Ann, Jennifer) $100.00

14", #1549, 1992 only, white/gold ballgown (Jennifer) $100.00

14", 1985, with trunk (see Enchanted Doll House under Special Events/Exclusives)

14", 1994, has two outfits (see Disney World under Special Events/Exclusives)

14", 1996, #87002, white gown, gold crown (Mary Ann) $100.00

14", #25940, 2001 (Margaret), long pink ballgown $125.00

10", 1989 (see Disney Annual Showcase of Dolls under Special Events/Exclusives)

10", #1137, 1990 – 1991, Portrette, dressed in all pink (Cissette) $90.00

10", #34950, 2002 – 2004, blue ballgown with three mice, long white gloves $150.00

10", #36240, 2004, vinyl, blue satin gown $35.00

Cinderella's Carriage — #13460, 1999 – 2000, white metal carriage $150.00

Cinderella's Footmouse — 8", #13470, 1999 – 2000, painted face $100.00

Cissy, 21", 1955, jointed knees and elbows, high heel feet, tagged dress.

Cinderella's Prince — 8", #35630, 2003 – 2004, white hat, blue pants $80.00

Cissette — 10" – 11" h.p., 1957 – 1963, high heel feet, jointed elbows
and knees, must have good face color, in various street dresses.
Allow more for M.I.B., rare outfits, and fancy hairdos $450.00

In formals, ballgowns ....$550.00 up

Coats and hats $350.00

1961 only, beauty queen with trophy $375.00

Special gift set/three wigs ....$950.00 up

Doll only, clean with good face color $125.00

1957, Queen/trunk/trousseau ....$1,200.00 up

Slacks or pants outfits $375.00

Cissette Barcelona — 10", Spanish costume, black lace, 1999 ....$125.00

Cissette Shadow Yardley — 10", #36605, blonde, blue dress,
perfume bottle $150.00

Cissy — 20" h.p. (also 21"), 1955 – 1959, jointed elbows and knees,
high heel feet, must have good face color, in various street dresses $750.00

Dress and full-length coat ....$800.00 up

In ballgowns ....$1,000.00 up

Trunk/wardrobe ....$1,400.00 up

Pants set ....$750.00 up

1950s magazine ads using doll (add $10.00 if framed) ....$30.00 up

21", reintroduced in the following 1996 MA Couture Collection

#67303, aquamarine evening column and coat $300.00

#67302, cafe rose and ivory cocktail dress $325.00

#67306, cafe rose and ivory cocktail dress, African-American $550.00

#67301, coral and leopard travel ensemble $350.00

#67601, ebony and ivory houndstooth suit $650.00

#67603, ebony and ivory houndstooth suit, African-American $750.00

#67304, onyx velvet lace gala gown and coat $375.00

#67602, pearl embroidered lace bridal gown $650.00

#86003, limited edition red sequin gown $375.00

21", 1997 MA Couture Collection

#22210, daisy resort ensemble, limited to 2,500 ....$450.00

#22230, tea rose cocktail ensemble $375.00

#22220, calla lily evening ensemble $475.00

#22290, gardenia gala ballgown $500.00

#22250, Cissy's secret armoire trunk set (1997 – 1998) $1,100.00

21", 1998 MA Couture, each limited to 1,500

#22300, Cissy Paris, gold houndstooth outfit, sable, feathered hat $600.00

#22330, Cissy Barcelona, coral charmeuse with black lace $550.00

#22333, Cissy Barcelona, African-American $700.00

#22320, Cissy Milan, long fur coat and fur-trimmed hat $650.00

#22310, Cissy Venice, brocade gown, blue taffeta cape $600.00

#22340, Cissy Budapest, blue dress and coat trimmed with fur $650.00

21", 1999, Cissy Designer Originals (see Madame Alexander Doll Company under Special Events/Exclusives)

21", 2000, #25555, Rome Cissy $450.00

#26980, New York Cissy $425.00

#25585, Vienna Cissy $450.00

#25560, Cairo Cissy $475.00

#25565, Shanghai Cissy $350.00

#26865, Hollywood Cissy $450.00

Dating Cissette Dolls

Eyelids: 1975, beige; 1958, pale pink; 1959 – 1963, beige

Clothes: 1957 – 1958, darts in bodice; 1959 – 1963, no darts except ballgowns

Fingernails: 1962 – 1963, polished

Eyebrows: 1957 – 1963, single stroked

Body and legs: 1957 – 1963, head strung with hook and rubber band, legs jointed with plastic socket

Feet: 1957 – 1963, high heels

Wigs: 1957 – 1958, three rows of stitching; 1959 – 1963, zigzag stitches except 1961 – 1962 with fancy hairdos, then three rows; 1963, few have rooted hair in cap, glued to head or removable wigs

Tags: 1957 – 1962, turquoise; 1963, dark blue

Portrette: 1968 – 1973, two or three stroke eyebrows, blue eyelids, no earrings, strung head with hook, high heels

Jacqueline: 1961 – 1962, two or three stroke eyebrows, side seam brunette wig, small curl on forehead, blue eyelids, eyeliner, painted lashes to sides of eyes, polished nails, head strung, socket jointed hips with side seams, high heels

Sleeping Beauty: 1959 only, three stroke eyebrows, pink eyelids, no earrings, mouth painted wider, no knee joints, flat feet, jointed with metal hooks

Sound of Music: 1971 – 1973 (Brigitta, Liesl, Louisa), two stroke eyebrows, the rest same as Portrettes

Tinker Bell: 1969 only, two stroke eyebrows, blue eyelids, painted lashes to side of eyes, no earrings, hair rooted into wig cap, head and legs strung with metal hooks

Margot: 1961, same as Jacqueline, except has three stroke eyebrows and elaborate hairdos

Cissy

#26866, Hollywood Cissy, African-American $500.00
#27005, Romantic Dreams Cissy $400.00
#28450, Peacock Rose, limited to 600 ....$900.00
#27370, Yardley Cissy, blue dress, blonde $650.00
21", 2001, all limited to 500 pieces
   #28415, Society Stroll Cissy (Caucasian) $450.00
   #28415, Society Stroll Cissy (African-American) $550.00
   #28441, Royal Reception Cissy $550.00
   #28430, Black and White Ball Cissy $450.00
   #28420, A Day in the Life of Cissy, trunk set $500.00
   #28435, Haute Couture, black suit, hat with feathers $450.00
   #28440, On the Avenue Yardley Cissy, green suit, plush dog $450.00
   #31235, Promise of Spring Cissy $700.00
21", Cissy Amethyst, #32070, 2001, limited to 350 ....$450.00
21", Manhattan Gothic, #31965, 2001, limited to 100 ....$1,200.00
21", Madame Du Pompador Cissy, #31520, 2001, limited to 100 ....$1,700.00
21", Prima Donna Cissy, #31970, 2001, limited to 100 ....$1,200.00
21", #33175, 2002, Maimey Cissy, blue dress, white sweater, limited to 350 ....$500.00
   #33165, 2002, Blue Bird Cissy, embroidered bluebird skirt $450.00
   #33166, 2002, Blue Bird Cissy, African-American, limited to 150 ....$500.00
Renaissance Garden Cissy, 21", #33200, 2002, evening gown, embroidered skirt, limited to 350 ....$500.00
Taffeta Romance Cissy, 21", #33160, 2002, pink ballgown, black trim, limited to 350 ....$450.00
Dance the Night Away Cissy, 21", #33160, 2002, black fitted long gown, black gloves and purse, limited to 350 ...$450.00
Cissy's European Holiday Trunk set, 21", #33190, 2002, trunk, two dresses, ballgown, wigs, etc., limited to 350 .$500.00
Equestrian Cissy, 21", #33965, 2002, black hat, jodhpurs, brocade vest, limited to 200 ....$475.00
Baby Doe Cissy, 21", #33960, 2002, blue plaid bustle dress, umbrella, limited to 200 ....$650.00
Pompadour Cissy, 21", #34400, 2002, vintage eighteenth century design, green jacket, straw hat $850.00
Sitting Pretty Yardley Cissy, 21", #33185, 2002, slack set, chair, pillows $375.00
80th Anniversary Cissy, 21", #34980, 2002, black top and crochet long skirt, limited to 200 ....$550.00
Fifties Swing Cissy, 21", #36090, 2003, black dress and hat with flowers, limited to 350 ....$500.00
Sixties Go-Go Cissy, 21", #36095, 2003, red, white, and black short dress, limited to 350 ....$400.00
Seventies Strut Cissy, 21", #36100, 2003, hot pants, long black coat, limited to 250 ....$500.00
Seventies Strut Cissy, 21", #36101, 2003, African-American, limited to 350 ....$500.00
Eighties Elegance Cissy, 21", #36105, 2003, ballgown, red shawl, limited to 350 ....$500.00
Dressed to the Nines Cissy, 21", #36110, 2003, black cocktail dress, limited to 350 ....$500.00
Center Stage Cissy 2000, 21", #36255, 2003, pink ruffle dress, limited to 350 ....$450.00
Pocahontas, 21", 2003, #36080, English Court costume, limited to 200 ....$550.00
Cocktails, 21", 2003, #36070, copper cocktail dress, black hat, limited to 200 ....$500.00
Pompadour Cissy Summer, 21", #36745, 2003, gold court gown, limited to 200 ....$700.00
In Her Honor, 21", #36140, 2003, blue long gown, pink cape, limited to 350 ....$550.00
Lavensque Yardley Cissy, 21", #36085, 2003, black suit, table, cup, bowl $450.00
English Waltz Cissy, 21", #36065, 2003, lacy white ballgown, limited to 350 ....$600.00
Curtain Call Cissy, 21", #36060, 2003, blue ballet outfit, limited to 350 ....$400.00
Cissy Boutique, 21", #38010, 2003, black dress, accessories, limited to 250 ....$500.00
Dorothy Cissy, 21", #36355, 2003, flat chested torso, Toto in basket $325.00
Pompadour Cissy "Fall" and Louis XV, 21", #38300, 2004, lavish court costumes, three dogs $1,500.00
Smokin', 21", #38305, 2004, silk plaid long skirt over pants, 1950s style, limited to 200 ....$400.00
The Sweet Life Cissy, 21", #38320, 2004, green silk sheath dress, straw hat $400.00
Opulent Shimmer Boutique Cissy, 21", #38375, 2004, blue hair, long sequin sparkle dress $400.00
Object of Desire Cissy, 21", #38330, 2004, long red gown with bustle, black hat $400.00
Cissy and The City, 21", #38325, 2004, pants, long brown trench coat $400.00
Life in the Limelight Cissy, 21", #38345, 2004, long gold silk dress $400.00
Life in the Limelight Cissy African-American, 21", #38348, 2004 ....$400.00
Romancing the Railway Cissy, 21", #38315, 2004, suit, trunk with extra clothes $400.00
Cissy Bride — 21", #52011, porcelain portrait, 1994 only $350.00
Cissy by Scassi — (see FAO Schwarz under Special Events/Exclusives)

Cissy Godey Bride — 21", #011, porcelain, 1993 only $400.00

Civil War — 18" h.p., #2010B, 1953 only, Glamour Girls Series, white taffeta with red roses (Margaret) . . . . .$1,800.00 up

Clara — 8", #25330, 2000 – 2001, long blue gown with nutcracker $90.00

Clara & the Nutcracker — 14", #1564, 1992 only (Louisa/Jennifer) $85.00

Clarabell Clown — 19", 1951 – 1953 . . . .$350.00

    29" $575.00

    49" $1,000.00

Clara's Party Dress — 8", #14570, 1995, Nutcracker Series $70.00

Classic Ballerina — 16", #22700, white tulle and satin (1999) $125.00

Classic Bride — 16", #22690, white tulle and lace gown (1999) $125.00

Claudette — 10", #1123 (in peach), 1988 – 1989, Portrette (Cissette) $85.00

Claudia — 14", #34360, 2003, blue dress with lace $90.00

Cleopatra — 12", #1315, 1980 – 1985, Portraits of History series $65.00

    10", #86002, 1996 Platinum Collection $90.00

Cleveland, Frances — 1985 – 1987, fourth set Presidents' Ladies/First Ladies Series (Mary Ann) $100.00

Clover Kid — 7" compo., 1935 – 1936 (Tiny Betty) $375.00

Clown — 8", #305, 1990 – 1992 only, Americana Series, has painted face (Wendy) $70.00

    Baby — 8", #464 – 1955, has painted face (Wendy) . . . .$1,000.00 up

    Bobo — 8" h.p., #310, 1991 – 1992 (Wendy Ann) $100.00

    Pierrot — 8", #561, 1956 only (Wendy Ann) . . . .$1,000.00 up

        14", 1991 only, #1558, white costume with red trim $90.00

    Stilts — 8", #320, 1992 – 1993, doll on stilts $125.00

Clue Game Doll — 8", #25255, 2000, maid costume $65.00

Coca-Cola Carhop — 10", #17400, 1997 – 2000, roller skates, #17401, brunette $90.00

Coca-Cola Celebrates American Aviation — 10", #17380, 1998 – 1999 . . . .$125.00

Coca-Cola Fantasy — 10", #31210 – white, #31213 – black, 1997 – 1998 . . . .$140.00

Coca-Cola 1920s — 10", #28280, 2001, long white dress with lace $125.00

Coca-Cola Nostalgia — 16", #17490, 1999, white lace dress $175.00

Coca-Cola Off to the North Pole — 8", #25245, 2001, with bear $100.00

Coca-Cola School Days — 8" #28275, 2001 – 2002, includes lunchbox $100.00

Coca-Cola Sock Hop — 10", #26255, 2001, red checked skirt $125.00

Coca-Cola Victorian Calendar Doll — 10", #17360, 1998 – 1999 . . . .$150.00

Coca-Cola Winter Fun Wendy — 8", #17370, 1999, red ski outfit $90.00

Coco — 21" plastic/vinyl, 1966, in various clothes (other than Portrait) . . . .$2,000.00 up

    In sheath style ballgown . . . .$2,200.00 up

    14", #1558, 1991 – 1992, Classic Series (Mary Ann) $85.00

    10", #1140, 1989 – 1992, Portrette, dressed in all black (Cissette) $75.00

    16", #31240, 1997 – 1998, travel wardrobe and dog, Cleo $375.00

    16", #22400, 1998, Belle Epoque, includes houndstooth and glitter gown outfits $275.00

Collecting Bears Teddy and Me — 8", #33020, 2002 – 2003, 8" doll and 5" bear in matching blue outfits $120.00

Collecting Butterflies — 8", #28240, 2001, lavender dress with butterflies $55.00

Collecting Buttons — 8", #28245, 2001, white dress trimmed in pink $55.00

Collecting Dolls — 8", #30940, 2001 – 2002, pink lacy dress with doll and dollhouse case $80.00

Collecting Seashells — 8", #28250, 2001, yellow dress with seashells $55.00

Collecting Trains — 8", #28585, 2001 – 2002, striped overalls with Bachmann train $100.00

Collector Pin Series — 1999, 2½" polyresin miniature doll $10.00

Collectors United — (see Special Events/Exclusives)

Colleen — 10", #1121, 1988 only, Portrette, in green (Cissette) $85.00

Colonial — 7" compo., 1937 – 1938 (Tiny Betty) $325.00

    9" compo., 1936 – 1939 (Little Betty) $350.00

    8" h.p., BKW, #389, #789, 1962 – 1964 (Wendy Ann) $325.00

Columbian Sailor — (see U.F.D.C. under Special Events/Exclusives)

Columbine — 8", #14575 – 1995, Nutcracker Series $60.00

Columbus, Christopher — 8" h.p., #328, 1992 only, Americana Series $125.00

Comedienne — 10", #20120, clown, 1996 Cirque du Soleil Series $90.00

Computer Age Wendy — 8", #17820, 1999, comes with laptop and cell phone $70.00

Confederate Officer

Confederate Officer — 12", 1990 – 1991, Scarlett Series (Nancy Drew) $85.00
    8" h.p., 1991 – 1992, Scarlett Series (see Ashley)
Congratulations — 8" h.p., #21180, 1998 (Maggie), pink dress, balloons $60.00
Contemporary Bride — 10", 2001 ....$135.00
Cookie — 19" compo./cloth, 1938 – 1940, must be in excellent condition $650.00
Coolidge, Grace — 14", 1989 – 1990, sixth set Presidents' Ladies/First Ladies Series (Louisa) $100.00
Coppelia — 16", #28390, 2001, pink ballerina $175.00
Coppertone Beach Set — 8", #12110, 1998 – 1999, bikini, umbrella, suntan lotion $125.00
Coquette — 10", #39255, pants, sweater, purse $80.00
    10", #39600, red suit $80.00
Coral and Leopard Travel Ensemble — 10", #22180, 1997 ....$125.00
Cornelia — Cloth and felt, 1930s ....$700.00 up
    21", #2191, 1972, Portrait, dressed in pink with full cape (Jacqueline) $425.00
    #2191, 1973, pink with ¾ length jacket $400.00
    #2296, 1974, blue with black trim $350.00
    #2290, 1975, rose red with black trim and hat $325.00
    #2293, 1976, pink with black trim and hat $325.00
    #2212, 1978, blue with full cape $325.00
Coroner — 8", #38395, 2004, Wizard of Oz series $85.00
Cossack — 8" h.p., #511, 1989 – 1991 (Wendy Ann) $65.00
Costume Party — #37785, 2003 – 2004, mask, dog, black hat $85.00
Country Christmas — 14", #1543, 1991 – 1992 only, Classic Series (Mary Ann) $125.00
    8", #20190, 1999 – 2000, calico dress, snowman $65.00
Country Club — 8", #37980, Latin, 2004, blue flower dress, large straw hat $90.00
Country Cousins — 10" cloth, 1940s $575.00
    26" cloth, 1940s $650.00
    30" cloth, 1940s $750.00
    16½", 1958, mint (Mary-Bel) $375.00
Country Fair — (see Wendy Loves)
Count Your Blessings Angel — 10", #36575, 2004, pink costume $140.00
Courtney and Friends — (see Madame Alexander Doll Company under Special Events/Exclusives)
Courtyard — 8", #38840, 2004, pink elaborate gown, limited to 1,000 ....$140.00
Cousin Grace — 8" h.p., BKW, #432, 1957 only (Wendy Ann) ....$1,900.00 up

Cowboy, 8" (Wendy), BK, 1967 – 1969.

Cowgirl, 8", BK (Wendy), 1967 – 1970.

Cousin Karen — 8" h.p., BKW, #620, 1956 only (Wendy Ann) . . . .$1,800.00 up
Cousin Marie & Mary — 8" h.p. (Marie, #465; Mary, #462), 1963 only (Wendy Ann), each . . . .$1,000.00 up
Cowardly Lion — 8", #431, 1993, Storybook Series, #140431, 1994 – 1996 . . . .$75.00
   #13220, 1997, 2003 – 2004 (Wizard of Oz), tan lion costume $70.00
   5", #28695, 2001 – 2002, porcelain $85.00
Cowboy — 8" h.p., BK, #732, 1967 – 1969, Americana Series (Wendy Ann) $375.00
   8", 1987 (see M.A.D.C. under Special Events/Exclusives)
Cowgirl — 8" h.p., BK, #724, 1967 – 1970, Americana/Storybook Series (Wendy Ann) $350.00
   10", #1132, 1990 – 1991, Portrette, white/red outfit (Cissette) $75.00
Crayola, Americana — 8", #17840 – 17873, felt outfits, with Crayolas . . . .$45.00 ea.
Crayola Meagan — 14", #25470, 2000, brown dress, with Crayolas $75.00
Crete — 8" straight leg, #529, 1987 only $75.00
Croatia — 8" h.p., #110543, 1994 (Wendy Ann) $65.00
Crockett, Davy, Boy or Girl — 8" h.p., 1955 only (Boy – #446; Girl – #443) (Wendy Ann) . . . .$700.00 up ea.
Cruella DeVille — 10", #38370, 2004, with three 2" puppies $150.00
Cry Dolly — 14" – 16" vinyl, 1953, 12-piece layette $250.00
   14", 16", 19", in swimsuit . . . .$100.00 – 185.00
   16" – 19" all vinyl, dress or rompers . . . .$125.00 – 250.00
Cuba — 8", #11548, 1995 only, has round brown face $65.00
   8", #38600, 2004, includes maracas $90.00
Cuddly — 10½" cloth, 1942 – 1944 . . . .$375.00
   17" cloth, 1942 – 1944 . . . .$400.00
Cupid — 8", #13860, 1998 – 1999 (Maggie), white costume, bow, arrow $75.00
Curly Locks — 8" h.p., #472, 1955 only (Wendy Ann) . . . .$950.00 up
   8" straight leg, #421, 1987 – 1988, Storybook Series, 1997 (Wendy Ann) $65.00
   8", #28315, 2001 – 2002, print dress with flowers $85.00
Cute Little Baby — 14", 1994 – 1995, doll only, $85.00. With layette and basket $200.00
Cutie Patootie — 18", #28320, 2001, cloth, Mary Engelbreit, pink dress $45.00
Cynthia — 15" h.p., 1952 only (black "Margaret") . . . .$850.00 up
   18", 1952 only . . . .$900.00 up
   23", 1952 only . . . . $1,200.00 up
Cyrano — 8" h.p., #140505, 1994 only, Storyland Series (Pinocchio) $65.00
Czarina Alexandra — 8", #12620, 1999, blue satin and gold $75.00
Czechoslovakia — 7" compo., 1935 – 1937 (Tiny Betty) $325.00
   8" h.p., BK, #764, 1972 (Wendy Ann) $100.00
      Straight leg, #0764, #564, 1973 – 1975, marked "Alex" $70.00
      Straight leg, #536, 1976 – 1987, marked "Alexander" $55.00
   8", #536, 1985 – 1987 . . . .$55.00
   8", #521, reintroduced 1992 – 1993 only (Wendy Ann) $55.00
Daddy's Little Princess — 8", #38920, 2004, pink dress, tiara $85.00
Daddy's My Hero — 8", #36765, 2003 – 2004, blue pleated dress, police hat $80.00
Daffy Down Dilly — 8" straight legs, #429, 1986 only, Storybook Series (Wendy Ann or Maggie) $60.00
Dahl, Arlene (Pink Champagne) — 18" h.p., 1950 – 1951, red wig, lavender gown (Maggie), mint . . . . .$6,500.00 up
Daisy — 10", #1110, 1987 – 1989, Portrette Series, white lace over yellow (Cissette) $70.00
Daisy Fairy — 8", #36890, 2003 – 2004, pink long dress, yellow petal trim $90.00
Daisy Munchkin — 8", #28770, 2001, white outfit with daisies $75.00
Daisy Resort Cissette Ensemble — 10", #22380, 1998, silk, linen outfit, chair $150.00
Dance of the Flowers — 8", #25225, 2000 – 2001, blue embroidered tutu $65.00
Dancing Clara — 8", #34305, 2002, pink dress, holding nutcracker $85.00
Dancing Princess Blue — 10", #32050, 2000, blue tulle gown $100.00
Dancing Princess Gold — 10", #32055, 2000, gold tulle gown $100.00
Dancing Princess Magenta — 10", #32045, 2000, tulle and lace gown $100.00
Dancing Queen Total Moves Wendy — 8", #38265, 2004 . . . .$95.00
Danger's Bath — 8", #38490, 2004, swimsuit with dog, tub, etc. $95.00
Danish — 7" compo., 1937 – 1941 (Tiny Betty) $325.00
   9" compo., 1938 – 1940 (Little Betty) $350.00

Dare, Virginia

Dare, Virginia — 9" compo., 1940 – 1941 (Little Betty) $450.00
Darlene — 18" cloth/vinyl, 1991 – 1992 ....$100.00
Darling Little Dancer — 8", #30335, 1999, pink tulle, limited to 2,500 ....$90.00
David and Diana — 8" (see FAO Schwarz under Special Events/Exclusives)
David Copperfield — 7" compo., 1936 – 1938 (Tiny Betty) $350.00
   14" compo., 1938 only (Wendy Ann) $750.00
   16" cloth, early 1930s, Dickens character ....$850.00 up
David Quack-a-Field or Twistail — cloth/felt, 1930s ....$700.00 up
David, The Little Rabbi — 8" (see Celia's Dolls under Special Events/Exclusives)
Day of Week Dolls — 7", 1935 – 1940 (Tiny Betty) ....$350.00 ea.
   9" – 11" compo., 1936 – 1938 (Little Betty) ....$375.00 ea.
   13" compo., 1939 (Wendy Ann) $450.00
Day to Remember — 10", 2001, bride $125.00
Dear America Series — 18" re-creations from *Dear America* Book Series
   Abigail Jane Stewart, 1999 – 2000, 18", blue print dress $80.00
   Catherine Carey Logan, 1999 – 2000, 18", Pilgrim costume $80.00
   Margaret Ann Brady, 1999 – 2000, 18", pink dress $80.00
   Remember Patience Whipple, 1999 – 2000, 18", red vest, skirt $80.00
   Clotee, a Slave Girl, 2000, #25665, African-American, brown outfit $80.00
   Emma Simpson, a Southern Belle, 2000, #25660, long beige dress $80.00
   Sara Nita, a Navajo Girl, 2000, #25655, black Indian outfit $80.00
   Zipporah Feldman, a Jewish Immigrant, 2000, #25650 ....$80.00
Dearest — 12" vinyl baby, 1962 – 1964 ....$125.00 – 175.00
Deborah Bride — 16", #25595, 2000, remake of 1949 – 1951 costume $185.00
Debra (Deborah) — 21", 1949 – 1951, Portrette, ballerina with extra make-up (Margaret) ....$6,500.00 up
   21", 1949 – 1951, bride with five-piece layered bustle in back ....$7,500.00 up
Debutante — 18" h.p., 1953 only (Maggie) ....$1,250.00 up
December — 14", #1528, 1989 only, Classic Series (Mary Ann) $100.00
Deck the Halls — 8", #35990, 2003 – 2004, red print dress with garland $85.00
DeFoe, Dr. Allen — 14" – 15" compo., 1937 – 1939 ....$1,600.00 up
Degas — 21" compo., 1945 – 1946, Portrait (Wendy Ann) ....$2,250.00 up
Degas Ballerina (The Star) — 10", #13910, 1998 – 1999 (Cissette), white tutu $85.00
   10", #25305, 2000 – 2001, long pink tutu with flowers $90.00
Degas "Dance Lesson" — 14", #241598, 1994 ....$80.00

Danish, 7", composition (Tiny Betty), original clothes.

Degas Girl — 14", #1475 (#1575 from 1974), 1967 – 1987 (20-year production), Portrait Children and Fine Arts Series (Mary Ann) $65.00
Degas' Rehersal Shadow Box — 10", 2001, #28410, white costume, gold shadow box $150.00
Delightful Afternoon — 10", #30410, 2001, long pink gown $120.00
Delilah — 8" h.p., #14583, 1995 only, Bible Series $90.00
Denmark — 10" h.p., 1962 – 1963 (Cissette) $700.00
   8" h.p., BK, #769, 1970 – 1972 (Wendy Ann) $100.00
   8" h.p., straight leg, #0769 – 569, 1973 – 1975, marked "Alex" (Wendy) $65.00
   8" h.p., straight leg, #546, 1976 – 1989, marked "Alexander" (1985 –1987 white face) (Wendy) $60.00
   8" reintroduced, #519, 1991 only (Wendy Ann) $55.00
Desert Storm — (see Welcome Home)
Dewdrop Fairy — 8", #28495, 2001 – 2002, blue tulle costume $85.00
Diamond Beauty — 21", 1998, black gown $900.00
Diamond Dance — 8", #26030, 2000, long pink gown, rhinestones .$100.00
Diamond Lil — 10" (see M.A.D.C. under Special Events/Exclusives)
Diana — 14", 1993 – 1994, Anne of Green Gables Series, trunk and wardrobe $225.00
   Tea dress, came with tea set, 1993 only $125.00

Sunday Social, 8", #260417, 1994 – 1995 (Wendy Ann) $125.00

Sunday Social, 14", #261503, 1994 ....$100.00

Dickinson, Emily — 14", #1587, 1989 only, Classic Series (Mary Ann) $90.00

Dicksie & Ducksie — Cloth/felt, 1930s ....$700.00 up

Dietrich, Marlene Shanghai Express — 16", #33485, 2002, long red coat dress, limited to 1,500 ....$160.00

Dilly Dally Sally — 7" compo., 1937 – 1942 (Tiny Betty) $325.00

9" compo., 1938 – 1939 (Little Betty) $350.00

Ding Dong Bell — 7" compo., 1937 – 1942 (Tiny Betty) $325.00

Dinner at Eight — 10", #1127, 1989 – 1991, Portrette, black/white dress (Cissette) $60.00

Dinosaur — 8" h.p., #343, 1993 – 1994, Americana Series $70.00

Dion, Celine — 10", 1999 (Cissette), long gown, heart necklace $110.00

Dionne Furniture — (no dolls)

Scooter, holds five ....$325.00 up

Basket case, holds five $250.00

Divided high chair, holds five ....$325.00 up

Table and chairs, five-piece set $450.00

Ferris wheel, holds five ....$500.00 up

Bath/shower ....$250.00 up

Wagon, holds five ....$425.00 up

Playpen, holds five ....$300.00 up

Crib, holds five ....$300.00 up

Tricycle ....$175.00 up

Merry-go-round, holds five ....$400.00 up

High chair for one $150.00

Dionne Quints — Original mint or very slight craze. Each has own color: Yvonne – pink, Annette – yellow,
Cecile – green, Emilie – lavender, Marie – blue

20" compo. toddlers, 1938 – 1939 ....$700.00 ea., $4,200.00 set

19" compo. toddlers, 1936 – 1938 ....$700.00 ea., $4,200.00 set

16" – 17" compo. toddlers, 1937 – 1939 ....$650.00 ea., $3,600.00 set

11" compo. toddlers, 1937 – 1938, wigs and sleep eyes ....$400.00 ea., $2,200.00 set

11" compo. toddlers, 1937 – 1938, molded hair and sleep eyes ....$400.00 ea., $2,200.00 set

11" compo. babies, 1936, wigs and sleep eyes ....$400.00 ea., $2,200.00 set

Dionne Quint, 14", 1937 – 1938, all composition, original clothes and name pin.

Dionne Quints, 8", composition.

Dionne Quints

11" compo. babies, 1936, molded hair and sleep eyes ....$400.00 ea., $2,200.00 set
8" compo. toddlers, 1935 – 1939, molded hair or wigs and painted eyes ....$300.00 ea., $1,500.00 set
8" compo. babies, 1935 – 1939, molded hair or wigs and painted eyes ....$300.00 ea., $1,500.00 set
14" cloth/compo., 1938 ....$475.00 ea., $3,100.00 set
17" cloth/compo., 1938 ....$575.00 ea., $3,600.00 set
22" cloth/compo., 1936 – 1937 ....$750.00 up
24" all cloth, 1935 – 1936, must be mint ....$1,200.00 ea.
16" all cloth, 1935 – 1936, must be mint ....$900.00 up
8" h.p., 1998, 75th Anniversary Set with carousel, #12230 ....$450.00
8" Yvonne, Marie, Annette, Cecile, Emilie, 1998 ....$85.00 ea.
Nursery (cardboard) with Dr. Dafoe, nurse, 8" quints, and furniture $7,000.00
Disney — (see Special Events/Exclusives)
Dogs — (see Poodles)
Doll Finders — (see Special Events/Exclusives)
Doll Hospital Nurse — 8" #33575, 2002, red dress and nurse's hat with 2½" doll $80.00
Dolls of the Month — 7" – 8" compo., 1937 – 1939, Birthday Dolls (Tiny Betty) $350.00
Dolls 'n Bearland — (see Special Events/Exclusives)
Dolly — 8", #436, 1988 – 1989, Storybook Series (Wendy Ann), 1997 ....$75.00
Dolly Dears — (see Special Events/Exclusives)
Dolly Dryper — 11" vinyl, 1952 only, seven-piece layette $300.00
Dolly Levi (Matchmaker) — 10" Portrette, 1994 only $75.00
Dominican Republic — 8" straight leg, #544, 1986 – 1988 (1985 – 1986 white face) $60.00
Dormouse — 8", #13090, 1998 – 2000, mouse in sugar bowl with spoon $100.00
Dorothy — 14", #1532, 1990 – 1993, Wizard of Oz, all blue/white check dress and solid blue pinafore (Mary Ann) $100.00
8" h.p., #464, 1991 – 1993, #140464, 1994 – 1995, blue/white check, white bodice (Wendy Ann),
    Wizard of Oz $100.00
8" h.p., emerald green dress special, mid-year special (see Madame Alexander Doll Co. under Special Events/Exclusives)
8" h.p., #13200, 1997 – 1999, blue check dress, basket with Toto, #13201, 2000 – 2001 ....$80.00
8", #13202, 2003 – 2004, ruby slippers, Toto in basket, blue check dress $60.00
8", #38715, 2004, limited to 1,000, blue check silk dress $95.00
14" plastic/vinyl, #87007, 1996 ....$125.00
15" cloth, #25545, 2000 – 2001, blue check dress, with Toto $50.00
5" porcelain, #27065, 2000 – 2004, blue check dress, with Toto $85.00
10", #36775, 2003 – 2004, blue check dress with 5" Lullaby, Flower Bonnet and Mayor Munchkin, Toto $180.00
21", #36355, Dorothy Cissy, flat chested torso, Toto in basket $350.00

Dionne Quintuplets, 8", with Quint furniture, 1930s, composition.

Dominican Republic, 8", #544, 1986 – 1988 (Wendy).

Dottie Dumbunnie — cloth/felt, 1930s ....$800.00 up

Dream Dance — 10", #26180, 2000 (Cissette), blue, short party dress $80.00

    10", #26175, 2000 (Cissette), black bodice, long tulle gown $90.00

Dressed for Opera — 18" h.p., 1953 only (Margaret) ....$1,800.00 up

Dressed Like Daddy — 8", #17002, 1996, white or black $75.00

Dressed Like Mommy — 8", #17001, 1996 – 1998, white or black $75.00

Drucilla — (see M.A.D.C. under Special Events/Exclusives)

Drum Majorette — (see Majorette)

Duchess Eliza, The — 10", #20114, 1996 Classics $90.00

Duchess, The — 8", #14613, 1996, Alice in Wonderland Series $95.00

Dude Ranch — 8" h.p., #449, 1955 only (Wendy Ann) ....$750.00 up

Dudley Do-Right and Nell — 8", #15140, 1999, Dudley in Mounty outfit (Maggie), Nell,

    (Wendy) includes rope, train track, and backdrop $165.00

Dumplin' Baby — 20" – 23½", 1957 – 1958 ....$175.00

Dutch — 7" compo., 1935 – 1939 (Tiny Betty) $300.00

    9" compo. boy or girl, 1936 – 1941 ....$325.00

    8" h.p., BKW, #777, 1964, boy* (Wendy) $150.00

      BK, #777, #0777, 1965 – 1972 ....$100.00

    8" h.p., straight leg, #777, *0777, 1972 – 1973, marked "Alex" $75.00

    8" h.p., BKW, #391 – 791, 1961 – 1964, girl* $125.00

    8" h.p., BK, #791, 1965 – 1972 ....$100.00

    8" BKW, #791, 1964 only (Maggie) $150.00

Dutch Lullaby — 8", #499, 1993, #140499, 1994, Wynkin, Blynkin & Nod, in wooden shoe ...$200.00

Easter — 8" h.p. #21020, 1998, hat with bunny ears, floral dress $65.00

Easter Bonnet — 14", #1562, 1992 (Louisa/Jennifer) $100.00

    8" h.p., #10383 – 10385, 1995 – 1996, three hair colors, Special Occasions Series $65.00

    8" h.p., #10401, 1996, African-American $65.00

Easter Bunny — 8" (see Child at Heart under Special Events/Exclusives)

    8", #26675, 2001, blue dress, hat, basket with bunny $100.00

Easter Doll — 8" h.p., 1968 only, special for West Coast, in yellow dress (Wendy Ann), limited to 300 ....$1,400.00 up

    7½" SLNW, #361, 1953, organdy dress, doll carries basket with chicken ....$925.00 up

    14" plastic/vinyl, 1968 only (Mary Ann), limited to 300 ....$600.00 up

Easter Egg Hunt — 8", #25020, 2000 – 2001, white dress, straw hat, basket $90.00

Easter Hop — 8", #37965, 2004, pink check dress, bunny $70.00

Easter Morning — 8", #34090, 2002, pink smocked dress, bunny purse $80.00

Easter of Yesterday — 1995 (see C.U. under Special Events/Exclusives)

Easter Splendor — 8", #35445, 2003 – 2004, pink hat, white dress, basket, eggs, Bible $80.00

Easter Sunday — 8" h.p., #340 or #340-1, 1993 only, Americana Series, black or white doll ...$65.00

    8", #21510 (white), #21513 (black), 1998 – 2000, yellow print dress, straw hat, basket ...$80.00

Ebony and Ivory Houndstooth Suit — 10", #22190, 1997 – 1998 ....$150.00

Ecuador — 8" h.p., BK & BKW, #878, 1963 – 1966 (Wendy Ann) $350.00

Edith and The Duckling — 8", #31800, with duck and Mr. Bear $85.00

Edith, The Lonely Doll — 16" plastic/vinyl, 1958 – 1959 (Mary-Bel) $350.00

    22", 1958 – 1959 ....$400.00

    8" h.p., #850, 1958 only (Wendy Ann) ....$700.00 up

    8", #34025, 2003 – 2004, pink check dress, 3" Mr. Bear $85.00

    8", #36930, 2004, wood doll, 3" Mr. Bear, limited to 750 ....$250.00

    8", #37205, 2004, Holiday Trunk Set, four outfits, Mr. Bear $220.00

Edith with Golden Hair — 18" cloth, 1940s $675.00

Edwardian — 18" h.p., #2001A, 1953 only, pink embossed cotton, Glamour Girl Series (Margaret) ...$2,200.00 up

    8" h.p., #0200, 1953 –1959 (Wendy Ann) ....$1,000.00 up

80th Anniversary Cissette — 10", #34985, 2003, pink dress $150.00

80th Anniversary Cissy — 21" #34980, 2003, black crochet dress $550.00

80th Anniversary Wendy — 8", #34975, 2002, pink dress $75.00

Eisenhower, Mamie — 14", 1989 – 1990, sixth set Presidents' Ladies/First Ladies Series (Mary Ann) ...$100.00

* Both became Netherlands in 1974.

Egypt

Egypt — 8" straight leg, #543, 1986 – 1989 (round brown face) $65.00
Egyptian — 7" – 8" compo., 1936 – 1940 (Tiny Betty) $350.00
    9" compo., 1936 – 1940 (Little Betty) $375.00
Egypt with Sarcophagus — 8", #24110, 1998 – 2000, pharaoh costume $100.00
Elaine — 18" h.p., 1954 only, Me and My Shadow Series, blue organdy dress (Cissy) ....$1,800.00 up
    8" h.p., #0035E, 1954 only, matches 18" (Wendy Ann) ....$950.00 up
Elegant Emerald — 8", #32085, 2000 – 2002, long green ballgown $95.00
Elise — 16½" h.p./vinyl arms (18", 1963 only), 1957 – 1964, jointed ankles and knees, face color
    In street clothes or blouse, slacks, and sash ....$475.00 up
    In ballgown, formal, or Portrait ....$750.00 up
    In riding habit, 1963 (Mary-Bel head) $425.00
    Ballerina, rare yellow tutu, red hair $900.00
    With Mary-Bel head, 1962 only $425.00
    18", 1963 only, with bouffant hairstyle $450.00
    17" h.p./vinyl, 1961 – 1962, one-piece arms and legs, jointed ankles and knees $350.00
    18" h.p./vinyl, 1963 – 1964, jointed ankles and knees $375.00
        In riding habit $375.00
    17" plastic/vinyl, 1966 only, street dress $375.00
    17", 1966 – 1972, in trunk/trousseau ....$650.00 up
    17", 1972 – 1973, Portrait $250.00
    17", 1966, 1976 – 1977, in formal $175.00
    17", 1966 – 1987, Bride $150.00
    17", 1966 – 1991, Ballerina $125.00
    17", 1966 – 1989, in any discontinued costume ....$100.00 up
    16", 1997, #22060, Firebird, red and gold tutu $125.00
    16", 1997, #22050, Giselle, aqua tutu, rose tiara $125.00
    16", 1997, #22040, Swan Lake, white tulle tutu $125.00
Elise/Leslie — 14", #1560, 1988 only (Mary Ann) $80.00
Eliza — 14", #1544, 1991 only, Classic Series (Louisa) $100.00
Elizabethan Bride — 10", #25005, 2000, Cissette $150.00
Elizabethan Pin Cushion — 2000 – 2001, pink #26480, gold #25645, 8", Wendy, brocade as a pin cushion $100.00
Eliza the Flower Girl — 10", #20113, 1996 Classics $100.00
Eloise — 8", #80680, 2000 – 2002, vinyl, Eloise lace, white blouse, navy pleated skirt $40.00
    8", #33405, 2002, vinyl, Eloise in Paris, gray check coat $45.00
    8", #27701, 2001 – 2002, Eloise at Christmastime $45.00
    18", #80690, 2000 – 2003, cloth, Eloise face, same costume as 8" doll $45.00

    36", Just Like Me, #30936, 2001, cloth with rag doll $200.00
    8", Eloise Tea Party, #30810, 2001 – 2002, vinyl, white dress $45.00
    8", Eloise Loves to Dance, #30815, 2001, ballet $45.00
    12", Eloise Loves to Dance, #30935, 2001, cloth $40.00
    12", #27225, 2000 – 2003, poseable cloth $30.00
    8", #33410, 2002, Eloise in Moscow, gold coat, black hat $45.00
    8", #31670, Tea Party Trunk Set, trunk, tea set, clothes $150.00
    12", #31855, 2002 – 2003, Eloise in Paris, blue coat, travel bag,
        passport $75.00
    8", #27710, 2000 – 2003, overnight kit, sleeping bag, clothes ...$100.00
Emerald City Guard — 8", #31395, 2001 – 2002, black costume
    with sequin hat $95.00
Emerald City and Wizard Chamber — folding playscape, #25945,
    15" tall $350.00
Emerald Lass — 8", #27870, 2001, green dress $80.00
Emily — cloth/felt, 1930s $600.00
    14", #34350, 2002 – 2003, black and white dress $90.00
    5", #27420, 2003, petite, pink dress $20.00
Emily Elizabeth — 8", #26370, 2000 – 2002 (Maggie), with cloth
    16" Clifford dog $90.00
    5" petite Emily Elizabeth and 10" plush red Clifford dog $45.00

Elise, 17", #1755, 1970. Was also made in blue.

38

Emma — 10", #25335, 2000 (Cissette) long blue gown, straw hat $125.00
Emperor and Nightingale — 8", #33700, 2002, with bird cage $90.00
Empire Bride — 10" (Cissette), white lace gown (1999) $125.00
Empress Elizabeth of Austria — 10" (see My Doll House under Special Events/Exclusives)
Enchanted Doll House — (see Special Events/Exclusives)
Enchanted Evening — 21" Portrait, 1991 – 1992 only, different necklace than shown in catalog (Cissy) $325.00
England — 8", #24040, 1997 – 1999, Beefeater guard outfit $75.00
   8", #28560, 2001, Queen costume $70.00
English Guard — 8" h.p., BK, #764, 1966 – 1968, Portrait Children Series (Wendy Ann) $350.00
   8", #515, reintroduced 1989 – 1991, marked "Alexander" (Wendy Ann) $65.00
Entertaining the Troops — 8", #17550, 1999, red outfit, microphone $70.00
Equestrian Wendy — 8", #35575, 2003 – 2004, red jacket, crop, plush horse $95.00
Eskimo — 8" h.p., BK, #723, 1967 – 1969, Americana Series (Wendy Ann) $375.00
   9" compo., 1936 – 1939 (Little Betty) $350.00
   With Maggie Mixup face $375.00
Estonia — 8" straight leg, #545, 1986 – 1987 only (Wendy Ann) $65.00
Estrella — 18" h.p. (Maggie), lilac gown, 1953 . . . .$1,200.00 up
Eva Lovelace — 7" compo., 1935 only (Tiny Betty) $375.00
   Cloth, 1935 only $600.00
Evangeline — 18" cloth, 1930s . . . .$650.00 up
Eva Peron — 10", #22030, 1997, long white lace dress (Cissette) $100.00
Evening Cissette — 10", #38745, 2004, white dress, lavender trim $150.00
Evening of Romance — 10", #27010, 2000 (Cissette) black lace gown $125.00
Evening Star — 15" porcelain, black lace over pink satin (1999 – 2000) $140.00
Evil Sorceress — 8", #13610, 1997, long black velvet dress $75.00
Fairie-ality Trunk Set — 8", #31825, log trunk, three outfits, accessories, 2003 – 2004 . . . .$240.00
Fairy Godmother — 14", #1550, #1551, #1568, 1983 – 1992, Classic Series (Mary Ann, Louisa) $100.00
   Fairy Godmother outfit, 1983, M.A.D.C. (see Special Events/Exclusives)
   10" Portrette, #1156, 1993 only, blue/gold gown (Cissette) $90.00
   10", #14549, 1995 only, purple gown, white wig (Cissette) $80.00
   8", #13430, 1997 – 1999, dark blue hooded cloak $75.00
   8", #25920, 2000 – 2001 (Maggie), dark blue over light blue gown $80.00
Fairy of Beauty — 8", #13620, 1997 – 2003, pink tulle gown, wand with hearts, pointed hat $85.00
Fairy of Song — 8", #13630, 1997 – 2003, green tulle gown, wand with music notes $85.00
Fairy of Virtue — 8", #13640, 1997 – 2003, blue tulle gown, wand with stars, pointed hat $85.00
Fairy Princess — 7" – 8" compo., 1940 – 1943 (Tiny Betty) $375.00
   9" compo., 1939 – 1941 (Little Betty) $400.00
   11" compo., 1939 only (Wendy Ann) $400.00
   15" – 18" compo., 1939 – 1942 (Wendy Ann) $650.00
   21" – 22" compo., 1939, 1944 – 1946 (Wendy Ann) $900.00
Fairy Queen — 14½" compo., 1940 – 1946 (Wendy Ann) $700.00
   18" compo., 1940 – 1946 (Wendy Ann) $800.00
   14½" h.p., 1948 – 1950 (Margaret) $800.00
   18" h.p., 1949 – 1950 (Margaret) $950.00
Fairy Tales – Dumas – 9" compo., 1937 – 1941 (Little Betty) $375.00
Faith — 8" h.p., #486, 1961 only, Americana Series, plaid jumper/organdy blouse (Wendy Ann) . . . .$1,800.00 up
   8" h.p. (see Collectors United under Special Events/Exclusives)
Fall Angel — 8", #28360, 2001 – 2002, rust gown with leaves $80.00
Fannie Elizabeth — 8" (see Belks & Leggett under Special Events/Exclusives)
Fantasy — 8", 1990 (see Doll Finders under Special Events/Exclusives)
FAO Schwarz — (see Special Events/Exclusives)
Farmer In The Dell — 8", #37990, with dog, cat, mouse, and cheese $90.00
Farmer's Daughter — 8", 1991 (see Enchanted Doll House under Special Events/Exclusives)
Fashions of the Century — 14" – 18" h.p., 1954 – 1955 (Margaret, Maggie) . . . .$2,500.00 up
Father Christmas — 8" h.p., #100351, Americana Series $75.00

Father of the Bride

Father of the Bride — 10", #24623, 1996, white satin wedding gown $90.00
Father of Vatican City, The — 8", #24190, 1999, gold silk robe $75.00
50th Birthday Wendy — 8", #34710, 2002, blue dress $90.00
50 Years of Friendship — 8", #37950, 2003, two dolls, pink print $145.00
    8", blue print, magnetic kiss $145.00
Figure Eight Total Moves Wendy — 8", #39135, 2004, blue ice skating costume $90.00
Figurines — 1999, 6", polyresin replica of Alexander dolls . . . .$20.00 – 30.00
Fiji — 8", #38605, 2004, with plush shark $90.00
Fillmore, Abigail — 1982 – 1984, third set Presidents' Ladies/First Ladies Series (Louisa) $100.00
Fill My Heart — 8", #28745, 2002 – 2003, pink lace trimmed dress, large hat $85.00
    8", #28746, 2002 – 2003, African-American $85.00
Fill My Stocking — 8", #36000, 2003, cream dress, gold check apron, Lenox stocking ornament $90.00
Findlay, Jane — 1979 – 1981, first set Presidents' Ladies/First Ladies Series (Mary Ann) $100.00
Finland — 8" h.p., BK, #767, 1968 – 1972 (Wendy Ann) $100.00
    8" h.p., straight leg, #0767 – 567, 1973 – 1975, marked "Alex" $65.00
    8" h.p., straight leg, #567, 1976 – 1987, marked "Alexander" $55.00
Finnish — 7" compo., 1935 – 1937 (Tiny Betty) $300.00
Fire Fighter Wendy — 8", #31270, 1998 – 1999, yellow coat, red hat, and dog $85.00
Fireplace Stocking Holder — #91005, 6¼", red fireplace $50.00
First Communion — 8" h.p., #395, 1957 only (Wendy Ann) $675.00
    8" h.p., reintroduced 1994, #100347, Americana Series $65.00
    8", #10347 – 10349, 1995, three hair colors, Special Occasions Series $65.00
    8", #17012 – 17015, 1996, black, three hair colors (Wendy Ann) #21100, 1997 – 1998 . . . .$65.00
    8", #21530 (white), #21534 (black), white dress, veil, Bible, 1999 – 2000 . . . .$70.00
    8", #30656, 2001 – 2003, Latin American, lacy white dress, veil $75.00
    8", #30655, 2001 – 2003, Caucasian, white dress, veil, gold necklace with cross $75.00
    8", #30658, 2002 – 2003, African-American, #30657, brunette $75.00
    14", #1545, 1991 – 1992 only, Classics Series (Louisa) $100.00
First Dance — 10", #36175, 2003, long black dress, red gloves $150.00
First Dance Pair — 8", 1996 . . . .$140.00
First Day at School — 8", #32995, 2002 – 2003 (Maggie), sweater, plaid skirt, book $75.00
First Ladies — (see Presidents' Ladies and individual names)
First Modern Doll Club — (see Special Events/Exclusives)

Flora McFlimsey, 14", 1939, composition, cotton dress, pinafore, and original shoes.

First Recital — 8", #17024 (white), #17037 (black), lacy dress $60.00
Fischer Quints — 7" h.p./vinyl, 1964 only, one boy and four girls
(Little Genius) . . . .$600.00 set
Five Little Peppers — 13" and 16" compo., 1936 only . . . .$750.00 ea.
Flapper — 10" Portrette, 1988 – 1991 (Cissette), red dress $60.00
    10", #1118, 1988, black dress (all white dress in 1991) (see M.A.D.C.
    under Special Events/Exclusives)
    8", #14105, 1995, three-tiered rose colored dress with matching headband,
    Nostalgia Series $60.00
Flies A Kite — 8", #33030, 2002 – 2003, red, white, blue dress, patriotic outfit,
with kite $75.00
Flora McFlimsey — (with and without "e")
    9" compo., 1938 – 1941 (Little Betty) $425.00
    22" compo., 1938 – 1944 (Princess Elizabeth) . . . .$800.00 up
    15" – 16" compo., 1938 – 1944 (Princess Elizabeth) . . . .$650.00 up
    16" – 17" compo., 1936 – 1937 (Wendy Ann) $600.00
    14" compo., 1938 – 1944 (Princess Elizabeth) . . . .$500.00 up
    12" compo., 1944 only, holds 5" "Nancy Ann" doll, tagged "Margie Ann"
    (Wendy Ann) . . . .$950.00 up
    15" Miss Flora McFlimsey, vinyl head (must have good color), 1953 only
    (Cissy) . . . .$750.00 up
    14", #25502, 1995, tiers of pink, white, and black, Buttons & Bows Series
    (Mary Ann) $125.00

Flower Child — 8", #17790, 1999 (Maggie) $60.00

Flower For the Bride — 8", #36880, 2003 – 2004, pale pink short dress, with lace $80.00

Flowergirl — 16" – 18" compo., 1939, 1944 – 1947 (Princess Elizabeth) $650.00

    20" – 24" compo., 1939, 1944 – 1947 (Princess Elizabeth) . . . .$650.00 – 850.00

    15" – 18" h.p., 1954 only (Cissy) . . . .$450.00 – 950.00

    15" h.p., 1954 only (Margaret) . . . .$800.00 up

    8" h.p., #602, 1956 (Wendy Ann) . . . .$950.00 up

    8" h.p., #445, 1959 (Wendy), blue nylon pleated dress . . . .$675.00 up

    8" h.p., #334, 1992 – 1993, Americana Series, white doll (Wendy Ann) $70.00

    8", #334-1, 1992 only, black doll $70.00

    10", #1122, 1988 – 1990, Portrette, pink dotted Swiss dress (Cissette) $85.00

    8", #22620, 1999, mauve satin, rose crown, limited to 2,700 . . . .$90.00

Follow Your Dreams Angel — 8", #38580, 2004, white and gold $90.00

Forget-Me-Not — 8", #28465, 2001 – 2002, yellow, pink dress with flowers, hat $90.00

    8", #37890, 2004, blue dress, holding flowers $85.00

Forrest — 8" h.p., #10750, 1998, Tyrolean outfit $65.00

Four-leaf Clover Fairy — 8", #35930, 2003 – 2004, green costume $90.00

Four of Us, The — 8", #37215, 2003 – 2004, pink dress, green sweater, bear, dog, and cat $125.00

France — 7" compo., 1936 – 1943 (Tiny Betty) $300.00

    9" compo., 1937 – 1941 (Little Betty) $325.00

    8" h.p., BKW, #390, #790, 1961 – 1965 (Wendy Ann) $125.00

    8" h.p., BK, #790, 1965 – 1972 . . . .$100.00

    8" h.p., straight leg, #0790, #590, 1973 – 1975, marked "Alex" $65.00

    8" straight leg, #590, #552, #517, #582, 1976 – 1993, marked "Alexander."

        (1985 – 1987) 1985 – 1987, #590, #552 . . . .$60.00

    8" h.p., reissued 1994 – 1995, #110538 (Wendy) $60.00

    8" h.p., #11557, 1996 International, Cancan costume (#24020 – 1998) $60.00

French Aristocrat — 10" Portrette, #1143, 1991 – 1992 only, bright pink/white (Cissette) $175.00

French Blue Godey — 10", #33565, 2002, long blue dress, striped top, limited to 750 . . . .$100.00

French Flowergirl — 8" h.p., #610, 1956 only (Wendy Ann) . . . .$800.00 up

French White Godey — 10", #33560, 2002, white dress, pink trim, limited to 750 . . . .$100.00

Friar Tuck — 8" h.p., #493, 1989 – 1991, Storybook Series (Maggie Mixup) $65.00

Friday's Child — 8", #27790, 2001, lavender dress $100.00

Friedrich — (see Sound of Music)

Frog Princess — 8", #27755, 2001 – 2002, includes frog, pink dress, puff sleeves $90.00

Frost Fairy Boy — 8", #25140, 2000, silver costume and crown $65.00

Frost Fairy Girl — 8", #25145, 2000, silver ballerina costume $65.00

Frou-Frou — 40" all cloth, 1951 only, ballerina with yarn hair, dressed in

    green or lilac . . . .$800.00 up

Fun Fun Chloe — 14", #30115, 2001, vinyl $65.00

Funny — 18" cloth, 1963 – 1977 . . . .$65.00

Funny Maggie — 8" (Maggie), #140506, 1994 – 1995, Storyland Series,

    yarn hair $60.00

Gainsborough — 20" h.p., 1957, Models Formal Gowns Series, taffeta gown,

    large picture hat (Cissy) . . . .$1,700.00 up

    #2184, 21" h.p./vinyl arms, 1968, blue with white lace jacket

        (Jacqueline) $650.00

    #2192, 21", 1972, yellow with full white lace overskirt (Jacqueline) $675.00

    #2192, 21", 1973, pale blue, scallop lace overskirt (Jacqueline) $525.00

    #2211, 21", 1978, pink with full lace overdress (Jacqueline) $350.00

    10" pink gown and hat, 1957 Portrette (Cissette) $750.00

    10", #45201, 1995, pink with lace overlay, Madame's Portfolio Series . . .$100.00

Garbo, Greta Grand Hotel — 16", #33480, 2002 – 2003, wool dress, coat,

    limited to 1,500 . . . .$160.00

    16", #31555, 2003, Greta Garbo Camille, pink gown,

    limited to 500 . . . .$200.00

Gainsborough, 21", #2192, 1972
(Jacqueline). Mint and all original.

Garden Fairy

Garden Fairy — 8", #28500, 2001 – 2002, pink costume with roses $80.00

Gardenia — 10", #22360, 1998 (Cissette), yellow satin long gown $100.00

Garden Party — 18" h.p., 1953 only (Margaret) . . . . $1,700.00 up

    20" h.p., 1956 – 1957 (Cissy) . . . . $1,600.00 up

    8" h.p., #488, 1955 only (Wendy Ann) . . . . $1,800.00 up

Garden Rose — 10" (Cissette), #22530, 1999, pink tulle with roses $125.00

Garfield, Lucretia — 1985 – 1987, fourth set Presidents' Ladies/First Ladies Series (Louisa) $100.00

Garland, Judy Meet Me in St. Louis — 16", #32175, 2002 – 2003, white dress, limited to 1,500 . . . . $160.00

Gemini — 8", #21350, 1998, African-American, two dolls, yellow outfit $150.00

    8", #21351, 1998, white, two dolls $150.00

Genius Baby — 21" – 30" plastic/vinyl, 1960 – 1961, has flirty eyes . . . . $125.00 – 250.00

    Little, 8" h.p. head/vinyl, 1956 – 1962 (see Little Genius)

Geppetto — 8", #478, 1993, #140478, 1994, Storybook Series $70.00

Geppetto and Pinocchio — 8", 5", #32130, 2000, navy jacket, hat $100.00

Geranium — 9" early vinyl toddler, 1953 only, red organdy dress and bonnet $125.00

German (Germany) — 8" h.p., BK, #763, 1966 – 1972 (Wendy Ann) $100.00

    8" h.p., straight leg, #0763 – 563, 1973 – 1975, marked "Alex" $70.00

    10" h.p., 1962 – 1963 (Cissette) $925.00

    8" straight legs, #563, #535, #506, 1976 – 1989, marked "Alexander" $65.00

    8", 1990 – 1991, marked "Alexander" $60.00

    8", #535, 1986 . . . . $60.00

    8" h.p., #110542, 1994 – 1995, outfit in 1994 Neiman-Marcus trunk set (Maggie) $60.00

    8", #25800, 2000 – 2001 (Maggie), blue print dress, beer stein $125.00

Get Well — 8" h.p., #21090, 1998 – 1999, red stripe outfit, vase of flowers $70.00

Get Well Wishes — #10363 – 10365, 1995, three hair colors,

        nurse with bear, Special Occasions Series $60.00

Ghost of Christmas Past — 8", #18002, 1996, Dickens, long white gown $60.00

Ghost of Christmas Present — 14", #18406, 1996, Dickens, sold as set only with

    8" Ignorance (boy) and 8" Want (girl) $275.00

Gibson Girl — 10" h.p., 1962, eyeshadow (Cissette) . . . . $800.00 up

    10", 1963, plain blouse with no stripes . . . . $800.00 up

    16" cloth, 1930s $850.00

    10", #1124, 1988 – 1990, Portrette, red and black (Cissette) $65.00

    10", #17750, 1999, navy blue gown $90.00

Gidget — 14" plastic/vinyl, #1415, #1420, #1421, 1966 only (Mary Ann) $275.00

Gift from Grandma — 8", #38195, 2004, pink check dress $85.00

Gift of Beauty Fairy — 8", #39045, 2004, pink outfit $85.00

Gift of Song Fairy — 8", #39055, 2004, blue gown $85.00

Gift of Virtue Fairy — 8", #39050, 2004, blue gown $85.00

Gigi — 14", #1597, 1986 – 1987, Classic Series (Mary Ann) $100.00

    14", #87011, 1996, plaid dress, straw hat (Mary Ann) $100.00

    8" h.p., #13990, 1998 – 1999, pleated plaid dress, straw hat (Maggie) $70.00

Gilbert — 8", #260420, 1994 – 1995, Anne of Green Gables Series $90.00

Gingerbread House — Candy-trimmed house, #26595, 2001 – 2003 . . . . $130.00

Girl on Flying Trapeze — 40" cloth, 1951 only, dressed in pink satin tutu (sold at FAO Schwarz) $950.00

Girl on a Swing — 8", #28640, 2001 – 2002, white dress with swing, flower rope $80.00

Giselle — 16", #22050, 1998, aqua tutu $125.00

Glamour Girl 1953 — 10" h.p., 2000, (Cissette) pink and black gown $100.00

Glamour Girls — 18" h.p., 1953 only (Margaret, Maggie) . . . . $1,800.00 up

Glinda, The Good Witch — 8", #473, 1992 – 1993, Storyland Series (Wendy Ann), #140473, 1994 – 1995 . . . . . $125.00

    14" plastic/vinyl, #141573, 1994 only $100.00

    10", #13250, 1997 – 2001 – 2004, pink tulle and taffeta dress (Cissette), silver crown $150.00

    15", #25546, 2001, cloth, pink gown $65.00

    5", #33765, 2002, porcelain, pink dress $85.00

Glorious Angel — 10½" h.p., #54860 (see Tree Toppers)

Godey — 21" compo., 1945 – 1947 (Wendy Ann), white lace over pink satin . . . . $2,700.00 up

14" h.p., 1950 – 1951 (Margaret) . . . .$1,500.00 up

21" h.p., 1951 only, lace ¾ top with long sleeves, pink satin two-tiered skirt (Margaret) . . . .$1,800.00 up

18" h.p., #2010A, 1953 only, Glamour Girl Series, red gown with gray fur stole (Maggie) . . . .$1,700.00 up

21" h.p., vinyl straight arms, 1961 only, lavender coat and hat (Cissy) $1,600.00

21", 1962, bright orange gown, white lace ruffles on bodice $1,600.00

21", #2153, 1965, dressed in all red, blonde hair (Jacqueline) $800.00

21" plastic/vinyl, 1966 only, red with short black jacket and hat (Coco) . . . .$2,300.00 up

21" h.p., vinyl arms, #2172, 1967, dressed in pink and ecru (Jacqueline) $600.00

#2195, 1969, red with black trim $650.00

#2195, 1970, pink with short burgundy jacket $325.00

#2161, 1971, pink, black trim, short jacket $425.00

#2298, 1977, ecru with red jacket and bonnet $300.00

8" SLW, #491, 1955 only (Wendy Ann) . . . .$1,400.00 up

10" h.p., #1172, 1968, dressed in all pink with ecru lace, with bows down front (Cissette) $450.00

#1172, 1969, all yellow with bows down front $450.00

#1183, 1970, all lace pink dress with natural straw hat $450.00

Godey Bride — 14" h.p., 1950, lace ¾ top over satin gown with long train (Margaret) . . . .$1,000.00 up

18" h.p., 1950 – 1951 (Margaret) . . . .$1,400.00 up

21" porcelain, 1993 (Cissy) $400.00

Godey Groom/Man — 14" h.p., 1950, has curls over ears, wearing black jacket and tan pants (Margaret) . . . . .$975.00 up

18" h.p., 1950 – 1951 (Margaret) . . . .$1,300.00 up

Godey Lady — 14" h.p., 1950, green velvet dress with pink/bright orange pleated ruffles,

    peach/white bodice (Margaret) . . . .$1,000.00 up

18" h.p., 1950 – 1951 (Margaret) . . . .$1,500.00 up

Golden Christmas Angel — 10", #38565, 2004, white and gold costume $150.00

Golden Girl 1920 — 10", #17740, 1999, black and gold dress $100.00

Goldfish — 8" h.p., #344, Americana Series, 1993 – 1994 . . . .$70.00

Goldilocks — 18" cloth, 1930s $875.00

7" – 8" compo., 1938 – 1942 (Tiny Betty) $325.00

18" h.p., 1951 only (Maggie) $1,200.00

14" plastic/vinyl, #1520, 1978 – 1979, Classic Series, satin dress (Mary Ann) $80.00

14", #1520, 1980 – 1983, blue satin or cotton dress (Mary Ann) $80.00

14", #1553, 1991 only, Classic Series, long side curls tied with ribbon (Mary Ann) $90.00

8", #497, 1990 – 1991 only, Storyland Series (1991 dress in different plaid) (Wendy Ann) $70.00

8", #140500, 1994 – 1995, Storyland Series, floral print dress, has bear $70.00

8", #25965, 2000 – 2003 (Wendy), blue dress, eyelet apron with bear $60.00

Gold Rush — 10" h.p., 1963 only (Cissette) $1,400.00

Golf Boy — 8", 1998, #16402 (Maggie) green coat, checked hat, pants,

    golf club $70.00

Golf Girl — 8", 1998, #16412 (Wendy) ivory sweater, navy skirt, golf club . .$70.00

Gone Fishing — 8", #28190, 2001, green dress, hat, fishing pole $80.00

Gone With the Wind (Scarlett) — 14", #1490, #1590, 1969 – 1986,

    all white dress/green sash, made 17 years without a change (Mary Ann)

    (dress must be mint) $125.00

Good Fairy — 14" h.p., 1948 – 1949 (Margaret) . . . .$725.00 up

Good Little Girl — 16" cloth, 1966 only, mate to "Bad Little Girl,"

    wears pink dress $185.00

Goya — 8" h.p., #314, 1953 only (Wendy Ann) . . . .$1,100.00 up

21" h.p./vinyl arms, #2183, 1968, multi-tiered pink dress (Jacqueline) . . .$550.00

21", #2235, 1982 – 1983, maroon dress with black Spanish lace

    (Jacqueline) $275.00

Grace — 14" vinyl, #34320, 2002 – 2003, African-American baby, pajamas .$90.00

Graceful Garnet — 8", #32170, 2000 – 2002, red and gold ballgown,

    garnet jewelry $90.00

Graduation — 8" h.p., #399, 1957 only (Wendy Ann) . . . .$900.00 up

12", 1957 only (Lissy) . . . .$1,000.00 up

Goya, 21", 1982 – 1983 (Jacqueline).

Graduation

8", #307, 1990 – 1991, Americana Series (white doll only) (Wendy Ann) $60.00
8", #307, #307-1, 1991 – 1992, Americana Series, white or black doll $65.00
8", #10307 – 10309 (black), #10310 (white), 1995, blue robe, Special Occasions Series $65.00
8", #26105 (blonde), #26106 (brunette), #26107 (African-American), 2000 – 2003, white robe, hat, red dress, diploma $90.00
8", #38895, 2004, blonde, white dress, blue robe, hat $85.00
8", #38896, 2004, brunette, white dress, blue robe, hat $85.00
8", #38897, 2004, African-American, white dress, blue robe, hat $85.00
Grandma Jane — 14" plastic/vinyl, #1420, 1970 – 1972 (Mary Ann) $225.00
Grand Ole Opry Boy — 8", #77005, 1996 Classic $70.00
Grand Ole Opry Girl — 8", #77004, 1996 Classic $70.00
Grant, Julia — 1982 – 1984, third set Presidents' Ladies/First Ladies Series (Louisa) $100.00
Grave, Alice — 18" cloth, 1930s . . . .$750.00 up
Grayson, Kathryn — 20" – 21" h.p., 1949 only (Margaret) . . . .$6,000.00 up
Great Britain — 8" h.p., #558, 1977 – 1988 (Wendy Ann) $55.00
Great Gatsby Pair — 10", #15310, 1997, Classic characters $150.00
Greece — 8", #35970, 2003 – 2004, blue and red cultural costume, bouzaki $85.00
Greece Boy — 8" h.p., #527, 1992 – 1993 only (Wendy Ann) $55.00
Greek Boy — 8" h.p., BK, 1965, & BKW, 1966 – 1968, #769 (Wendy Ann) $300.00
Greek Girl — 8" h.p., BK, #765, 1968 – 1972 (Wendy Ann) $100.00
8" h.p., straight leg, #0765, #565, 1973 – 1975, marked "Alex" $65.00
8" h.p., straight leg, #565, #527, 1976 – 1987 (1985 – 1987), marked "Alexander" $60.00
Gretel — 7" compo., 1935 – 1942 (Tiny Betty) $325.00
9" compo., 1938 – 1940 (Little Betty) $350.00
18" h.p., 1948 only (Margaret) . . . .$1,000.00 up
7½" – 8" h.p., SLW, #470, 1955 (Wendy Ann) . . . .$575.00 up
8" h.p., BK, #754, 1966 – 1972, Storybook Series (Wendy) $100.00
8" h.p., straight leg, #0754, #454, 1973 – 1975, marked "Alex" $65.00
8" h.p., straight leg, #454, 1976 – 1986, marked "Alexander" $60.00
8" h.p., #462, 1991 – 1992 only, Storyland Series, reintroduced doll (Wendy Ann) $60.00
8" h.p., #26600, 2001 – 2003, red stripe skirt, eyelet apron, green felt hat $80.00
Gretel Brinker — 12", 1993 only (Lissy) $175.00
8", #14650, 1996 . . . .$60.00
Gretl — (see Sound of Music)
Groom — 18" – 21" compo., 1946 – 1947, mint (Margaret) . . . .$975.00 up
18" – 21" h.p., 1949 – 1951 (Margaret) . . . .$975.00 – 1,500.00
14" – 16" h.p., 1949 – 1951 (Margaret) . . . .$750.00 up
7½" h.p., SL & SLW, #577, #464, #466, 1953 – 1955 (Wendy Ann) . . . .$550.00 up
8" BKW, #577, 1956 . . . .$425.00
8" BKW, #377, 1957 . . . .$425.00
8" BKW, #572, 1958 . . . .$400.00
8" h.p., BKW, #421, #442, 1961 – 1963 (Wendy Ann) $375.00
8", #488, #388, reintroduced 1989 – 1991 only (Wendy Ann) $70.00
8", #339, 1993, black pants, peach tie, white jacket $70.00
8", #17020, 1996, black velvet tails, black pants, pink tie $70.00
8", #17023, 1996, black velvet tails, etc., black doll $65.00
8", #21071, 1997 – 2003, velvet tailcoat, top hat, #21073 – 21074, African-American (1997 – 2003) $90.00
Groovy Girl 1970 — 8", #17800, 1999, BK, denim pants, hat $65.00
Guardian Angel — 10", #10602 – 1995, first in series, 100th Anniversary Special, all pink with white wings $125.00
10", #10720, 1998, rose print brocade gown, feather wings $100.00
10", of Harmony, #10691, 1996 . . . .$100.00
10", of Hope, #10609, 1996 . . . .$100.00
10", of Love, frosted ivy, #10605, 1996 . . . .$100.00
10", of Love, heather blue #10607, 1996 . . . .$100.00
10", of Love, misty rose, #10603, 1996 . . . .$100.00
10", Pink Pristine, #10700, 1997 – 2000, pink tulle dress $100.00

10", #10720, 1999, pink print brocade gown, feather wings $100.00

Guatemala — 8", #24180, 1999, red and black outfit $65.00

Guinevere — 10", #1146, 1992 only, Portrette, forest green/gold $100.00

    8", #13570, 1999, blue dress with white brocade over dress $80.00

Gypsy of the World — 8", #28570, 2001, purple costume, tarot cards $80.00

Hairdresser — 8", #33585, 2003 (Wizard of Oz), green dress, mini scissors, blonde with curls $75.00

Halloween Treats — 8", #38590, 2004, with bear and treat bag $85.00

Halloween Witch — 8" (see Collectors United under Special Events/Exclusives)

Hamlet — 12", Romance Series (Nancy Drew) $80.00

    12", 1993 only (Lissy) $100.00

Hannah — 10", #28310, 2002 – 2004, jeans, sweater, hat $40.00

    10", #28300, 2002 – 2004, skirt, striped jacket $40.00

Hannah Pepper Trunk Set — 10", #35450, 2003 – 2004, clothes, trunk $120.00

Hans Brinker — 12", 1993 only (Lissy) $125.00

    8", #14649, 1996 . . . .$60.00

Hansel — 7" compo., 1935 – 1942 (Tiny Betty) $325.00

    9" compo., 1938 – 1940 (Little Betty) $350.00

    18" h.p., 1948 only (Margaret) . . . .$900.00 up

    8" h.p., SLW, #470, 1955 only (Wendy Ann) . . . .$650.00 up

    8" h.p., BK, #753, 1966 – 1972, Storybook Series (Wendy Ann) $100.00

    8" h.p., straight leg, #0753, #543, 1973 – 1975, marked "Alex" $70.00

    8" h.p., straight leg, #543, 1976 – 1986 (1986 white face), marked "Alexander" $65.00

    8" h.p., #461, 1991 – 1992 only, Storyland Series, reintroduced doll (Wendy Ann) $60.00

    8" h.p., #26605, 2001 – 2003, green costume $80.00

Happy — 20" cloth/vinyl, 1970 only $200.00

Happy Birthday — 1985 (see M.A.D.C. under Special Events/Exclusives)

    8" h.p., #325, #325-1, 1992 – 1993, Americana Series, black or white doll (Wendy Ann) $65.00

    8" h.p., #100325, 1994, white only $65.00

    8", #10325 – 10327, 1995, three hair colors, Special Occasions Series $65.00

    8", #17004 – 17010, 1996, three hair colors, black or white doll (Wendy, Maggie) $65.00

    14" plastic/vinyl, #241596, 1994 only $85.00

    8", #21520 (blonde), #21521 (brunette), #21523 (black), pink print dress, 1999 – 2000 . . . .$70.00

    8", #27240 (blonde), #27241 (brunette), #27242, African-American, 2001 – 2002 . . . .$80.00

    8", #35925 (blonde), 2003 – 2004, pink dress, slice of cake $70.00

    8", #35926 (brunette), 2003 – 2004, with gift $70.00

    8", #35927, African-American, 2003 – 2004, with gift $70.00

Happy Birthday Billie — 8" h.p., #345, #345-1, Americana Series, black or white boy, 1993 only $60.00

Happy Birthday Maggie — 8", #21080 – white, #21083 – black, 1997 – 1998 . . . .$70.00

Happy Chanukah — 8", #10367, 1996 Holiday, #19630, 1997 – 1999 . . . .$75.00

Happy the Clown — 8", #10414, 1996 Classic Circus $65.00

Harding, Florence — 1988, fifth set Presidents' Ladies/First Ladies Series (Louisa) $100.00

Harlequin — 8", #14574, 1995, Nutcracker Series $70.00

Harley-Davidson — 8" h.p., #77002, 1996 (Wendy) Classic American, #17420, 1997 . . . .$100.00

    8" h.p., #77005, 1996 (Billy), Classic American, #17410, 1997 . . . .$100.00

    10" h.p. #77102, 1996, pictured 1996 catalog . . . . .not available for sale

    10", #17440, 1997, Cissette, black leather coat, boots $175.00

    10", #17430, 1997, David, jeans, black leather jacket $125.00

    10", #17390, 1998, Cissette, faux leather halter and skirt and backpack $150.00

Harriet The Spy — 12", #38565, 2004, cloth dog $30.00

Harrison, Caroline — 1985 – 1987, fourth set Presidents' Ladies/First Ladies Series (Louisa) $100.00

Harry Potter — 8", #38415, 2004, with broom $85.00

Hats Off to Wendy — 8", #37800, 2003, white dress, pink trim $85.00

Hawaii — 8", #301, 1990 – 1991 only, Americana Series (Wendy Ann) $60.00

Hawaiian — 8" h.p., BK, #722, 1966 – 1969, Americana Series (Wendy Ann) $350.00

    7" compo., 1936 – 1939 (Tiny Betty) $325.00

    9" compo., 1937 – 1944 (Little Betty) $350.00

Hayes, Lucy

Hayes, Lucy — 1985 – 1987, fourth set Presidents' Ladies/First Ladies Series (Louisa) $100.00
Heather — 18" cloth/vinyl, 1990 only $90.00
    8" h.p., #10760, 1998, Tyrolean outfit with basket $80.00
Heavenly Pink Angel — 8", #26285, 2000 – 2001, pink costume, white feather wings $100.00
Heidi — 7" compo., 1938 – 1939 (Tiny Betty) $325.00
    8" h.p., #460, 1991 – 1992, Storyland Series (Maggie) $70.00
    14" plastic/vinyl, #1480, #1580, #1581, 1969 – 1985 (16-year production), Classic Series (Mary Ann) $75.00
    14", #1581, 1986 – 1988, solid green dress, floral apron $75.00
    14", #25503, 1995, Ribbons & Bows Series (not on order sheet) ....not available for sale
    8" h.p., #15100, 1998 – 2000, green dress, lace apron, straw hat, goat $75.00
Hello Baby — 22", 1962 only $175.00
He Loves Me, He Loves Me Not — 8", #37895, 2004 (Wendy) $85.00
Henie, Sonja — 13" – 15" compo., 1939 – 1942 ....$675.00
    7" compo., 1939 – 1942 (Tiny Betty) $450.00
    9" compo., 1940 – 1941 (Little Betty) $575.00
    11" compo. (Wendy Ann) $650.00
    14" compo. $650.00
    14" in case/wardrobe ....$1,800.00 up
    17" – 18" compo. $950.00
    20" – 23" compo. ....$1,200.00 – 1,600.00
    13" – 14" compo., jointed waist $750.00
    15" – 18" h.p./vinyl, 1951 only, no extra joints, must have good face color (Madeline) $750.00
Her First Day at School — (see Wendy Loves Series)
Her Lady and Child (Thumbelina) — 21" porcelain, 8" h.p., #010, 1992 – 1994, limited to 2,500 ....$500.00
Hermione Granger — 8", #38420, 2004, with books $85.00
    10", #38640, 2004, vinyl $35.00
Hershey's Kisses Doll — 8", #17880, 2000, pink and silver costume $70.00
Her Sunday Best — (see Wendy Loves Series)
Hiawatha — 8" h.p., #720, 1967 – 1969, Americana Series (Wendy Ann) $375.00
    7" compo. (Tiny Betty) $325.00
    18" cloth, early 1930s $800.00

Heidi, 14" (Mary Ann), made between 1974 and 1985 in a variety of prints.

Sonja Henie, 21", composition. Mint original doll in original box.

Hickory Dickory Dock — 8", #11650, 1998 – 1999, clock costume $75.00
Highland Fling — 8" h.p., #484, 1955 only (Wendy Ann) $750.00
Holiday Ballerina — 8", #28525, 2001, white long dress with gold and red trim $70.00
Holiday on Ice — 8" h.p., #319, 1992 – 1993 only, red with white fur hat and muff, some tagged "Christmas on Ice" . .$125.00
Holiday Snowflake Skater — 8", #28520, 2001 – 2002 (Maggie), red skating outfit $95.00
Holland — 7" compo., 1936 – 1943 (Tiny Betty) $325.00
   8", #33490, 2002, blue print pinafore, with spoon $100.00
Holly — 10", #1135, 1990 – 1991, Portrette, white/red roses Cissette $100.00
Hollywood Glamour 1930 — 10", #17760, 1999, blue taffeta dress $100.00
Hollywood Trunk Set — 8", #15340, 1997 . . . .$250.00
Homecoming — 8", 1993 (see M.A.D.C. under Special Events/Exclusives)
Home for Holidays — 14", #24606, 1995, Christmas Series $100.00
Homefront Pals — 8", pair, #34335, 2002, boy, denim, girl, star dress $175.00
Honeybea — 12" vinyl, 1963 only $175.00
Honeybun — 18" – 19", 1951 – 1952 only $225.00
   23" – 26" $300.00
Honeyette Baby — 16" compo./cloth, 1941 – 1942 . . . .$225.00
   7" compo., 1934 – 1937, little girl dress (Tiny Betty) $275.00
Honeymoon in New Orleans — 8" (see Scarlett)
Hoover, Lou — 14", 1989 – 1990, sixth set Presidents' Ladies/First Ladies Series (Mary Ann) $100.00
Hope — 8" (see Collectors United under Special Events/Exclusives)
Hot Cross Buns — 8", #33055, 2002, pink dress, buns on tray $65.00
How Does Your Garden Grow — 8", #34085, 2002, with watering can $75.00
How Much Is That Doggie in the Window — 8", #38780, 2004, with store front and dog $95.00
Howdy Doody Time, It's — 8", #15230, 1999 – 2000, marionette $100.00
Huckleberry Finn — 8" h.p., #490, 1989 – 1991 only, Storybook Series (Wendy Ann) $75.00
Huggums, Big — 25", 1963 – 1979, boy or girl $100.00
Huggums, Little — 14", 1986 only, molded hair $50.00
   12", 1963 – 1995, molded hair, available in 7 – 10 outfits (first black version available in 1995) $50.00
   12", 1963 – 1982, 1988, rooted hair $50.00
   1991, special outfits (see Imaginarium Shop under Special Events/Exclusives)
   1996 – 2003, variety of outfits . . . .$40.00 – 65.00
   12", #29700, 1998, 75th Anniversary Huggums, white dress with
     flowers . . . .$40.00 – 75.00
Huggums, Lively — 25", 1963 only, knob makes limbs and head move . . .$150.00
Huggums Man in the Moon Mobile — #14700, 8" boy, star costume,
   cloth moon, star mobiles $70.00
Hug Me Pets — #76001 – 76007, plush animal bodies, Huggums face $50.00
Hulda — 18" h.p., 1949 only, lamb's wool wig, black doll
   (Margaret) . . . .$1,900.00 up
   14" h.p., 1948 – 1949, lamb's wool wig, black doll . . . .$1,300.00 up
Humpty Dumpty — 8", #13060, 1997 – 1998, plaid tailcoat, brick wall . . .$70.00
Hungarian (Hungary) — 8" h.p., BKW, #397, #797, 1962 – 1965
   (Wendy Ann) $150.00
   BK, #397, with metal crown $125.00
   BK, #797, 1965 – 1972 . . . .$100.00
   8" h.p., straight leg, #0797, #597, 1973 – 1976, marked "Alex" $70.00
   8" h.p., straight leg, #597, 1976 – 1986, marked "Alexander" $60.00
   8" h.p., #522, reintroduced 1992 – 1993 only (Wendy) $60.00
   8", #11547, 1995 only $60.00
Hush-You-Bye — 8", #25235, 2000 – 2001, comes with rocking horse . .$100.00
Hyacinth — 9" early vinyl toddler, 1953 only, blue dress and bonnet $150.00
Ibiza — 8", #510, 1989 only (Wendy Ann) $75.00
I Can Tie My Shoes — 8", #36185, 2003, pink checked dress $80.00

Summer Salute Huggable Huggums, 14", cloth body, vinyl head, arms, and legs, 2003.

Ice Capades

Ice Capades — 1950s (Cissy) . . . . $1,600.00 up
 960s (Jacqueline) . . . . $1,600.00 up
Iceland — 10", 1962 – 1963 (Cissette) . . . . $750.00 up
Ice Skater — 8" h.p., BK & BKW, #555, 1955 – 1956 (Wendy Ann) . . . . $700.00 up
 8", #303, 1990 – 1991 only, Americana Series, purple/silver (Wendy Ann) $75.00
 8", #16371, 1997, boy, brocade vest, black pants $65.00
 8", #16361, 1997 – 1998, girl, pink knit and silver outfit $65.00
Ignorance — 8", #18406 (see Ghost of Christmas Present) (sold as set)
I'll Love You Forever Valentine — 8", #25025, 2000, pink dress, lace front $70.00
I Love My Kitty — 8", #30420, 2001– 2002, blue checked dress, kitty $70.00
I Love My Puppy — 8", #30430, 2001, red checked dress, puppy $65.00
I Love My Teddy — 8", #30425, 2001 – 2003, white, red dress, with teddy $75.00
I Love You — 8", #10386 – 10388, 1995, three hair colors, Special Occasions Series $55.00
I. Magnin — (see Special Events/Exclusives)
Imaginarium Shop — (see Special Events/Exclusives)
I'm a Little Teapot — 8", #28870, 2001 (Maggie), blue print teapot with tea bag $60.00
I'm Gonna Like Me — 12", #35805, 2003 – 2004, cloth, Jamie Lee Curtis $35.00
I'm So Tall — 8", #38500, 2004, pink doll, doll and child growth charts $120.00
India — 8" h.p., BKW, #775, 1965 (Wendy Ann) $125.00
 8" h.p., BK, #775, 1965 – 1972 (Wendy) $100.00
 8" h.p., straight leg, #0775, #575, 1973 – 1975, marked "Alex" $65.00
 8" h.p., straight leg, #575, #549, 1976 – 1988, marked "Alexander" (1985 – 1987) $60.00
 8" h.p., straight leg, #11563, 1996 International, #24030, 1997 . . . . $60.00
 8" h.p., #39060, 2004, Henna painted hands and plush elephant $90.00
Indian Boy* — 8" h.p., BK, #720, 1966 only, Americana Series (Wendy Ann) $425.00
Indian Girl* — 8" h.p., BK, #721, 1966 only, Americana Series (Wendy Ann) $400.00
Indonesia — 8" h.p., BK, #779, 1970 – 1972 (Wendy) $100.00
 8" h.p., straight leg, #779, #0779, #579, 1972 – 1975, marked "Alex" $75.00
 8" h.p., straight leg, #579, 1976 – 1988, marked "Alexander" $60.00
 8" BK, with Maggie Mixup face $150.00

Isolde, 14" (Mary Ann), #1413, 1985 – 1986.

Italy, 8", left, BK Walker; right, straight legs (Wendy).

*Became Hiawatha and Pocahontas in 1967.

Ingalls, Laura — 14", #1531, 1989 – 1991, Classic Series, burnt orange dress/blue pinafore (Mary Ann) $100.00

14", #24621, 1995, green with rose floral, Favorite Books Series (Mary Ann) $100.00

Ingres — 14" plastic/vinyl, #1567, 1987 only, Fine Arts Series (Mary Ann) $80.00

Iris — 10" h.p., #1112, 1987 – 1988, pale blue (Cissette) $65.00

Irish (Ireland) — 8" h.p., BKW, #778, 1965 only (Wendy Ann) $125.00

8" BK, #778, 1966 – 1972, long gown $100.00

8" straight leg, #0778, #578, 1973 – 1975, marked "ALEX," long gown $65.00

8" straight leg, #578, #551, 1976 – 1985, marked "Alexander" $60.00

8" straight leg, #551, 1985 – 1987, short dress $60.00

8" straight leg, #551, 1987 – 1993, marked "Alexander," short dress (Maggie) $60.00

8" h.p., #100541, re-issued 1994 only, green skirt with white top $55.00

8" h.p., #17028, 1996 International, leprechaun outfit, #21000, 1997 – 1999 . . . .$55.00

Irish Lass — 8", #11555, 1995 only $60.00

Isabelle — 14", #34345, 2002 – 2003, African-American, print dress $90.00

Isolde — 14", #1413, 1985 – 1986 only, Opera Series (Mary Ann) $80.00

Israel — 8" h.p., BK, #768, 1965 – 1972 (Wendy Ann) $100.00

8" h.p., straight leg, #0768, 1973 – 1975, marked "Alex" $75.00

8" h.p., straight leg, #568, 1976 – 1989, marked "Alexander" $65.00

Italy — 8" h.p., BKW, #393, 1961 – 1965 (Wendy Ann) $150.00

8" h.p., BK, #793, 1965 – 1972 . . . .$100.00

8" h.p., straight leg, #0793, #593, 1973 – 1975, marked "ALEX" $65.00

#593, 1985 . . . .$65.00

8" straight leg, #593, #553, #524, 1976 – 1994 (#110524), marked "Alexander" $60.00

8", #11549, 1995 only $60.00

8", #24050, 1997 – 1998, gondolier outfit, with decorated oar $65.00

8", #37095, 2003 – 2004, red costume, gold mask, hat with scarf $95.00

It's Good to Be Queen — 8", #25270, 2000 – 2001 (Maggie) Mary Engelbreit $90.00

It's My Birthday — 8", #37070, 2003, brunette, blue dress with lace pinafore $100.00

It's Raining, It's Pouring — 8", #34175, 2002 – 2003, yellow raincoat, umbrella, boots, pink print dress $50.00

Itsy, Bitsy Spider — 8", #38785, 2004 (Wendy) $50.00

Ivana — 16", #25635, 2000 – 2001, Ivana Trump in black velvet gown $175.00

Ivory Victorian Lady — 5" porcelain, #27030, 2000, long white gown $60.00

Jabberwocky — 8", #13580, 1999 – 2000, gold costume, comes with brick tower $75.00

Jack and Beanstalk — 8", #35615, 2003 – 2004, white dress, checked top $80.00

Jack & Jill — 7" compo., 1938 – 1943 (Tiny Betty) . . . .$325.00 ea.

9" compo., 1939 only (Little Betty) . . . .$350.00 ea.

8" straight leg (Jack – #455, #457; Jill – #456, #458), 1987 – 1992, Storybook Series (Maggie) . . . .$60.00 ea.

8" straight leg, sold as set, #14626, 1996 (Wendy) $100.00

Jack Be Nimble — 8" (see Dolly Dears under Special Events/Exclusives)

Jackie — 10", #45200, 1995, Madame's Portfolio Series, pink suit $90.00

10" h.p., #20115, 1996, wedding gown, Classic American $100.00

21", #17450, 1997, three outfits, three pieces luggage, jewelry, etc. $650.00

10", #17460, 1997 – 1998, pink luncheon suit $100.00

10", #17470, 1998, opera coat, evening dress $100.00

10", #17480, 1998, beaded cocktail dress $100.00

10", #39095, suit, hat, purse (Coquette) $80.00

Jackie and John — 10", #20117, 1996, limited edition . . . .$225.00 set

Jackson, Sarah — 1979 – 1981, second set Presidents' Ladies/First Ladies Series (Louisa) $100.00

Jacqueline — 21" h.p./vinyl arms, 1961 – 1962, street dress or suit, pillbox hat . . . .$950.00 up

In sheath dress and hat or slacks and top $750.00

In gown from cover of 1962 catalog $950.00

Ballgown other than 1962 catalog cover $900.00

10" h.p., 1962 only (Cissette) $700.00

1962, 1966 – 1967, exclusive in trunk with wardrobe . . . .$1,800.00 up

Jamaica — 8" straight leg, #542, 1986 – 1988 (round brown face) $65.00

Janie

Janie — 12" toddler, #1156, 1964 – 1966 only $250.00
    Ballerina, 1965 only $275.00
  14" baby, 1972 – 1973 ....$65.00
  20" baby, 1972 – 1973 ....$75.00
Japan — 8" h.p., BK, #770, 1968 – 1972 (Wendy) $100.00
  8" h.p., straight leg, #0770, #570, 1973 – 1975, marked "Alex" $65.00
  8" h.p., straight leg, #570, 1976 – 1986, marked "Alexander" $60.00
  8", #570, 1987 – 1991 (Maggie) $60.00
  8" BK, #770, 1960s (Maggie Mixup) $150.00
  8" h.p., #526, reintroduced 1992 – 1993 only, white face (Wendy Ann) $60.00
  8", #28545, 2001 – 2002, Geisha costume, includes tea set $110.00
Japanese Bride — 10", #28590, kimono $125.00
Jasmine — 10", #1113, 1987 – 1988, Portrette, burnt orange (Cissette), 1997 ....$70.00
Jeannie Walker — 13" – 14" compo., 1940s, unique jointed legs, excellent face color, mint condition ....$675.00 up
  18" compo., 1940s ....$750.00 up
Jennifer's Trunk Set — 14" doll, #1599, 1990 only $225.00
Jessica — 18" cloth/vinyl, 1990 only $125.00
Jewelry Angel — 10", #28375, 2002, long pink dress $260.00
Jingle Bell Skater — 8", #33460, 2002 – 2003, white skating costume, fur hat $80.00
Jingles the Juggler — 8", #10404, 1996, jester's outfit $75.00
Jo — (see Little Women)
Jo Goes to New York — 8", #14522, 1995 only, trunk set, Little Women Series ......$250.00 set
Joanie — 36" plastic/vinyl, 1960 – 1961, allow more for flirty eyes, 36", 1960,
    nurse dressed in all white with black band on cap ....$475.00 up
  36", 1961, nurse in colored uniform, all white pinafore and cap ....$425.00 up
John — 8", #440, 1993 only, Peter Pan Series, wears glasses $70.00
John Powers Models — 14" h.p., 1952 only, must be mint (Maggie & Margaret) ....$1,700.00 up
  18", 1952 only ....$1,900.00 up
Johnson, Lady Bird — 14", 1994 only $100.00
Jolly Old Saint Nick — 16", #19620, 1997 ....$175.00
Jones, Casey — 8" h.p., Americana Series, 1991 – 1992 only (Wendy Ann) $60.00
Josephine — 12", #1335, 1980 – 1986, Portraits of History (Nancy Drew) $65.00
  21" Portrait, 1994 only $325.00
Joseph, The Dream Teller — 8", #14580, 1995 only, Bible Series $100.00

Left: Japan, 8", Maggie. Right: Wendy face. Made 1968 – 1991.

Jeannie Walker, 1940s, composition, all original. Her unique walker mechanism is patented.

Joy — 12" (see New England Collectors Society under Special Events/Exclusives)

Joy Noel — 8" (see Spiegel's under Special Events/Exclusives)

Joyous Tulip Ball Gown — 10", 2001, #28515, fancy ballgown $125.00

Judy — 21" compo., 1945 – 1947, pinch pleated flowers at hem (Wendy Ann) ....$3,200.00 up

    21" h.p./vinyl arms, 1962 only (Jacqueline) ....$1,800.00 up

Judy Loves Pat the Bunny — 14", blue dress, plush bunny $95.00

Jugo-Slav — 7" compo., 1935 – 1937 (Tiny Betty) $275.00

Julia — 10", #31455, 2002, tan pants, print top $40.00

    10", #35820, 2003 – 2004 (Hannah), Let's Celebrate, yellow dress, blue trim $40.00

Juliet — 21" compo., 1945 – 1946, Portrait (Wendy Ann) ....$2,500.00 up

    18" compo., 1937 – 1940 (Wendy Ann) ....$1,250.00 up

    8" h.p., #473, 1955 only (Wendy Ann) ....$950.00 up

    12" plastic/vinyl, 1978 – 1987, Portrait Children Series (Nancy Drew) $65.00

    12", reintroduced 1991 – 1992, Romance Collection (Nancy Drew) $65.00

    8" (see Madame Alexander Doll Co. under Special Events/Exclusives)

Jumping Rope — 8", #38015, Caucasian, pastel dress, jumprope $85.00

    8", #38016, African-American, pastel dress, jumprope $85.00

June Bride — 21" compo., 1939, 1946 – 1947, Portrait Series, embroidered flowers near hem (Wendy Ann) .$2,500.00 up

June Wedding — 8" h.p., 1956 (Wendy Ann) $750.00

Just Because You're Special — 8", #35935, 2003 (Maggie), blue dress, bouquet $75.00

Just Grape — 8", #31305, 2002, lavender checked dress, red hair $80.00

Just Heavenly — 8", #37880, carcoat set, 2004 ....$90.00

Just Like Mommy — 8", #39240, 2004, pink frilly dress $90.00

Karen — 15" – 18" h.p., 1948 – 1949 (Margaret) ....$850.00 up

Karen Ballerina — 15" compo., 1946 – 1949 (Margaret) ....$950.00 up

    18" compo., 1948 – 1949 (Margaret) ....$1,200.00 up

    18" – 21" h.p., can be dressed in pink, yellow, blue, white, or lavender ....$950.00 up

    15" porcelain (1999 – 2000), #90200, remake of 1940s Ballerina $150.00

    10" h.p., 2000, #25551 (Cissette), remake of 1940s Ballerina $100.00

Kate Greenaway — 7" compo., 1938 – 1943 (Tiny Betty) $400.00

    9" compo., 1936 – 1939 (Little Betty) $450.00

    16" cloth, 1936 – 1938 ....$900.00

    13", 14", 15" compo., 1938 – 1943 (Princess Elizabeth) $800.00

    18", 1938 – 1943 (Wendy Ann/Princess Elizabeth) $900.00

    24", 1938 – 1943 (Princess Elizabeth) ....$950.00 up

    14" vinyl, #1538, 1993 only, Classic Series $100.00

Kathleen Toddler — 23" rigid vinyl, 1959 only $200.00

Kathy — 17" – 21" compo., 1939, 1946 (Wendy Ann) ....$650.00 – 850.00

    15" – 18" h.p., 1949 – 1951, has braids (Maggie) ....$550.00 – 750.00

Kathy Baby — 13" – 15" vinyl, 1954 – 1956, has rooted or molded hair ......$75.00 – 125.00

    11" – 13" vinyl, 1955 – 1956, has rooted or molded hair ....$75.00 – 125.00

    18" – 21", 1954 – 1956, has rooted or molded hair ....$100.00 – 150.00

    11" vinyl, 1955 – 1956, doll has molded hair and comes with trousseau $200.00

    21", 1954 only $175.00

    21" and 25", 1955 – 1956 ....$100.00 – 175.00

Kathy Cry Dolly — 11" – 15" vinyl nurser, 1957 – 1958 ....$75.00 – 175.00

    18", 21", 25" ....$100.00 – 250.00

Kathy Tears — 11", 15", 17" vinyl, 1959 – 1962, has closed mouth ....$75.00 – 150.00

    19", 23", 26", 1959 – 1962 ....$100.00 – 175.00

    12", 16", 19" vinyl, 1960 – 1961 (new face) ....$75.00 – 175.00

Katie (black Smarty) — 12" plastic/vinyl, 1963 only $325.00

    12" (black Janie), #1156, #1155, 1965 only $325.00

    12" h.p., 1962, 100th Anniversary doll for FAO Schwarz (Lissy) $800.00

    12", Shopping in Paris, 2000, #26475, white dress, red checked jacket $60.00

Keane, Doris — cloth, 1930s $750.00

    9" – 11" compo., 1936 – 1937 (Little Betty) ....$250.00 – 350.00

Keepsake Silk Victorian

Keepsake Silk Victorian — 8", #28725, 2001 – 2002, cream silk dress $95.00
Kelly — 12" h.p., 1959 only (Lissy) ....$500.00 up
    15" – 16", 1958 – 1959 (Mary-Bel) $300.00
    16", 1959 only, in trunk/wardrobe $800.00
    18", 1958 ....$375.00
    22", 1958 – 1959 ....$400.00
    8" h.p., #433, 1959, blue/white dress (Wendy Ann) $575.00
    15", Shopping in Paris, #26470, 2000, black checked outfit $85.00
Kelly and Kitty — 20", #29770, 1999, pink checked outfit with kitten $125.00
Kelly Blue Dupionne — 20", #29380, 1998, blue silk dress $125.00
Kelly Blue Gingham — 18", #29100, 1997 – 1998, vinyl $125.00
Kelly Good Morning — 20", #29930, 1999, white dress trimmed in blue $100.00
Kelly Happy Birthday — 18", #29230, 1997, vinyl $125.00
Kelly Pink Butterfly — 20", #29920, 1999, pink dress and pinafore $100.00
Kelly Pink Dot Tulle — 18", #29230, 1997, vinyl $125.00
Kelly Pink Snowflake — 18", #29110, 1997, vinyl $125.00
Kelly's Little Sister, Katie — 12", #29940, 1999, pink plaid dress $55.00
Kelly Teacher's Pet — 15", #29760, 1999, plaid dress and hat $75.00
Kelly Teatime — 15", #29300, 1998, blue dress, straw hat $75.00
Kelly Tree Trimming — 18", #29240, 1997, vinyl $125.00
Kelly White Floral Party — 15" vinyl #29390, 1998 – 1999 ....$100.00
Kennedy, Jacqueline — 14", 1989 – 1990, sixth set Presidents' Ladies/First Ladies Series (Mary Ann) $175.00
Kenya — 8", 1994, outfit tagged, in Neiman-Marcus trunk set $70.00
    8", issued 1995 only, same outfit but sold as Nigeria ....no price available
Kick It — 8", #38890, 2004, with soccer ball $50.00
King — 21" compo., 1942 – 1946 , extra make-up, red chest ribbon, gold trimmed cape (Wendy Ann) ......$2,700.00 up
King of Hearts — 8", #14611, 1996, Alice in Wonderland Series $60.00
Kitten — 14" – 18" cloth/vinyl, 1962 – 1963 ....$50.00 – 95.00
    24", 1961 only, has rooted hair $95.00
    20" nurser, 1968 only, has cryer box, doesn't wet $100.00
    20", 1985 – 1986 only, dressed in pink $90.00
    8", 1998, #29310 Powder Pink or #29423 Sunny $60.00
Kitten Kries — 20" cloth/vinyl, 1967 only $100.00
Kitten, Littlest — (see Littlest Kitten)
Kitten, Lively — 14", 18", 24", 1962 – 1963, knob moves head and limbs ....$100.00 – 250.00
Kitten, Mama — 18", #402, 1963 only, same as "Lively" but also has cryer box $150.00
Kitty Baby — 21" compo., 1941 – 1942 ....$175.00
Klondike Kate — 10" h.p., 1963 only, Portrette (Cissette) ....$1,500.00 up
Knave — 8", #13040, 1997 – 1998, brocade suit, large playing card, 5 of spades $70.00
Knight — 8", #25915 (Wendy), 2000 – 2001 Alice in Wonderland Series $75.00
Korea — 8" h.p., BK, #772, 1968 – 1970 (Wendy) $200.00
    BKW & BK, #772 (Maggie Mixup) $225.00
    #522, reintroduced 1988 – 1989 (Maggie Mixup) $60.00
Kukla — 8", #11101, 1995 only, International Folk Tales (Russia) (Wendy) $65.00
Kwanzaa Celebration — 10" h.p., #10368, 1996 Holiday $100.00
Lady and Her Child — 21" porcelain, 8" h.p., 1993 ....$500.00 set
Lady Bird — 8", #438, 1988 – 1989, Storybook Series (Maggie) $60.00
Ladybug — 8", #27725, 2001 – 2002, red checked dress, green jacket and hat $85.00
Lady Hamilton — 20" h.p./vinyl arms, 1957 only, Models Formal Gowns Series, picture hat, blue gown with
    shoulder shawl effect (Cissy) ....$1,300.00 up
    11" h.p., 1957, pink silk gown, picture hat with roses (Cissette) ....$750.00 up
    21", #2182, 1968, beige lace over pink gown (Jacqueline) $475.00
    12" vinyl, #1338, 1984 – 1986, Portraits of History (Nancy Drew) $70.00
Lady in Red — 20", #2285, 1958 only, red taffeta (Cissy) ....$2,900.00 up
    10", #1134, 1990, Portrette (Cissette) $90.00
Lady in Waiting — 8" h.p., #487, 1955 only (Wendy Ann) ....$1,700.00 up

Lady Lee — 8", #442, 1988 only, Storybook Series $60.00
Lady Lovelace — cloth/felt, 1930s $650.00
Lady Valentine — 8", #140503, 1994 only (Wendy Ann) $65.00
Lady Windermere — 21" compo., 1945 – 1946, extra make-up, Portrait Series . . . .$2,500.00 up
Lancelot — 8", #79529, 1995, 100th Anniversary (copy of 1995 Disney auction doll) $100.00
   8", #13550, 1999, blue and black outfit with sword $75.00
Lane, Harriet — 1982 – 1984, third set Presidents' Ladies/First Ladies Series (Mary Ann) $125.00
Laos — 8" straight leg, #525, 1987 – 1988 . . . .$60.00
La Petite Mademoiselle — 8", #37210, 2003 –2004, toile dress, bear in wagon $90.00
Lapland — 8" h.p., #537, 1993 . . . .$60.00
Lassie — 8", #11102, 1995 only, International Folk Tales (Norway) $60.00
Latvia — 8" straight leg, #527, 1987 only $65.00
Laughing Allegra — cloth, 1932 . . . .$650.00
Laura Ingalls Wilder — 8", #14110, 1998 – 1999, patchwork print outfit $85.00
Laurie, Little Men — 8" h.p., BK, #781, #755, 1966 – 1972 (Wendy Ann) $175.00
   Straight leg, #0755, #416, 1973 – 1975, marked "Alex" $95.00
   Checked pants, marked "Alexander" $85.00
   Straight leg, #416, #410, 1976 – 1992 . . . .$75.00
   8", #14620, 1996, waistcoat, houndstooth trousers $60.00
   12" all h.p., 1966 only (Lissy) $600.00
   12" plastic/vinyl, 1967 – 1988 (Nancy Drew) $70.00
Laurie, Piper — 14" h.p., 1950 only (Margaret) . . . .$2,400.00 up
   21" h.p., 1950 only (Margaret) . . . .$2,900.00 up
Lavender Bouquet — 8", #30895, 2001 – 2002, white, long black gown with lavender flowers $80.00
Lavender Sachet — 8", #33645, 2004, lavender dress $90.00
Laverne and Shirley Set — 10", #25755, 2000, with Boo Boo Kitty $180.00
Lazy Mary — 7" compo., 1936 – 1938 (Tiny Betty) $275.00
Leaf Fairy — 8", #28505, 2001 – 2002, rust costume with leaves $85.00
Lemonade Girl — 8", #14130, 1998 – 1999 (Maggie), doll with stand, etc $80.00
Lena (Riverboat Queen) — (see M.A.D.C. under Special Events/Exclusives)
Lennox, Mary — 14" Classic Series, 1993 – 1994 . . . .$80.00
Leo — 8", #21370, 1998, golden lion costume $90.00
Leopard with Shopping Bag — 10", Cissette, 1997 – 1998 . . . .$100.00
Le Petit Boudoir — 1993 (see Collectors United under Special Events/Exclusives)

Leslie, 17", 1970, #1665, plastic/vinyl (Polly).

Lily, 10", #1114, 1987 – 1988 (Cissette). Portrette Series.

Jenny Lind, 21", #2191, 1969 (Jacqueline).

Leslie (black Polly)

Leslie (black Polly) — 17" vinyl, 1965 – 1971, in dress $275.00
   1966 – 1971, as bride $300.00
   1965 – 1971, in formal or ballgown $375.00
   In trunk with wardrobe . . . .$650.00 up
   1966 – 1971, as ballerina $400.00
Letty Bridesmaid — 7" – 8" compo., 1938 – 1940 (Tiny Betty) $350.00
Lewis, Shari — 14", 1958 – 1959 . . . .$675.00
   21", 1958 – 1959 . . . .$850.00
Liberace with Candelabra — 8", #22080, 1997, velvet cape $100.00
Liberty Angel — 10", #34300, 2002, white gown, feather wings with jewels $140.00
Libra — 8", #21390, 1998, balanced scale headpiece, purple costume $90.00
Liesl — (see Sound of Music)
Lila Bridesmaid — 7 – 8" compo., 1938 – 1940 (Tiny Betty) $325.00
Lilac Fairy — 21", 1993, Portrait Ballerina $300.00
Lilac Rococo Lady — 5", #27020, porcelain, 2000, embroidered gown $80.00
'Lil Christmas Candy — 8" h.p., #100348, 1994 only, Americana Series $65.00
'Lil Christmas Cookie — 8", #341, 1993 – 1994, Americana Series $70.00
'Lil Clara and the Nutcracker — 8", #140480, 1994, Storyland Series $70.00
Lilibet — 16" compo., 1938 (Princess Elizabeth) . . . .$750.00 up
'Lil Sir Genius — 7", #701 and #400701 vinyl, painted eyes, 1993, blue jumpsuit $45.00
Lily — 10", #1114, 1987 – 1988, red/black (Cissette) $70.00
Lily of the Valley — 10", satin gown with lilies of the valley $125.00
Lily of the Valley Fairy — 8", #36885, 2003 – 2004, lace and tulle gown $90.00
Lincoln, Mary Todd — 1982 – 1984, third set Presidents' Ladies/First Ladies Series (Louisa) $150.00
Lind, Jenny — 21" h.p./vinyl arms, #2191, 1969, dressed in all pink, no trim (Jacqueline) $1,400.00
   #2181, 1970, all pink with lace trim, 21" $1,500.00
   10", #1171, 1969, Portrette, all pink, no trim (Cissette) $575.00
   10", #1184, 1970, Portrette, pink with lace trim (Cissette) $650.00

Dating Lissy Dolls

12" Lissy and Lissy face dolls are all hard plastic with glued-on wigs. Lissy is not marked anywhere on the body. Only the clothes were tagged.

1956 – 1958: Lissy had jointed elbows and knees which allow her to sit. Her feet are slightly arched to wear sandals with hose or white socks. The 1957 – 1958 Lissy Little Women wear black sandals.

1959 – 1967: The Lissy face dolls have the Lissy face but have non-jointed arms and legs. The feet are flat.

1959 – 1967: Lissy face Little Women were made.

1959: Kelly (Lissy face) was produced in 1959 only in a variety of outfits.

1962: Pamela (Lissy face) had three interchangeable outfits with extra clothing in a gift set. Pamela has a Velcro strip to attach the wigs. Pamelas were made for several years as store specials. Pamela was also made with the later Nancy Drew vinyl head.

1962: Lissy face Katie and Tommy made for FAO Schwarz's 100th Anniversary.

1963: McGuffey Ana, Southern Belle, and Scarlett O'Hara were made using the Lissy face doll.

1965: Brigitta of the large set of the Sound of Music was made using the Lissy face doll in an Alpine outfit and the rare sailor costume.

1966: Lissy face Cinderella was available in "poor" outfit or in blue satin ballgown. A gift set featured the doll and both outfits.

1967: Only year Laurie of Little Women was made using the Lissy face.

1993: Nine Lissy face dolls were made for the regular line: Amy, Beth, Jo, Meg, Ballerina, Greta Brinker, Hans Brinker, Hamlet, and Ophelia.

1993: Special for Horchow. Pamela Plays Dress Up was a Lissy face doll with wigs, clothes, and a trunk. Lissy face Alice in Wonderland with Jabberwocky was made for Disney, and the Columbian Sailor was made for the U.F.D.C. Luncheon.

14" plastic/vinyl, #1491, 1970 only, Portrait Children Series (Mary Ann), pink, lace trim $350.00

10", #27375, 2000, long white gown $100.00

Lind, Jenny & Listening Cat — 14", #1470, 1969 – 1971, Portrait Children Series,
blue dot dress apron and holds plush kitten (must have kitten) (Mary Ann) $325.00

Linus — 10", #26435, 2001 – 2002, Peanuts Gang, red stripe shirt, blue blanket $30.00

10", #35895, 2003 – 2004, Trick or Treat, blanket, sign, pumpkin $45.00

Lion Tamer — 8", #306, 1990, Americana Series (Wendy Ann) $60.00

Lissy — 11½" – 12" h.p., 1956 – 1958, jointed knees and elbows

1956 – 1958, as ballerina $475.00

1956 – 1958, as bride ....$475.00 up

1956 – 1957, as bridesmaid ....$700.00 up

1958, dressed in formal ....$800.00 up

1956 – 1958, in street dresses ....$375.00 up

1956, in window box with wardrobe $1,600.00

21", one-piece arm, pink tulle pleated skirt (Cissy) $1,450.00

21", #2051, 1966, pink with tiara (Coco) $2,200.00

12" h.p., 1957, jointed elbows and knees, in window box with wardrobe (Lissy) ....$1,500.00 up

12" h.p., one-piece arms and legs in window box/wardrobe, 1959 – 1966 (Lissy) ....$1,000.00 up

Classics (see individuals, examples: McGuffey Ana, Scarlett, Cinderella)

Lithuania — 8" h.p., #110544, 1994 only (Maggie) $60.00

Little Angel — 9" latex/vinyl, 1950 – 1957 ....$200.00

Little Audrey — Vinyl, 1954 only ....$475.00 up

Little Betty — 9" – 11" compo., 1935 – 1943, must be mint ....$250.00 – 375.00

Little Bitsey — 9" all vinyl nurser, 1967 – 1968 (Sweet Tears) $150.00

Little Boop Beep — 10", #28970, 2001 (Betty Boop), pink dress $125.00

Little Bo Peep — (see Bo Peep, Little)

Little Boy Blue — 7" compo., 1937 – 1939 (Tiny Betty) $300.00

Little Butch — 9" all vinyl nurser, 1967 – 1968 (Sweet Tears) $150.00

Little Cherub — 11" compo., 1945 – 1946 ....$275.00

7" all vinyl, 1960 only $225.00

Little Christmas Princess — 8", #10369, 1996 Holiday $65.00

Little Colonel — 8½" – 9" compo. (rare size), 1935, closed mouth (Betty) $650.00

Lissy, 12", 1956 – 1958, jointed at elbows and knees. Tagged "Lissy," pink cotton dress, black taffeta pinafore, and hat.

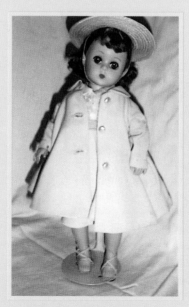

Lissy, 12", 1956 – 1958, all hard plastic jointed knees and elbows. Tagged outfit, probably from 1957.

Lissy, 12", 1956 – 1958, all hard plastic (Lissy). Mint and all original. Tagged "Lissy."

Little Colonel

11" – 13" compo. (rare size), closed mouth (Betty)	$550.00 – 750.00
17" compo., closed mouth (Betty)	$750.00 up
14", open mouth (Betty)	$650.00 up
17" – 23", open mouth	$700.00 – 950.00
26" – 27", open mouth	$1,300.00 up

Little Countess — 8", #28890, 2001, white lacy dress $100.00
Little Devil — 8" h.p., Americana Series, 1992 – 1993 only $75.00
Little Dorrit — 16" cloth, early 1930s, Dickens character $700.00
Little Edwardian — 8" h.p., SL, SLW, #0200, 1953 – 1955, long dotted navy gown ....$1,000.00 up
Little Emily — 16" cloth, early 1930s, Dickens character $650.00
Little Emperor — 8" (see U.F.D.C. under Special Events/Exclusives)
Little Gardenia Bridesmaid — 8", 2001, white dress $100.00
Little Genius — 12" – 14" compo./cloth, 1935 – 1940, 1942 – 1946 ....$250.00

16" – 20" compo./cloth, 1935 – 1937, 1942 – 1946	$250.00
24" – 25", 1936 – 1940	$275.00
8" h.p./vinyl, 1956 – 1962, nude (clean condition), good face color	$100.00
In cotton play dress	$200.00
In dressy, lacy outfit with bonnet	$325.00
In christening outfit	$375.00
Sewing or Gift Set, 1950s	$850.00 up
7" vinyl, 1993 – 1995, reintroduced doll with painted eyes	$45.00
#701 and #400701, 1993 – 1995, dressed in blue jumpsuit ('Lil Sir Genius)	$45.00
#702 and #400702, 1993 – 1995, dressed in pink lacy dress ('Lil Miss Genius)	$50.00
1993, extra packaged outfits	$30.00 ea.
Christening Baby, #400703, 1994 – 1995	$50.00
Super Genius, #400704, 1994 – 1995, dressed in Superman style outfit	$45.00
Birthday Party, #400705, 1994 only	$50.00
Genius Elf, #400706, 1994 – 1995, dressed in Christmas outfit	$50.00

Little Genius Toddler — 8" h.p., 1954 – 1955 (Wendy Ann), caracul hair $275.00
Little Girl with a Curl — 8", #28965, 2001, pink dress $75.00
Little Godey — 8" h.p., #491, 1953 – 1955 (Wendy Ann) ....$1,400.00 up
Little Granny — 14" plastic/vinyl, #1431, 1966 only, floral gown (Mary Ann) $200.00

   14", #1430, 1966 only, pinstriped gown (also variations) (Mary Ann) $225.00

Little Huggums — (see Huggums)
Little Irish Dancer — 8", #32125, 2000 – 2004, navy decorated dress, bend knees $90.00
Little Jack Horner — 7" compo., 1937 – 1943 (Tiny Betty) $300.00
Little Jumping Joan — 8", #487, 1989 – 1990, Storybook Series (Maggie Mixup) $65.00
Little Lady Doll — 8" h.p., #1050, 1960 only, Gift Set in mint condition (Maggie Mixup) ...$900.00 up

   8" doll only, must have correct hairdo and excellent face color $325.00
   21" h.p., 1949, has braids and colonial gown, extra make-up, Portrait Series (Wendy Ann) ...$2,400.00

Little Lord Fauntleroy — cloth, 1930s $750.00

   13" compo., 1936 – 1937 (Wendy Ann) ....$650.00 up

Little Love Angel — 8", #28350, 2001– 2002, pink costume with wings $100.00

   10", #28355, 2001, lavender dress, feather wings $110.00

Little Madeline — 8" h.p., 1953 – 1954 (Wendy Ann) ....$750.00 up
Little Maid — 8" straight leg, #423, 1987 – 1988, Storybook Series (Wendy Ann) $60.00
Little Men — 15" h.p., 1950 – 1952 (Margaret and Maggie) ....$850.00 up ea.
Little Men — Set with Tommy, Nat, and Stuffy, must be in excellent condition ....$2,600.00 set
Little Mermaid — 10", #1145, 1992 – 1993, Portrette, green/blue outfit (Cissette) $100.00

   8", #14531, 1995, Hans Christian Andersen Series, has long black hair $60.00

Little Minister — 8" h.p., #411, 1957 only (Wendy Ann) ....$3,200.00 up
Little Miss — 8" h.p., #489, 1989 – 1991 only, Storybook Series (Maggie Mixup) $65.00
Little Miss Godey — (see M.A.D.C. under Special Events/Exclusives)
Little Miss Magnin — (see I. Magnin under Special Events/Exclusives)
Little Miss Sunshine — 8", #35065, 2003 – 2004 (Maggie), yellow print dress $50.00
Little Nannie Etticoat — #428, 1986 – 1988, straight leg, Storybook Series $60.00

Little Nell — 16" cloth, early 1930s, Dickens character . . . .$650.00 up

    14" compo., 1938 – 1940 (Wendy Ann) $700.00

Little Orphan Annie — 8", #13740, 1999 – 2002, red dress, comes with dog Sandy $70.00

Little Pearl Bridesmaid — 8", 2001, white dress, rose crown $90.00

Little Princess — 14", #26415, 1995 only, has trunk and wardrobe (Louisa) $225.00

Little Princess, A — 8", #14120, 1998 – 1999, pink taffeta, with doll $85.00

Little Shaver — 10" cloth, 1940 – 1944 . . . .$475.00 up

    7" cloth, 1940 – 1944 . . . .$550.00

    15" cloth, 1940 – 1944 . . . .$650.00

    22" cloth, 1940 – 1944 . . . .$700.00 up

    12" cloth, 1941 – 1943 (see Baby Shaver)

    12" plastic/vinyl, 1963 – 1965, has painted eyes $225.00

    10", #26820, 2000, cloth, grey/cream, remake of 1940s $55.00

    10", #26825, 2000 – 2001, cloth, pink/cream, remake of 1940s $55.00

    6", #26830, 2000 – 2001, cloth, gray/cream, remake of 1940s $50.00

Little Southern Boy/Girl — 10" latex/vinyl, 1950 – 1951 . . . .$195.00 ea.

Little Southern Girl — 8" h.p., #305, 1953 only (Wendy Ann) . . . .$950.00 up

Littlest Kitten — 8" vinyl, 1963, nude, clean, good face color . . . .$125.00 up

    Dressed in lacy dress outfit with bonnet . . . .$275.00 up

    Dressed in christening outfit . . . .$350.00 up

    In sewing or Gift Set . . . .$750.00 up

    Dressed in play attire $175.00

Little Thumbkins — 8", #14532, Hans Christian Andersen Series, lavender/pink/yellow tiers $60.00

Little Victoria — 7½" – 8", #376, 1953 – 1954 only (Wendy Ann) . . . .$1,200.00 up

Little Women — Meg, Jo, Amy, Beth (Marme in sets when available)

    16" cloth, 1930 – 1936 . . . .$750.00 up ea.

    7" compo., 1935 – 1944 (Tiny Betty) . . . .$350.00 ea.

    9" compo., 1937 – 1940 (Little Betty) . . . .$325.00 ea.

    13" – 15" compo., 1937 – 1946 (Wendy Ann) . . . .$350.00 ea.

    14" – 15" h.p., 1947 – 1956, plus Marme (Margaret and Maggie) . . . .$450.00 ea., $2,200.00 set

    14" – 15" h.p., widespread fingers, ca. 1949 – 1952 . . . .$550.00 ea.

    14" – 15" h.p., BK, plus Marme (Margaret and Maggie) . . . .$450.00 ea., $2,200.00 set

    14" – 15" Amy with loop curls, must have good face color (Margaret) . . . .$550.00 ea.

    8" Amy with loop curls, 1991, #411 . . . .$100.00 ea.

Little Shaver, cloth, 1940 – 1944.

Jo, Little Women, 12", #1207, 1988 (Nancy Drew). All original.

Jo, Little Women, 16", cloth doll, 1930s.

Little Women

7½" – 8" h.p., SL, SLW, all #609, 1955, plus Marme (Wendy Ann) . . . .$400.00 ea., $2,000.00 set
8" h.p., BKW, all #609, all #409, all #481, 1956 – 1959 (Wendy Ann) . . . .$350.00 ea., $1,600.00 set
8" BKW, all #381, 1960 – 1963 (Wendy Ann) . . . .$250.00 ea., $1,200.00 set
    #781, 1966 – 1972 . . . .$125.00 ea., $650.00 set
    #7811 to #7815, 1973 . . . .$75.00 ea., $375.00 set
8" straight leg, #411 to #415, 1974 – 1986 . . . .$70.00 ea., $325.00 set
    #405 to #409, 1987 – 1990 . . . .$60.00 ea., $275.00 set
    #411 to #415, 1991 – 1992 . . . .$60.00 ea., $275.00 set
    #14523 – #14528, 1995 . . . .$60.00 ea., $275.00 set
    #33375, #33380, #33385, #33386, 2002, Amy, Meg, Jo, Beth . . . .$80.00 ea.
    #36120, Marmee, 2003, brown plaid dress $90.00
    #36125, Laurie, 2003, brown three-piece suit $80.00
    #33375, #33380, #33385, #33386, Amy, Meg, Jo, Beth, 2004 . . . .$90.00 ea.
    #39070, 2004, Amy's Party Dress, long pink party dress with roses $90.00
    Exclusive for FAO Schwarz (see Special Events/Exclusives)
    #28140 – #28180, 2000 . . . .$65.00 – $325.00 set
10", #14630 – #14633, 1996 . . . .$70.00 ea., $325.00 set
11½" – 12" h.p., jointed elbows and knees, 1957 – 1958 (Lissy) . . . .$400.00 ea., $2,000.00 set
11½" – 12" h.p., one-piece arms and legs, 1959 – 1968 (Lissy) . . . .$250.00 ea., $1,200.00 set
12" plastic/vinyl, 1969 – 1982 (Nancy Drew) . . . .$65.00 ea., $325.00 set
12" plastic/vinyl, 1983 – 1989, new outfits (Nancy Drew) . . . .$65.00 ea., $325.00 set
12", 1989 – 1990 only (see Sears under Special Events/Exclusives)
12", 1993 only, no Marme (Lissy) . . . .$100.00 ea.
16", 1997 – 2000, plastic/vinyl, Little Women Journal Series (no Marme) . . . .$85.00 ea.
16", 1999 – 2000, Marme, #28040, Little Women Journals $100.00
Lively Huggums — 25", knob makes limbs and head move, 1963 . . . .$150.00
Lively Kitten — 14", 18", 24", 1962 – 1963, knob makes limbs and head move . . . .$100.00 – 175.00
Lively Pussy Cat — 14", 20", 24", 1966 – 1969, knob makes limbs and head move . . . .$100.00 – 225.00
Lola and Lollie Bridesmaid — 7" compo., 1938 – 1940 (Tiny Betty) . . . .$350.00 up ea.
Lollie Baby — Rubber/compo., 1941 – 1942 . . . .$100.00
Lollipop Munchkin — (see Munchkin)
Looby Loo — 15½" h.p., ca. 1951 – 1954 . . . .$675.00 up

Little Women, 8", Marme, both BK walkers (Wendy).

Meg, Little Women, 12" (Nancy Drew), #1323, 1981.

Lord Fauntleroy — 12", 1981 – 1983, Portrait Children (Nancy Drew) $85.00
Lord Valentine — 8", #140502, 1994 only (Wendy Ann) $60.00
Louisa — (see Sound of Music)
Love — (see Collectors United under Specials Events/Exclusives), 8", made for public in 1994 (only differences on
   C.U. doll are gold locket, pearls set into cap, and gold metal braids on slippers, heart box) $75.00
Love Notes for Grandma – 8", #36915, 2003 – 2004, red checked dress, notes $80.00
   10", #35890, 2003, trick or treat, mask, bag with candy $120.00
Lovey Dove (Dovey) — 19" vinyl baby, 1958 – 1959, closed mouth, molded or rooted hair, few are mistagged $175.00
   19" h.p./latex, 1950 – 1951 ....$175.00
   12" all h.p. toddler, 1948 – 1951 (Precious) ....$375.00 up
   1951, dressed as "Ringbearer" ....$675.00 up
   "Answer Doll" with lever in back to move head ....$525.00 up
Lucinda — 12" plastic/vinyl, 1969 – 1970 (Janie) $275.00
   14" plastic/vinyl, #1435, #1535, 1971 – 1982 (11-year production), blue gown (Mary Ann) $65.00
   14", #1535, 1983 – 1986, Classic Series, pink or peach gown (Mary Ann) $75.00
Luck of the Irish — 8", #327, 1992 – 1993 only, Americana Series (Maggie Mixup) $65.00
   8", #38595, 2004, with 5" leprechaun and pot of gold $90.00
Lucy — 8" h.p., #488, 1961 only, Americana Series, strip cotton/poke bonnet (Wendy Ann) ....$1,800.00 up
   10", #26420, 2001 – 2004, Peanuts Gang, blue dress, includes backdrop $45.00
   10", #33715, 2002, School Days Lucy (Peanuts), plaid coat, books $45.00
Lucy Bride — 14" h.p., 1949 – 1950 (Margaret) ....$950.00 up
   18" h.p., 1949 – 1950 (Margaret) ....$950.00 up
   21" h.p., 1949 – 1950 (Margaret) ....$1,100.00 up
   21", #2155, 1955 (Cissy) pale pink gown, very red hair, heavily painted face ....$6,500.00 up
   14" compo., 1937 – 1940 (Wendy Ann) $450.00
   17" compo., 1937 – 1940 (Wendy Ann) $600.00
   21" compo., 1942 – 1944, Portrait, extra make-up (Wendy Ann) $2,500.00
Lucy Gets in Pictures — 10", #31450, 2001, long pink gown, feather headpiece $160.00
Lucy Locket — 8" straight leg, #433, 1986 – 1988, Storybook Series $60.00
   14", #25501, 1995, Ribbons & Bows Series, purple floral skirt (Louisa) $90.00
Lucy and Ricky — 9" set, Vitameatavegamin episode $200.00
Lucy Ricardo — (see FAO Schwarz under Special Events/Exclusives)
   9", 1950s gingham dress, with bottle and spoon $110.00
   21", #50003, 1996 Timeless Legends, black dress with black and white polka dot accents $350.00

Lucinda, 12", #1135, 1969 – 1970 (Janie).

Lucinda, 14" (Mary Ann). Left, 1971 – 1982;
right, 1983 – 1986.

Lucy Ricardo

10", #14071, Shadow Polka Dot Lucy, 1998 – 1999 . . . .$175.00
10", #15160, 1999 – 2000, Lucy's Italian Movie, peasant outfit, grape vat $160.00
Lucy's Rhumba — 10", #25760, 2001, Be a Pal episode, white dress, ruffles $130.00
Lullaby Munchkin — (see Munchkin)
Mad Hatter — 8", #14510, 1995, Alice in Wonderland Series $85.00
8", #38880, 2004, with teapot, cup, and mouse $85.00
Madame (Alexander) — 21", 1984 only, one-piece skirt in pink $275.00
21", 1985 – 1987, pink with overskirt that unsnaps $225.00
21", 1988 – 1990, blue with full lace overskirt $225.00
21", #79507, 1995, 100th Anniversary, pink with lace jacket, limited edition of 500 . . . .$425.00
8", 1993 only, introduced mid-year (see Madame Alexander Doll Co. under Special Events/Exclusives)
8" in blue gown (see Doll & Teddy Bear Expo. under Special Events/Exclusives)
8", #79527, 1995, 100th Anniversary $100.00
Madame Alexander Celebrates American Design — 10" h.p. (Cissette), 2000, pink gown $130.00
Madame Alexander Collector's Phonograph Album — 1978, Madame's voice reading children's stories $35.00
M.A.D.C. (Madame Alexander Doll Club) — (see Special Events/Exclusives)
Madame Butterfly — 10" (see Marshall Fields under Special Events/Exclusives)
8" h.p., #22000, 1997 – 1998, shadow, kimono $90.00
21", #22010, 1997, kimono over silk robe $325.00
Madame de Pompadour — 10", #25010, 1999 (Cissette), elaborate taffeta costume $175.00
Madame Doll — 21" h.p./vinyl arms, 1966 only, pink brocade (Coco) . . . .$2,300.00 up
14" plastic/vinyl, #1460, #1561, 1967 – 1975, Classic Series (Mary Ann) $225.00
Madame Pompadour — 21" h.p./vinyl arms, #2197, 1970, pink lace overskirt (Jacqueline) $425.00
Madame's Best — 8", #38045, 2004, dress and pinafore $95.00
Madame X, John Singer Sargent's — 10", #25300, 2000, long black gown $120.00
Madelaine — 14" compo., 1940 – 1942 (Wendy Ann) . . . .$650.00 up
8" h.p., 1954, FAO Schwarz special . . . .$800.00 up
Madelaine Du Bain — 11" compo., closed mouth, 1937 (Wendy Ann) $500.00
14" compo., 1938 – 1939 (Wendy Ann) . . . .$550.00 up
17" compo., 1939 – 1941 (Wendy Ann) $675.00
21" compo., 1939 – 1941 (Wendy Ann) . . . .$900.00 up
14" h.p., 1949 – 1951 (Maggie) . . . .$950.00 up

Madame, 14", 1967 – 1975 (Mary Ann).
Has pearl necklace hidden in slip pocket.

Madame's Best, 8", 2004, BK (Wendy),
pink and blue dress.

Madeline — 17" – 18" h.p./jointed elbows and knees, 1950 – 1953 ....$800.00 up
    18" h.p., 1961 only, vinyl head, extra jointed body, wears short dress, must be mint ....$700.00 up
    Ballgown 1961 only ....$800.00 up
Madison, Dolly — 1976 – 1978, first set Presidents' Ladies/First Ladies Series (Martha) $125.00
Madonna and Child — 10", #10600, 1995, Christmas Series $100.00
Maggie — 15" h.p., 1948 – 1954 (Little Women only to 1956) $550.00
    17" – 18", 1949 – 1953 ....$650.00 up
    20" – 21", 1948 – 1954 ....$750.00 up
    22" – 23", 1949 – 1952 ....$800.00 up
    17" plastic/vinyl, 1972 – 1973 only (Elise) $175.00
Maggie Elf — 8", #14585, 1995, Christmas Series $65.00
Maggie Mixup — 16½" h.p./vinyl, 1960 only (Elise body) $400.00
    17" plastic/vinyl, 1961 only $400.00
    8" h.p., #600, #611, #617, #627, 1960 – 1961, freckles $450.00
    8" Wendy Ann face, freckles ....$650.00 up
    8" h.p., #618, 1961, as angel $800.00
    8", #610, 1960 – 1961, dressed in overalls and has watering can $800.00
    8", #626, 1960 – 1961, dressed in skater outfit ....$750.00 up
    8", #634, 1960 – 1961, dressed in riding habit $550.00
    8", #593, 1960, dressed in roller skating outfit ....$750.00 up
    8", #598, #597, #596, 1960, wearing dresses or skirts/blouses ....$475.00 up
    8", #31000, 1997 – 1998, Post Office commemorative, blue gingham $55.00
Maggie's Best Memories — 8", #38905, 2004, plaid dress, scrapbook $90.00
Maggie Teenager — 15" – 18" h.p., 1951 – 1953 ....$475.00 – 650.00
    23", 1951 – 1953 ....$650.00 up
Maggie Walker — 15" – 18" h.p., 1949 – 1953 ....$400.00 – 650.00
    20" – 21", 1949 – 1953 ....$600.00
    23" – 25", 1951 – 1953 (with Cissy face) ....$650.00 up
Magnolia — 21", #2297, 1977 only, many rows of lace on pink gown $425.00
    21", #2251, 1988 only, yellow gown $275.00
Maid Marian — 8" h.p., #492, 1989 – 1991 only, Storybook Series (Wendy Ann) $135.00
    21", 1992 – 1993 only, Portrait Series (Jacqueline) $325.00
Maid of Honor — 18" compo., 1940 – 1944 (Wendy Ann) ....$700.00 up
    14" plastic/vinyl, #1592, 1988 – 1989, Classic Series, blue gown (Mary Ann) $90.00
    10", #28645, 2001 – 2002, long pink dress, limited to 1,000 ....$125.00
Maimey Shadow Wendy — 8", #38755, blue dress, white sweater $95.00
Majorette — 14" – 17" compo., 1937 – 1938 (Wendy Ann) ....$850.00 up
Majorette, Drum — 8" h.p., #482, 1955 only (Wendy Ann) ......$950.00 up
    8", #314, 1991 – 1992 only, Americana Series, no baton $65.00
Making Friends on Sesame Street — 8", #39086, #39085,
    2004 with Zoe, Cookie Monster, and Elmo $150.00
Making New Friends — 8", #37225, 2003 – 2004, African-American,
    pink dress, two dolls, #37226, Caucasian $80.00
Mali — 8", #11565, 1996 International, African-American print costume ...$60.00
Mambo — 8" h.p., #481, 1955 only (Wendy Ann) ....$850.00 up
Mammy — 8", #402, 1989 only, Jubilee II set (black "round" face) $150.00
    8" h.p., #635, 1991 – 1992 only, Scarlett Series (black Wendy Ann on
    Cissette body $100.00
    10" h.p., #15010, 1997 – 1999 (black Wendy Ann) $100.00
    #38825, 8", 2004, checked dress, white apron, hat $85.00
Manet — 21", #2225, 1982 – 1983, light brown with dark brown
    pinstripes (Jacqueline) $225.00
    14", #1571, 1986 – 1987, Fine Arts Series (Mary Ann) $75.00
Marcella Dolls — 13" – 24" compo., 1936 only, dressed in
    1930s fashions ....$650.00 – 900.00 ea.
March Hare — cloth/felt, mid-1930s $700.00

Manet, 14" (Mary Ann), #1571, 1986 – 1987.

Margaret (O'Brien)

Margaret (O'Brien) — 14" h.p., nude with excellent color $375.00

 18" h.p., nude with excellent color ....$600.00 up

 14" h.p., in tagged Alexander boxed clothes $800.00

 18" ....$750.00 up

 21" compo., tagged Alexander clothes ....$1,300.00 up

Margaret Ann — 15", #90100, 1999, blue dress, straw hat, porcelain $125.00

Margaret Rose — (see Princess Margaret Rose)

Margot — 10" – 11" h.p., 1961 only, in formals (Cissette) ....$500.00 up

 Street dresses, bathing suit, 1961 only $425.00

Margot Ballerina — 15" – 18", 1951 – 1953, dressed in various colored outfits (Margaret and Maggie) ....$650.00 – 850.00

 15" – 18" h.p./vinyl arms, 1955 only (Cissy) ....$350.00 – 700.00

Maria — (see Sound of Music)

Marie Antoinette — 21", #2248, 1987 – 1988, multi-floral print with pink front insert (Jacqueline) $350.00

 21" compo., 1944 – 1946, Portrait with extra make-up and in mint condition (Wendy Ann) ....$2,300.00 up

Marilla — 10", #261-168, 1994, Anne of Green Gables Series $85.00

Marine — 14" compo., 1943 – 1944 (Wendy Ann as boy) ....$800.00 up

Marionettes/Tony Sarg — 12" – 14" compo., 1934 – 1940 ....$450.00 up

 12" compo., Disney characters ....$550.00 up

Marionette Theatre — by Tony Sarg, 1938 ....$800.00 up

Marley's Ghost — 8", #18004, 1996, Dickens, silver chains $60.00

Marme — (see Little Women)

Marme Liza — 21" compo., 1938 and 1946, extra make-up, mint condition (Wendy Ann) ....$3,200.00 up

Marshall Fields — (see Special Events/Exclusives)

Marta — (see Sound of Music)

Martin, Mary — 14" – 17" h.p., 1948 – 1952, wearing jumpsuit (Margaret) ....$700.00 – 1,000.00

 14" – 17", 1948 – 1952, dressed in sailor suit or ballgown (Nell from South Pacific) ....$750.00 – 975.00

Mary Ann — 14" plastic/vinyl, 1965, tagged "Mary Ann," in red/white dress $225.00

 Dressed in skirt and sweater $250.00

 Ballerina $250.00

 14" ballerina, 1973 – 1982 ....$125.00

 14", reintroduced #241599, 1994 only $75.00

Mary-Bel, "The Doll That Gets Well" — 16" rigid vinyl, 1959 – 1965, doll only $200.00

 1959, 1961, 1965, doll in case $325.00

 1960 only, doll in case with wardrobe $350.00

 1965 only, doll with very long straight hair, in case $350.00

Alice, 12", Tony Sarg/Marionettes, comp., all original.

 75th Anniversary, Mary-Bel Returns, 1998, #12220 ....$150.00

Mary Cassatt Baby — 14" cloth/vinyl, 1969 – 1970 ....$175.00

 20", 1969 – 1970 ....$250.00

 14" plastic/vinyl child, #1566, 1987 only, Fine Arts Series (Mary Ann) ...$85.00

Mary Ellen — 31" rigid vinyl, walker, 1954 only ....$650.00 up

 31" plastic/vinyl arms, 1955 only, non-walker with jointed elbows ...$525.00 up

Mary Ellen Playmate — 16" plastic/vinyl, 1965 only, Marshall Fields exclusive (Mary Ann) $350.00

 12", 1965, in case with wigs (Lissy) ....$850.00 up

 17", 1965, exclusive $350.00

Mary Engelbreit Pink Flower Tea Set — #33850, 2002 ....$40.00

Mary Gray — 14" plastic/vinyl, #1564, 1988 only, Classic Series (Mary Ann) $75.00

Mary Had a Little Lamb — 8", #14623, 1996 Nursery Rhyme, #11610, 1997 – 1999 ....$70.00

Mary, Joseph, Baby Jesus in Manger — 8", #19470, 1997 – 2000, Nativity set $225.00

Mary Lennox — 14", #1537, 1993 – 1994, Classic Doll Series $85.00

 8" h.p., #13850, 1998 – 1999 (Secret Garden), plaid jumper, holds key ...$80.00

Mary Louise — 21" compo., 1938, 1946 – 1947, golden brown/burnt orange (Wendy Ann) $2,700.00

18" h.p., 1954 only, Me & My Shadow Series, burnt orange and olive green (Cissy) . . . . $1,800.00 up
8" h.p., #0035D, 1954 only, same as 18", Me & My Shadow Series (Wendy Ann) . . . . $1,200.00 up
Mary, Mary — 8" h.p., BKW, BK, #751, 1965 – 1972, Storybook Series (Wendy Ann) $125.00
    8" h.p., straight leg, #0751, #451, 1973 – 1975, marked "Alex" $70.00
    8" h.p., straight leg, #451, 1976 – 1987, marked "Alexander" (1985 – 1987 white face) $65.00
    8", #471, reintroduced 1992 only (Wendy Ann) $60.00
    8", #14556, 1996, floral dress, straw hat, #11600, 1997 – 1999, water can $65.00
    8", #25930, 2000 – 2001 (Maggie), pink print dress, straw hat $70.00
    14", #1569, 1988 – 1991, Classic Series (Mary Ann) $80.00
    14", #241595, reintroduced 1994 only $95.00
Mary Mine — 21" cloth/vinyl, 1977 – 1989 . . . . $125.00
    14" cloth/vinyl, 1977 – 1979 . . . . $100.00
    14", reintroduced 1989 . . . . $75.00
Mary Muslin — 19" cloth, 1951 only, pansy eyes $500.00
    26", 1951 only $575.00
    40", 1951 only $850.00
Mary Poppins Set - 10" Mary, 5" Michael and Jane, 2004, #38380 . . . . $220.00
Mary, Queen of Scots — 21", #2252, 1988 – 1989 (Jacqueline) $325.00
Mary Rose Bride — 17" h.p., 1951 only (Margaret) . . . . $850.00 up
Mary Sunshine, Little — 15" plastic/vinyl, 1961 (Caroline) $350.00
Marzipan Dancer — 10", #14573, 1995, Nutcracker Series (Cissette) $75.00
Matthew — 8", #26424, 1995, Anne of Green Gables Series $70.00
Mayor of Munchkinland — 8", #37125, 2004, Wizard of Oz $80.00
McElroy, Mary — 1985 – 1987, fourth set Presidents' Ladies/First Ladies Series (Mary Ann) $100.00
McGuffey Ana — 16" cloth, 1934 – 1936 . . . . $675.00 up
    7" compo., 1935 – 1939 (Tiny Betty) $350.00
    9" compo., 1935 – 1939 (Little Betty) $375.00
    15" compo., 1935 – 1937 (Betty) $675.00
    13" compo., 1938 (Wendy Ann) $650.00
    11", 1937 – 1939, has closed mouth $675.00
    11" – 13" compo., 1937 – 1944 (Princess Elizabeth) . . . . $675.00 – 750.00
    14" – 16" compo., 1937 – 1944 (Princess Elizabeth) . . . . $700.00 – 900.00
    17" – 20" compo., 1937 – 1943 (Princess Elizabeth) . . . . $700.00 – 1,200.00
    21" – 25" compo., 1937 – 1942 (Princess Elizabeth) . . . . $750.00 – 1,400.00

McGuffey Ana, 9", comp. All original
with original box.

McGuffey Ana, 25" (Princess
Elizabeth), comp. All original.

McGuffey Ana, comp., 1939.
Red plaid dress, white pinafore,
and red straw hat.

McGuffey Ana

28" compo., 1937 – 1939 (Princess Elizabeth) $1,400.00
17" compo., 1948 – 1949 (Margaret) $900.00
14½" compo., 1948, wears coat, hat and muff $950.00
18", 25", 31", 1955 – 1956, has flat feet (Cissy) ....$500.00 – 950.00
18" h.p., 1949 – 1950 (Margaret) $900.00
21" h.p., 1948 – 1950 (Margaret) $1,400.00
12" h.p. (rare doll), 1963 only (Lissy) ....$2,300.00 up
8" h.p., #616, 1956 only (Wendy Ann) $750.00
8" h.p., #788, #388, 1963 – 1965 (was "American Girl" in 1962 – 1963) $325.00
8", #496, 1990 – 1991 only, Storybook Series (Wendy Ann) $75.00
29" cloth/vinyl, 1952 only (Barbara Jane) $650.00
15" porcelain, #90110, 1999 – 2000 ....$150.00
14" plastic/vinyl, #1450, 1968 – 1969, Classic Series, wears plaid dress/eyelet apron (Mary Ann) $100.00
14" plastic/vinyl, #1525, 1977 – 1986, Classic Series, wears plaid dress (Mary Ann) $75.00
14" plastic/vinyl, #1526, 1987 – 1988, mauve stripe pinafore, Classic Series (Mary Ann) $75.00
14", #24622, 1995, red plaid dress, Nostalgia Series (Mary Ann) $75.00

McKee, Mary — 1985 – 1987, fourth set Presidents' Ladies/First Ladies Series (Mary Ann) $100.00
McKinley, Ida — 1988, fifth set Presidents' Ladies/First Ladies Series (Louisa) $100.00
Meagan — 14", #29990 or #30000, 1999 ....$80.00
Me and My Scassi — (see FAO Schwarz under Special Events/Exclusives)
Medici, Catherine de — 21" porcelain, 1990 – 1991 ....$400.00
Meg — 8", #79530, 100th Anniversary, two-tiered blue gown with white and rose trim (also see Little Women) $100.00
Melanie — 21" compo., 1945 – 1947 (Wendy Ann) ....$2,300.00 up

21" h.p./vinyl arms, 1961, lace bodice and overdress over satin (Cissy) ....$1,500.00 up
21", #2050, 1966, blue gown with wide lace down sides (Coco) ....$2,200.00 up
#2173, 1967, blue dress with white rick-rack around hem ruffle (Jacqueline) $575.00
#2181, 1968, rust brown dress and hat $575.00
#2193, 1969, blue gown, white trim, many rows of lace, bonnet $500.00
#2196, 1970, white gown with red ribbon trim $500.00
#2162, 1971, blue gown, white sequin trim $450.00
#2195, 1974, white gown, red jacket and bonnet $425.00
#2220, 1979 – 1980, white dotted Swiss gown with pink trim $350.00
1981, pink nylon with blue ribbon $350.00
#2254, 1989, all orange with lace shawl $300.00

Melanie, 21" (Jacqueline), #32220, 1979 – 1981.

Melanie, 21" (Jacqueline), #32193, 1969.

10", #1173, 1968 – 1969, pink multi-tiered skirt (Cissette) $400.00

10", #1182, 1970, yellow multi-tiered skirt $450.00

8" h.p., #633, 1955 – 1956, green velvet (Wendy Ann) . . . .$1,300.00 up

12", 1987 only, Portrait Children Series, aqua green gown, brown trim (Nancy Drew) $75.00

10", #1101, 1989 only, Jubilee II, royal blue dress with black trim (Cissette) $100.00

8", #627, 1990, Scarlett Series, lavender/lace (Wendy Ann) $90.00

8", #628, 1992, peach gown/bonnet with lace $80.00

8", #25775, 2000, blue gown and hat trimmed in lace $85.00

10", #16555, 1996, Melanie's Sewing Circle, blue dress $100.00

Melinda — 10" h.p., 1968 – 1969, blue gown with white trim (Cissette) $425.00

10" h.p., 1970, yellow multi-tiered lace skirt $400.00

22", #1912, 1962 only, wears white organdy dress with red trim $350.00

14", 16", 22" plastic/vinyl, 1962 – 1963, cotton dress $250.00

14", 16", 22" plastic/vinyl, 1963, party dress . . . .$275.00 – 475.00

14", 1963 only, as ballerina $300.00

Melody and Friend — 25" and 8" (see Madame Alexander Doll Co. under Special Events/Exclusives)

Merlin — 8", #13560, 1999, red velvet robe and crystal ball $75.00

Merry Angel — 8" (see Spiegel's under Special Events/Exclusives)

Metroplex Doll Club — (see Special Events/Exclusives)

Mexico — 7" compo., 1936 (Tiny Betty) $300.00

9" compo., 1938 – 1939 (Little Betty) $325.00

8" h.p., BKW, #776, 1964 – 1965 (Wendy Ann) $125.00

8" h.p., BK, #776, 1965 – 1972 . . . .$100.00

8" straight leg, #0776, 1973 – 1975, marked "ALEX" $70.00

8" straight leg, #576, #550, #520, 1976 – 1991, marked "Alexander" (1985 – 1987) $65.00

8", #11551, 1995 only (Maggie) $60.00

8", #24100, 1997 – 1998, Mariachi outfit, guitar $70.00

8", #38915, 2004 (Wendy), white blouse, red skirt $90.00

Michael — 11" plastic/vinyl, 1969 only (Janie) (Peter Pan set), with teddy bear $375.00

8", #468, 1992 – 1993, Storybook Series (Peter Pan set) (Wendy) $70.00

Mickey Mouse and Minnie Mouse — 8", 31601, 2003 – 2004, mouse ears, yellow shoes $100.00

Midnight — 21", #2256, 1990, dark blue/black (Jacqueline) $300.00

Midnight Angel — 8", #33135, 2002 – 2003, black gown and fur wings $90.00

Millennium Princess — 8", #25810, 2000 only, lavender gown $100.00

Miller's Daughter — 14" with 8" Rumpelstiltskin, #1569, 1992 only,

limited to 3,000 sets . . . .$300.00 set

Milly — 17" plastic/vinyl, 1968 only (Polly) $375.00

Mimi — 30" h.p. in 1961 only, multi-jointed body, dressed in formal $950.00

Dressed in romper suit/skirt $600.00

Dressed in Tyrolean outfit $950.00

Dressed in slacks, stripe top, straw hat $650.00

Dressed in red sweater, plaid skirt $650.00

21" h.p./vinyl arms, #2170, 1971, vivid pink cape and trim on white gown

(Jacqueline) $600.00

14", #1411, 1983 – 1986, Opera Series (Mary Ann) $85.00

Minister, Little — 8" h.p., #411, 1957 only . . . .$3,200.00 up

Miracle Santa — 10", 1996, with street sign $100.00

Miracle Wendy — 8", 1996 . . . .$100.00

Miss America — 14" compo., 1941 – 1943, holds flag . . . .$850.00 up

Miss Eliza Doolittle — 10", #20112, 1996 Classic $100.00

Miss Gulch with Bicycle, Toto — 10", #13240, 1997 – 2001,

Wizard of Oz Series $125.00

Miss Leigh — 8", 1989, made for C.U. Gathering (see Special Events/Exclusives)

Miss Liberty — 10" (see M.A.D.C. under Special Events/Exclusives)

Miss Magnin — 10" (see I. Magnin under Special Events/Exclusives)

Michael, 11", #1120, 1969, Peter Pan set (Janie), vinyl jointed body.

Miss Muffet, Little

Miss Muffet, Little — 8" h.p., BK, #752, 1965 – 1972, Storybook Series (Wendy Ann) $125.00

    8" straight leg, #0752, #452, 1973 – 1975, marked "Alex" $75.00

    8" straight leg, #452, 1976 – 1986 (1985 – 1986 white face), marked "Alexander" (Wendy) $65.00

    8" straight leg, #452, 1987 – 1988 (Maggie) $65.00

    8", #493, 1993, Storybook Series, #140493, 1994 . . . .$65.00

    8", #13500, 1998 – 2000, comes with bowl, spoon, and pillow $85.00

    8", #38790, 2004 (Wendy), with spider $80.00

Miss Scarlett — 14" (see Belk & Leggett under Special Events/Exclusives)

Miss Smarty — 8", #17610, 1999 – 2001, Mary Engelbreit (Maggie), pink check outfit $75.00

Miss Unity — 10" (see U.F.D.C. under Special Events/Exclusives)

Miss U.S.A. — 8" h.p., BK, #728, 1966 – 1968, Americana Series (Wendy Ann) $350.00

Miss Victory — 20" compo., 1944 – 1946, magnets in hands (Princess Elizabeth) . . . .$750.00 up

Misterioso — 10" h.p., #20119, 1996 Cirque du Soleil Series $90.00

Mistletoe and Holly — 10", #38555, 2004, long plaid dress, fur collar and hat $150.00

Mistress Mary — 7" compo., 1937 – 1941 (Tiny Betty) $375.00

Molly — 14", #1561, 1988 only, Classic Series (Mary Ann) $75.00

Molly Cottontail — cloth/felt, 1930s $650.00

Mommy & Me — 14" and 7" compo., 1948 – 1949 (Margaret and Tiny Betty) . . . .$1,700.00 up set

Mommy & Me at Home — 8", 10", h.p., #11009, 1997 – 1998, pink floral outfits $125.00

Mommy & Me On-the-Go — 8", 10", h.p., #11010, 1997 – 1998 . . . .$150.00

Mommy's Pet — 14" – 20", 1977 – 1986 . . . .$50.00 – 175.00

Mona Lisa, DaVinci's — 8", h.p., 1997, #22140, green velvet dress $80.00

Monday's Child — 8", #27770, 2001, pink dress, mirror $100.00

    10", #28860, 2001, print skirt, 10" goose $135.00

Monet — 21", #2245, 1984 – 1985, black and white check gown with red jacket (Jacqueline) $225.00

Monique — 8" (see Disney under Specials Events/Exclusives)

Monkeying Around — 8", #38510, 2004, comes with knit monkey $85.00

Monroe, Elizabeth — 1976 – 1978, first set Presidents' Ladies/First Ladies Series (Mary Ann) $125.00

Moonlight Dance — 10", #28900, 2001, blue tulle and brocade dress $125.00

Mop-Top Annie — 8", #14486, 1995, red dress with white dots $65.00

Mop-Top Baby Girl — 12", #29030, 1998, yarn hair, patchwork dress $50.00

Mop-Top Billy — 8", #140485, 1993 – 2000, Toy Shelf Series $65.00

Mop-Top Wendy — 8", #140484, 1993 – 2000, Toy Shelf Series $70.00

Morisot — 21", #2236, 1985 – 1986 only, lime green gown with white lace (Jacqueline) $275.00

Morning Glory — 14", #25505, Ribbons & Bows Series, floral dress with lace (Mary Ann) $100.00

    8", #28476, 2001– 2002, lavender dress, bonnet with flowers $90.00

Morocco — 8" h.p., BK, #762, 1968 – 1970 (Wendy Ann) $275.00

    8" h.p., #11559, 1996 International, belly dancer $60.00

    8", #33510, 2002, Maroon belly dancer, plush camel $70.00

Moss Rose — 14", #1559, 1991 only, Classic Series (Louisa) $100.00

Mother & Me — 14" – 15" and 9" compo., 1940 – 1943, mint condition

    (Wendy Ann and Little Betty) . . . .$1,400.00 up

Mother Goose — 8" straight leg, #427, #459, 1986 – 1992,

    Storybook Series (Wendy Ann) $65.00

    8", #11620, 1997 – 1999, with goose and book of rhymes $65.00

    10", #28860, 2001 – 2003, print dress with 10" goose $125.00

Mother Gothel and Rapunzel — 8" and 14", #1539, 1993 – 1994,

    limited to 3,000 sets. . . . .$225.00 set

Mother Hubbard — 8", #439, #459, 1988 – 1989, Storyland Series

    (Wendy) $60.00

Mother's Day — 8", #10380 – 10382, 1995, three hair colors,

    Special Occasions Series $60.00

    8", #30265, 2001, pink, white dress with porcelain flower box $90.00

Mouseketeer — 8" (see Disney under Special Events/Exclusives)

Mr. and Mrs. Frankenstein Set — 8", 1996 . . . .$250.00

Mr. Monopoly — 8", #25260, 2000, tails, top hat, comes with game . .$75.00

Miss U.S.A., 8", BK, #728, 1966 – 1968
(Wendy Ann).

Mr. O'Hara — 8", #638, 1993 only, Scarlett Series (Wendy) $150.00
Mrs. Buck Rabbit — cloth/felt, mid-1930s $625.00
Mrs. Claus — (see mid-year specials for Madame Alexander Co. under Special Events/Exclusives)
 14", #24607, 1995, Christmas Series $100.00
Mrs. Darling — 10", 1993 – 1994, Peter Pan Series (Cissette) $125.00
Mrs. Fezziwig — 8", #18005, 1996, Dickens, moiré gown $60.00
Mrs. Malloy's Millinery Shop — 10" Portrette, #201167, 1995 only, trunk set with wardrobe and hats $250.00
Mrs. March Hare — cloth/felt, mid-1930s $650.00
Mrs. O'Hara — 8", #638, 1992 – 1993 only, Scarlett Series (Wendy) $150.00
Mrs. Quack-a-Field — cloth/felt, mid-1930s $625.00
Mrs. Snoopie — cloth/felt, 1940s $625.00
Muffin — 19" cloth, 1966 only $100.00
 14", 1963 – 1977 . . . .$75.00
 14" cloth, 1965 only, sapphire eyes $75.00
 14" black cloth, 1965 – 1966 only $100.00
 14" cloth, 1966 – 1970, cut slanted blue eyes $75.00
 14" cloth, eyes like sideways commas $55.00
 12" all vinyl, 1989 – 1990 (Janie) $55.00
 12", 1990 – 1992, in trunk/wardrobe $125.00
Mulan — 8", #36260, 2003, black wig, kimono, 2¼" Mushu $90.00
Munchkin Peasant — 8", #140444, 1993 – 1995, Wizard of Oz Series $100.00
 Daisy, 8", #28770, 2001 – 2002, daisies on costume $95.00
 Flower Bonnet, 8", #28775, 2001 – 2002, blue, white costume, ruffled flower trimmed hat $85.00
 Herald, 8", #140445, 1994 – 1995, Wizard of Oz Series $125.00
 Mayor, 8", #140443, 1993 – 1995, Wizard of Oz Series $125.00
 Lollipop, 8", #14513, 1995, Wizard of Oz Series, pink/white striped outfit $125.00
 Lullaby, 8", #14512, 1995, Wizard of Oz Series, white gown $100.00
 Lullaby, 8", #13300, 1999 – 2001, pink dress and hat $90.00
 Flower, 8", #27035, 2000 – 2001, Wizard of Oz Series $65.00
 Lullaby Munchkin, 5", #27070, porcelain, 2000 – 2002, pink costume $85.00
 Mayor of Munchkinland, 8", #37125, 2003, green coat, hat, watch $80.00
My Doll House — (see Special Events/Exclusives)
My Favorite Ballerina — 14", #25485, 2000, lilac, ballet outfit $75.00
 14", #25480, 2000, pink, ballet outfit $75.00
My First Christmas Tree — 8", #36875, 2002 – 2004, Spode ornament,
 green dress $85.00
My First Christmas with Lenox Ornament — 8", #34215, 2002 . . . . .$90.00
My Heart Belongs to Grandma — 8", #36165, 2003 – 2004, pink dress,
 red heart $70.00
My Heart Belongs to You — 8", #35440, brunette, #35441,
 African-American, red dress, 2003 . . . .$70.00
My Little Sweetheart — (see Child At Heart under Special
 Events/Exclusives)
Mystery Dance 1951 — 14", #26035, 2000, pink lace and tulle
 long gown $175.00
Nan McDare — cloth/felt, 1940s $625.00
Nana — 6" dog with bonnet, #441, 1993 only, Peter Pan Series $50.00
Nana/Governess — 8" h.p., #433, 1957 only (Wendy Ann) . . . . .$2,000.00 up
Nancy Ann — 17" – 18" h.p., 1950 only (tagged Nancy Ann) . . . . . .$975.00 up
Nancy Dawson — 8", #441, 1988 – 1989, Storybook Series (Maggie) $60.00
Nancy Drew — 12" plastic/vinyl, 1967 only, Literature Series . . . . . .$450.00 up
Nancy Jean — 8" (see Belks & Leggett under Special Events/Exclusives)
Napoleon — 12", #1330, 1980 – 1986, Portraits of History (Nancy Drew) .$65.00
Nashville Goes Country — 8" (1995, see C.U. under Special Events/Exclusives)
Nashville Skater — #1 (see Collectors United under Special Events/Exclusives)
 #2 (see Collectors United under Special Events/Exclusives)

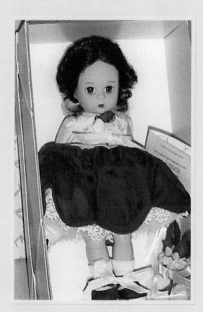

My Heart Belongs To You, 8" (Wendy), 2003, red velvet skirt.

Nat (Little Men)

Nat (Little Men) — 15" h.p., 1952 (Maggie) ....$850.00 up
Natasha — 21", #2255, 1989 – 1990, brown and paisley brocade (Jacqueline) $325.00
National Velvet — 12", 1991 only, Romance Series, no riding crop (Nancy Drew) $80.00
    8", #10409, 1996, riding habit $85.00
Nativity Set — 1997 – 2000, #19460, Mary, Joseph, Jesus, Angel, creche, Three Wise Men, Shepherd, Drummer .$950.00
    #38770, 2004, 8" Mary, Joseph, Jesus, creche, donkey, lambs $320.00
Neiman-Marcus — (see Special Events/Exclusives)
Nelson, Lord — 12" vinyl, #1336, 1984 – 1986, Portraits of History (Nancy Drew) $65.00
Netherlands Boy — Formerly "Dutch" (Wendy)
    8" h.p., straight leg, #577, 1974 – 1975, marked "Alex" $75.00
    8" h.p., straight leg, #577, 1976 – 1989, marked "Alexander" (1985 – 1987) $65.00
Netherlands Girl — 8" h.p., #591, #525, 1974 – 1992 (Wendy) $65.00
New Arrival — 19", #30290, 2001, stork with Baby Kisses 8" doll $50.00
New England Collector Society — (see Special Events/Exclusives)
Nicole — 10", #1139, 1989 – 1990, Portrette, black/off white outfit (Cissette) $80.00
Nigeria — 8", #11552, 1995 only (also in 1994 Neiman-Marcus trunk set as Kenya) $60.00
Nightingale, Florence — 14", #1598, 1986 – 1987, Classic Series $90.00
Nina Ballerina — 7" compo., 1940 (Tiny Betty) $350.00
    9" compo., 1939 – 1941 (Little Betty) $375.00
    14" h.p., 1949 – 1951 (Margaret) ....$575.00 up
    17", 1949 – 1951 ....$550.00
    15" h.p., 1951, came in various colors, all years (Margaret) $700.00
    19", 1949 – 1950 ....$850.00 up
    23", 1951 ....$850.00
1950s Cissette Trunk Set — 10", #38740, 2004, hat box, trunk, four outfits, BK Cissette $290.00
Nixon, Pat — (see Presidents' Ladies/First Ladies Series) 14", 1994 only $150.00
Noah's Ark — #33155, 2002, includes 8" Noah, wooden ark, pair zebras, camels, giraffes, resin doves $240.00
Nod — (see Dutch Lullaby)
Noel — 12" (see New England Collector Society under Special Events/Exclusives)
Normandy — 7" compo., 1935 – 1938 (Tiny Betty) $300.00
Norway — 8" h.p., BK, #584, 1968 – 1972 (Wendy Ann) $300.00
    8" straight leg, #584, 1973 – 1975, marked "Alex" $65.00
    8" straight leg, #584, 1976 – 1987, marked "Alexander" (1985 – 1987 white face) $60.00

Nina Ballerina, 14", hard plastic, 1949 –
1951. Tagged "Madame Alexander."

Nurse, BKW, 8", 1961 (Wendy). Tag:
"Alexander-Kin."

8" straight leg, #11566, 1996 International Viking costume $70.00

8", #35880, 2003 – 2004, red sweater, tweed skirt, troll $95.00

Norwegian — 7" – 8" compo., 1936 – 1940 (Tiny Betty) $300.00

9" compo., 1938 – 1939 (Little Betty) $325.00

Now I Lay Me Down to Sleep — 8", #28380, 2001– 2002, white gown, bonnet $85.00

Nurse — 16", 1930s, cloth and felt $675.00

7" compo., 1937, 1941 – 1943 (Tiny Betty) $350.00

9" compo., 1939, 1942 – 1943 ....$350.00

13" – 15" compo., 1936 – 1937 (Betty), all white outfit, Dionne nurse, mint in box ....$950.00 up

15" compo., 1939, 1943 (Princess Elizabeth) $550.00

14" h.p., 1948 (Maggie and Margaret) $850.00

8" h.p., #563, 1956 only, all white dress (Wendy Ann) ....$600.00 up

8", #429, 1961, all white dress, comes with baby ....$650.00 up

8" BKW, BK, #329, #460, #660, #624, 1962 – 1965, wears striped dress, comes with baby $525.00

8", #308, all white uniform, Americana Series, 1991 ....$70.00

8", #17620, 1999, World War II, brown, white costume with medicine bag $70.00

Nutcracker — 16", #21700, 1998 – 1999, Clara in rose embroidered costume $200.00

8", 2001 – 2002, #27560, silver pants, red jacket, black hat $90.00

Nutcracker Prince — 8", #14571, 1995, Nutcracker Series, has mask $70.00

O'Brien, Margaret — 14½" compo., 1946 – 1948 ....$750.00 up

17", 18", 19" compo., 1946 – 1948 ....$850.00 – 1,200.00

21" – 24" compo., 1946 – 1948 ....$900.00 – 1,500.00

14½" h.p., 1949 – 1951 ....$900.00 up

17" – 18" h.p., 1949 – 1951 ....$950.00 up

21" – 22" h.p., 1949 – 1951 ....$1,400.00 up

15" porcelain, #90100, white blouse, blue pinafore $130.00

O. E. O. Guard — 8", #33595, 2002 – 2004 (Wizard of Oz), blue fur coat, hat $85.00

Off to Class — 8", #35645, 2003, blue plaid dress, book bag and books $80.00

Off to the North Pole – Coca-Cola — 8", #25245, 2000, fur costume with white bear $100.00

Oktoberfest — 8" (see Collectors United under Special Events/Exclusives)

Old Fashioned Girl — 13" compo., 1945 – 1947 (Betty) ....$550.00 up

20" compo. (Betty) $700.00

20" h.p., 1948 only (Margaret) ....$850.00 up

14" h.p., 1948 only (Margaret) $650.00

Old McDonald — 8", #30785, 2001, red check dress $85.00

Olive Oyl — 10", #20126, 1996, Timeless Legends $90.00

Oliver Twist — 16" cloth, 1934, Dickens character $650.00

7" compo., 1935 – 1936 (Tiny Betty) $300.00

8", #472, 1992 only, Storyland Series (Wendy Ann) $65.00

Oliver Twistail — Cloth/felt, 1930s $650.00

Olivia and the Missing Toy — #36430, 2004, 8" $100.00

Olivia Saves the Circus — 8", #35115, 2003 – 2004, vinyl piglet, three costumes, lion, dog, and tent ..$100.00

8", At Home with Olivia Set — #35646, 2004, bed, table $100.00

8", Olivia vinyl piglet, #35105, 2003, red dress, purse $25.00

Olivia Trunk Set — 8", #31680, 2003, vinyl piglet, clothes, accessories, trunk $80.00

One Fish, Two Fish — 8", #34095, 2002 (Maggie), smocked dress with fish $80.00

One, Two, Buckle My Shoe — 14", #24640, Nursery Rhymes (Louisa) $85.00

Only Hearts — 8", #35940, 2003, pink stripe dress, tiny flower hat $80.00

On The Campaign Trail Maggie — 8", #39550, 2004 ....$80.00

On The Campaign Trail Wendy — 8", #39545, 2004 ....$80.00

Onyx Velvet and Lace Gala Gown and Coat — 10" h.p., #22170, 1997 – 1998 (Cissette) $125.00

Opening Night — 10", #1126, 1989 only, Portrette, gold sheath and overshirt (Cissette) $80.00

Ophelia — 12", 1992, Romance Collection (Nancy Drew) $100.00

12", 1993 only (Lissy) $125.00

Opulent Opal — 10", #33355, 2002, blonde, pink gown, jewel trim $150.00

Orchard Princess — 21" compo., 1939, 1946 – 1947, has extra make-up (Wendy Ann) ....$2,400.00 up

Orphan Annie

Orphan Annie — 14" plastic/vinyl, #1480, 1965 – 1966 only, Literature Series (Mary Ann) $325.00
  #1485, 1965 only, in window box with wardrobe . . . .$500.00 up
Our Song — 10", #36180, 2003, blue long ballgown with lace trim $125.00
Out for a Stroll — 10", #27815, 2001, pink long dress trimmed in lace $100.00
Oz Flower Munchkin — 8", #27035, 2000 – 2001, Wizard of Oz Series $50.00
Oz Scape — #33770, 2002, Artstone backdrop $120.00
Pakistan — 8" h.p., #532, 1993 only $60.00
Palace Guard — 8", #33395, 2002, beefeater costume, limited to 1,000 . . . .$80.00
Pamela — 12" h.p., 1962 – 1963 only, takes wigs, excellent condition, doll only (Lissy) . . . .$400.00 up
  12" h.p. in case, 1962 – 1963 . . . .$1,000.00 up
  12" h.p. in window box, 1962 – 1963 . . . .$1,000.00 up
  12" plastic/vinyl, 1969 – 1971, doll only (Nancy Drew) . . . .$225.00 up
  12" plastic/vinyl in case, 1969 . . . .$625.00 up
Pamela Plays Dress Up — 12" (see Horchow under Special Events/Exclusives)
Pan American – (Pollera) — 7" compo., 1936 – 1938 (Tiny Betty) $300.00
Panama — 8", #555, 1985 – 1987 . . . .$60.00
Pandora — 8" (see Dolls 'n Bearland under Special Events/Exclusives)
Pansy Fairy — 8", #38185, 2004, gold outfit, pansy trim $90.00
Parisian Chic 1940 — 10", #17770, 1999, dress, coat, hat, purse $125.00
Park Avenue Alex the Bellhop — 8" h.p., #31180, 1997 – 1999, burgundy uniform $75.00
Park Avenue Cissette — 10", #35585, 2003, gray check suit, plush puppy $135.00
Park Avenue Wendy — 8" h.p., #31060, 1997 – 1999, black and white ensemble $85.00
Parlour Maid — 8" h.p., #579, 1956 only (Wendy Ann) . . . .$950.00 up
Party Sun Dress — 8" h.p., #344, 1957, BKW, blue or red dress with gold accents (Wendy Ann) . . . .$550.00 up
Party Time Vintage — 8", #28910, white dress $80.00
Pat-A-Cake — 8", #12812, 1995, floral dress with white apron and chef's hat, Nursery Rhymes Series $65.00
Patchity Pam & Pepper — 15" cloth, 1965 – 1966 . . . .$175.00 ea.
Patriot — 8", #33506, 2002, African-American, red, white, blue dress, limited to 150 . . . .$90.00
  8", #33505, 2002, blonde, limited to 1,800 . . . .$90.00
Patterson, Martha Johnson — 1982 – 1984, third set Presidents' Ladies/First Ladies Series (Martha) $100.00
Patty — 18" plastic/vinyl, 1965 only $275.00
Patty Pigtails — 14" h.p., 1949 only (Margaret) . . . .$675.00 up

Pamela, 12", 1962 (Lissy face), original clothes, wig attached to Velcro strip on head.

Pamela, 12", 1962 (Lissy face), wig attached to Velcro strip on head.

Paulette — 10", #1128, 1989 – 1990 only, Portrette, dressed in pink velvet (Cissette) $110.00
Peachtree Lane — 8" in blue and 14" Scarlett in green/white stripes, #16551, limited to 2,500 . . . .$275.00 set
Pearl (June) — 10", #1150, 1992 only, Birthstone Collection, white/silver flapper doll $75.00
Pearl of the 1920s — 10", #79700 . . . .$200.00
Peasant — 7" compo., 1936 – 1937 (Tiny Betty) $300.00
    9" compo., 1938 – 1939 (Little Betty) $325.00
Peekaboos — 8" cloth baby, vinyl face, animal peekaboo cover . . . .$12.00 – 16.00
    8", cloth, vinyl face as Pooh, Piglet, Tigger, and Eeyore . . . .$16.00 ea.
Peggy Bride — 14" – 18" h.p., 1950 – 1951, very blonde hair (Margaret) . . . .$900.00 – 1,400.00
    21" h.p., 1950 . . . .$1,500.00 up
Penny — 34" cloth/vinyl, 1951 only . . . .$500.00 up
    42", 1951 only $800.00
    7" compo., 1938 – 1940 (Tiny Betty) $275.00
Pen Pals — 8", #38505, 2004, blue check dress, letter, photo $70.00
Peppermint Twist — 8", #14591, 1995, pink skirt and jacket in 1950s style, Nostalgia Series $55.00
Perfect Bouquet — 8", #36285, 2003 – 2004, pink pleats with roses $80.00
Perfect Pearl — 8", #33350, 2002, blonde, gold gown, pearl trim $95.00
Periwinkle Angel — 10", #35865, 2003, white wings, blue gown $140.00
Persia — 7" compo., 1936 – 1938 (Tiny Betty) $300.00
Peru — 8", #556, 1986 – 1987 . . . .$75.00
    8" h.p., #531, 1993 only (Wendy Ann) $65.00
    8" h.p., #35665, 2003 – 2004, colorful pink and brown costume, plush llama $100.00
Peruvian Boy — 8" h.p., BK, #770, 1966 (Wendy Ann) $400.00
    8" h.p., BKW, #770, 1965 . . . .$425.00
Peter Pan — 15" h.p., 1953 – 1954 (Margaret) . . . .$800.00 up
    8" h.p., #310, 1953 – 1954 (Wendy Ann), Quiz-Kin . . . .$850.00 up
    8" h.p., #465, reintroduced 1991 – 1993, #140465 in 1994, Storyland Series (Wendy Ann) $60.00
    8" h.p., #13660, 1999 – 2001, green costume with Tinker Bell pin and sword $60.00
    14" plastic/vinyl, #1410, 1969 only (Mary Ann) $225.00
    1969 only, complete set of four dolls – Peter, Michael (12" Jamie), Wendy (14" Mary Ann), Tinker Bell
    (10" Cissette) . . . .$1,000.00 up
Peter Pan's Wendy — 8", #13670, 1999 – 2001, blue gown and fuzzy shoes $70.00
Petite Playhouse — #28950, 2003, fold-up house with rooms $50.00

Perfect Bouquet, 8", 2003 – 2004
(Wendy), pink satin with bows.

Philippines, 8", #3531, 1987 only.
Difficult to find in yellow.

Petite Playhouse

5" dolls, 2002 – 2003, Kayla #27410, Emily #27420, Wendy #30360, Sarah #27415, Caitlin #27405 . . . .$20.00 ea

Philippines — 8" straight leg, #554, 1986 – 1987 (blue gown) $75.00

1987, #531, dressed in yellow gown $150.00

Picnic Day — 18" h.p., #2001C, 1953 only, Glamour Girl Series, leaves on pink or blue print dress

(Margaret) . . . .$1,900.00 up

Picnic Time for Teddy — 8", #34080, 2002 – 2003, smocked dress with bear and basket $90.00

Pierce, Jane — 1982 – 1984, third set Presidents' Ladies/First Ladies Series (Mary Ann) $100.00

Pierrot Clown — (see Clowns, 8" and 14")

Pig Brick — 8", #33655, vinyl, brick house bank, 2003 – 2004 . . . .$50.00

Pig Stick — 8", #33657, 2003 – 2004, vinyl, stick house bank $50.00

Pig Straw — 8", #33650, 2003 – 2004, vinyl, straw house bank $50.00

Pilgrim — 7" compo., 1935 – 1938 (Tiny Betty) $30.00

8" h.p., #100349, 1994, Americana Series $60.00

8", #10349, 1995, Special Occasions Series $60.00

Pink Butterfly Princess — 8", #25675, 2000 – 2001, pink wings $75.00

Pink Carnation — 10", #25615, 2000 (Cissette), pink tiered gown $125.00

Pink Champagne (Arlene Dahl) — 18" h.p., red hair/pink lace/rhinestone bodice gown . . . .$6,500.00 up

Pinkie — 12" plastic/vinyl, 1975 – 1987, Portrait Children Series (Nancy Drew) $70.00

8", 1997 – 1998, #22120, chiffon gown, pink hat $70.00

Pinking of You — 8", #37980, hot pink dress and hat, 2003 – 2004 . . . .$85.00

Pink Petals Fairy — 8", #33430 , 2002 – 2003, petal tutu, leaf wings $85.00

Pink Pirouette — 8", #33140, 2002 – 2003, pink tutu, rhinestones $85.00

8", #33141, 2002 – 2003, African-American $85.00

Pink Pristine Angel — 10", #10700, 1997 – 2000, pink feather wings $125.00

Pink Sparkle — Dragonfly Fairy, 8", #36030, 2003 – 2004, pink and blue costume $90.00

Pink Sparkle Princess — 15", #22670, 1999, porcelain, pink gown $150.00

Pinky — 16" cloth, 1940s . . . .$475.00 up

23" compo./cloth baby, 1937 – 1939 . . . .$300.00

13" – 19" vinyl baby, #3561, #5461, 1954 only, one-piece vinyl body and legs . . . .$100.00 – 150.00

Pinocchio — 8", #477, 1992 – 1993, Storyland Series (Wendy Ann), #140477, 1994 . . . .$75.00

8", #32130, 2001 – 2002, with 5" wooden Pinocchio $100.00

8", #38860, 2004, with 2" Jiminy Cricket $90.00

Pip — All cloth, early 1930s, Dickens character $800.00

7" compo., 1935 – 1936 (Tiny Betty) $300.00

Pippi Longstocking — 18", #16003, 1996, Rag Dolls (cloth doll) . . . . .not available for sale

8", #25975, 2000 – 2001 (Maggie), with monkey $60.00

14", #28780, 2001, cloth $35.00

Pisces — 8", #21320, 1998, blue fish costume $90.00

Pitty Pat — 16" cloth, 1950s $475.00

Pitty Pat Clown — 1950s $450.00

Place in the Sun, A — 10", #24624, lavender ballgown $100.00

Playmates — 29" cloth, 1940s . . . .$450.00 up

Pocahontas — 8" h.p., BK, #721, 1967 – 1970, Americana and Storyland Series, has baby (Wendy Ann) $375.00

8" h.p., #318, 1991 – 1992, Americana Series (Wendy Ann) $65.00

8" h.p., #100350, 1994 – 1995, Americana and Favorite Book Series (Wendy Ann) $60.00

10", #38390, 2004 (Cissette) with 2" raccoon, dog, and hummingbird $150.00

14", #24613, 1995, first dark skin doll this size, Favorite Books Series (Louisa) $80.00

Polish (Poland) — 7" compo., 1935 – 1936 (Tiny Betty) $300.00

8" h.p., BKW, #780, 1964 – 1965 (Wendy Ann) $150.00

8" BKW, #780, 1965 only (Maggie Mixup) $150.00

8" h.p., BK, #780, 1965 – 1972 . . . .$100.00

8" h.p., straight leg, #0780, #580, 1973 – 1975, marked "ALEX" $70.00

8" straight leg, #580, 1976 – 1988 (1985 – 1987 white face), marked "Alexander" $60.00

8", #523, reintroduced 1992 – 1993 (Maggie Mixup), 1994, #110523 . . . .$60.00

Polk, Sarah — 1979 – 1981, second set Presidents' Ladies/First Ladies Series (Martha) $100.00

Pollera (Pan American) — 7" compo., 1936 – 1938 (Tiny Betty) $275.00

72

Polly — 17" plastic/vinyl, 1965 only, dressed in ballgown $350.00
  Dressed in street dress $275.00
  Dressed as ballerina $275.00
  Dressed as bride $300.00
  1965 only, came in trunk with wardrobe . . . .$750.00 up
Pollyana — 16" rigid vinyl, 1960 – 1961, marked "1958" (Mary-Bel) $425.00
  16", dressed in formal $475.00
  22", 1960 – 1961 . . . .$500.00
  14", #1588, 1987 – 1988, Classic Series (Mary Ann) $90.00
  14", reintroduced 1994 only, #24159 . . . .$100.00
  8", #474, 1992 – 1993 only, Storyland Series (Wendy) $70.00
  8", #25210, 2000 – 2001 (Wendy), pink dress, straw hat $70.00
Polly Flinders — 8", #443, 1988 – 1989, Storybook Series (Maggie) $60.00
Polly Pigtails — 14½" h.p., 1949 – 1951 (Maggie) $500.00
  17" – 17½", 1949 – 1951 . . . .$625.00
  8" (see M.A.D.C. under Special Events/Exclusives)
Polly Put Kettle On — 7" compo., 1937 – 1939 (Tiny Betty) $325.00
  8" h.p., #11640, 1998 – 1999, teacup print dress, kettle $65.00
Poodles — 14" – 17", early 1950s, standing or sitting, named Ivy, Pierre, Fifi, and Inky . . . .$500.00 up
Poor Cinderella — (see Cinderella)
Popeye — 8", #10428, 1996, Timeless Legends $90.00
Popeye, Olive Oyl, and Sweet Pea — #20127, 1996 . . . .$175.00 set
Pop Goes the Weasel — 8", #35670, 2003, bench, monkey, and weasel $75.00
Poppy — 9" early vinyl, 1953 only, orange organdy dress and bonnet $125.00
Poppy Garden Ball Gown — 10", #34165, 2002, velvet, ruffled rose hem, limited to 1,000 . . . .$130.00
Portrait Elise — 17" plastic/vinyl, 1972 – 1973 . . . .$225.00
Portugal — 8" h.p., BK, #785, 1968 – 1972 (Wendy Ann) $100.00
  8" straight leg, #0785, #585, 1973 – 1975, marked "Alex" $75.00
  8" straight leg, #585, #537, 1976 – 1987, marked "Alexander" $60.00
  8", #537, 1986, white face $60.00
  8" h.p., #535, 1993, #110535, 1994 . . . .$60.00
  8" h.p., #35975, 2003 – 2004, red and black costume, folk rooster $85.00
Posey Pet — 15" cloth, 1940s, plush rabbit or other animals, must be clean . . . .$450.00 up
Pot of Gold — 8", #39260, 2004, green costume $80.00

Elizabeth Monroe, 14" (Mary Ann), first set of Presidents' Ladies, 1976 – 1978.

Sarah Jackson, 14" (Louisa), second set of Presidents' Ladies, 1979 – 1981.

Sarah Polk, 14" (Martha), second set of Presidents' Ladies, #1511, 1979 – 1981.

Practice Makes Perfect

Practice Makes Perfect — 8", #37885, 2004, with violin $85.00
Precious — 12" compo./cloth baby, 1937 – 1940 ....$275.00
    12" all h.p. toddler, 1948 – 1951 ....$350.00
Precious Peridot — 8", #33365, 2002, green gown, lace overskirt $90.00
Premier Dolls — 8" (see M.A.D.C. under Special Events/Exclusives)
Presidents' Ladies/First Ladies —
    First set, 1976 – 1978 ....$125.00 – 175.00 singles, 800.00 set
    Second set, 1979 – 1981 ....$100.00 singles, 600.00 set
    Third set, 1982 – 1984 ....$100.00 singles, 600.00 set
    Fourth set, 1985 – 1987 ....$100.00 singles, 600.00 set
    Fifth set, 1988 ....$100.00 singles, 600.00 set
    Sixth set, 1989 – 1990 ....$100.00 singles, 600.00 set
Pretty Head to Toe — 8", #37905, 2004, dress, coat, hat $90.00
Pretty Pals — 8", #26770, pink; #26835, ivory; 2001 – 2002, smocked dresses ....$95.00 ea.
Prince Charles — 8" h.p., #397, 1957 only (Wendy Ann) ....$750.00 up
Prince Charles and Princess Ann Set — 8", pair, #34150, 2002 ....$160.00 set
Prince Charming — 16" – 17" compo., 1947 (Margaret) $850.00
    14" – 15" h.p., 1948 – 1950 (Margaret) $850.00
    17" – 18" h.p., 1948 – 1950 (Margaret) $950.00
    21" h.p., 1949 – 1951 (Margaret) ....$1,100.00 up
    12", 1990 – 1991, Romance Collection (Nancy Drew) $85.00
    8", #479, 1993, Storybook Series, royal blue/gold outfit $70.00
    8", #14541, 1995, Brothers Grimm Series, braid trimmed jacket with brocade vest $70.00
Prince Phillip — 17" – 18" h.p., 1953 only, Beaux Arts Series (Margaret) ....$900.00 up
    21", 1953 only ....$1,000.00 up
    8", #33495, 2002, navy blue suit, red robe, limited to 500 ....$125.00
Princess — 12", 1990 – 1991 only, Romance Collection (Nancy Drew) $85.00
    14", #1537, 1990 - Mary Ann, 1991 - Jennifer, Classic Series $100.00
Princess — 13" – 15" compo., 1940 – 1942 (Princess Elizabeth) ....$550.00 up
    24" compo., 1940 – 1942 (Princess Elizabeth) ....$850.00 up
Princess Alexandria — 24" cloth/compo., 1937 only ....$300.00 up
Princess and the Dragon — pink and purple costume, silver dragon, 2001 – 2002 ....$130.00
Princess and the Pea — 8", #27745, 2001 – 2002 (Maggie), includes mattress and pea $100.00
Princess Ann — 8" h.p., #396, 1957 only (Wendy Ann) ....$900.00 up
Princess Budir Al-Budor — 8", #483, 1993 – 1994 only, Storybook Series $60.00
Princess Diana — 10", #22500, 1998 (Cissette), white satin gown $175.00
Princess Diana Birthday — 10", white satin and gold gown $170.00
Princess Elizabeth — 7" compo., 1937 – 1939 (Tiny Betty) $375.00
    8", 1937, with Dionne head (rare) $400.00
    9" – 11" compo., 1937 – 1941 (Little Betty) ....$350.00 – 500.00
    13" compo., 1937 – 1941, with closed mouth (Betty) ....$625.00 up
    14" compo., 1937 – 1941 ....$600.00 up
    15" compo., open mouth ....$600.00 up
    18" – 19" compo., 1937 – 1941, open mouth ....$750.00 up
    24" compo., 1938 – 1939, open mouth ....$900.00 up
    28" compo., 1938 – 1939, open mouth ....$1,000.00 up
Princess Flavia (also Victoria) — 21" compo., 1939, 1946 – 1947 (Wendy Ann) ....$2,000.00 up
Princess Margaret Rose — 15" – 18" compo., 1937 – 1938 (Princess Elizabeth) ....$800.00 up
    21" compo., 1938 ....$975.00
    14" – 18" h.p., 1949 – 1953 (Margaret) ....$650.00 – 975.00
    18" h.p. #2020B, 1953 only, Beaux Arts Series, pink taffeta gown with red ribbon, tiara (Margaret) ....$1,600.00 up
    8", #35535, 2002, pink dress, red cape $125.00
Princess of Quite a Lot — 8", #25275, 2000 – 2001 (Maggie), Mary Engelbreit,
    yellow dress, crown, limited to 2,800 ....$80.00
Princess of Storyland — 8", #25990, 2000, long pink gown $75.00
Princess Rosetta — 21" compo., 1939, 1946 – 1947 (Wendy Ann) $2,300.00

Priscilla — 18" cloth, mid-1930s $625.00
    7" compo., 1935 – 1938 (Tiny Betty) $325.00
    8" h.p., BK, #729, 1965 – 1970, Americana and Storybook Series (Wendy Ann) $300.00
Prissy — 8", #630, 1990 only, Scarlett Series (Wendy Ann) $100.00
    8", #637, reintroduced 1992 – 1993 . . . .$100.00
    8", #16650, 1995, Scarlett Series, floral gown $100.00
Pristine Angel — 10", #10604, 100th Anniversary, second in series, white/gold $100.00
Prom Queen (Memories) — 8" (see M.A.D.C. under Special Events/Exclusives)
Psycho — 10", #14810, doll in shower, pictured in 1998 catalog . . . . .not available for sale
Puddin' — 14" – 21" cloth/vinyl, 1966 – 1975 . . . .$75.00 – 165.00
    14" – 18", 1987 . . . .$65.00 – 100.00
    14" – 21", 1990 – 1993 . . . .$65.00 – 125.00
    14" only, 1994 – 1995 . . . .$75.00
    21", 1995 . . . .$125.00
Puerto Rico — 8", 1998 – 1999, #24120, red outfit, carries flag and frog $70.00
Pumpkin — 22" cloth/vinyl, 1967 – 1976 . . . .$125.00
    22", 1976 only, with rooted hair $150.00
Pumpkin Patch Treats — 8", #26350, 2001, one doll with three Halloween costumes $190.00
Pumpkin Pie — 8", #38180, 2003 – 2004, black jumper with pumpkin $50.00
Puppet, Hand (also see Marionettes) — Compo. head, cloth hand mitt body, by Tony Sarg, ca. 1936 . . . . .$475.00 up
Puppy Love — 8", #35825, 2003 – 2004, black check dress, Scottie dog $80.00
Purple Petals Fairy — 8", #33425, 2002, purple petal tutu, leaf wings $85.00
Purple Sparkle Dragonfly Fairy — 8", #35580, 2003 – 2004, green wings, costume $90.00
Puss 'n Boots — 8", #14552, Fairy Tales Series $65.00
Pussy Cat — cloth/vinyl
  White dolls:
    14", 1965 – 1985 (20-year production) $60.00
    14", 1987 – 1995 . . . .$60.00
    14", 1966, 1968, in trunk/trousseau . . . .$250.00 up
    18", 1989 – 1995 . . . .$100.00
    20", 1965 – 1984, 1987 – 1988 (20+ year production) $100.00
    24", 1965 – 1985 (20-year production) $135.00
    14", 1998, variety of outfits . . . .$75.00 – 100.00
    14", 2000, #25510, pink knit layette, pink outfit $120.00
    14" – 18", 2002 – 2004, variety of outfits . . . .$100.00 – 225.00
  Black dolls:
    14", 1970 – 1976 . . . .$85.00
    14", 1984 – 1995 (12-year production) $85.00
    20", 1976 – 1983 . . . .$125.00
Pussy Cat, Lively — 14", 20", 24", 1966 – 1969 only, knob makes head and limbs move . . . .$75.00 – 175.00
Queen — 18" h.p., #2025, 1953 only, Beaux Arts Series, white gown, long velvet cape trimmed
    with fur (Margaret) . . . .$1,800.00 up
    18" h.p., 1953 only, Glamour Girl Series, same gown/tiara as above but no cape (Margaret) . . . .$1,600.00 up
    18" h.p., 1954 only, Me & My Shadow Series, white gown, short Orlon cape (Margaret) . . . .$1,600.00 up
    8" h.p., 1954, #0030C, #597, Me & My Shadow Series, Orlon cape attached to purple robe (Wendy Ann) .$1,000.00 up
    8", #499, 1955 only, scarlet velvet robe $800.00
    10" h.p., #971, #879, #842, #763, 1957 – 1958, 1960 – 1961, gold gown with blue ribbon $450.00
    #742, #765, 1959, 1963, white gown with blue ribbon $450.00
    #1186, #1187, 1972 – 1973, white gown with red ribbon $325.00
    1959, in trunk with wardrobe, must be mint . . . .$1,000.00 up
    14", #1536, 1990 only, Classic Series (Louisa, Jennifer) $90.00
    20" h.p./vinyl arms, 1955, Dreams Come True Series, white brocade gown (Cissy) . . . .$1,200.00 up
    1957, Fashion Parade Series, white gown . . . .$950.00 up
    1958, 1961 – 1963 (1958 – Dolls to Remember Series), gold gown . . . .$950.00 up
    18", 1963 only, white gown with red ribbon (Elise) $750.00
    With vinyl head (Mary-Bel) $875.00

Queen

18" vinyl, same as 1965 (21" with rooted hair, 1966 only), gold brocade gown, rare doll (Elise) $975.00
   #2150, 21" h.p./vinyl arms, 1965, white brocade gown (Jacqueline) $750.00
      1968, gold gown $750.00
   #33660, 8", 2002, Crowning Glory, gold robe, limited to 500 . . . . $190.00
   #33525, 21", 2002, Recessional, purple robe, limited to 250 . . . . $950.00
   #33530, 10", 2002, Processional, red robe, limited to 500 . . . . $150.00
Queen Alexandrine — 21" compo., 1939 – 1941 (Wendy Ann) . . . .$1,975.00 up
Queen Charlotte — 10" (see M.A.D.C. under Special Events/Exclusives)
Queen Elizabeth I — 10" (see My Doll House under Special Events/Exclusives)
   8", #12610, 1999, red velvet trimmed in gold $100.00
Queen Elizabeth II — 8", 1992 only (mid-year issue), commemorating reign's 40th anniversary $150.00
Queen Esther — 8", #14584, 1995 only, Bible Series $125.00
Queen Isabella — 8" h.p., #329, 1992 only, Americana Series $125.00
Queen Mother — 10", #35715, 2002, red cape $100.00
Queen of Hearts — 8" straight leg, #424, 1987 – 1990, Storybook Series (Wendy Ann) $60.00
   8", #14511, 1995, Alice in Wonderland Series $80.00
   8", #38410, 2004, includes flamingo, mallet, and hedgehog $80.00
   10" (see Disney under Special Events/Exclusives)
Queen of Storyland — 10", #26025, 2000, long white gown, limited to 2,600 . . . . $100.00
Queen of the Roses — 10", #22660, 1999, long yellow satin dress, limited to 1,500 . . . . $100.00
Quintuplets (Fischer Quints) — 7" h.p. and vinyl, 1964 (Genius), with original box . . . . $550.00 set
Quiz-Kins — 8" h.p., 1953, bald head, in romper only (Wendy Ann) . . . . $500.00 up
   1953 Peter Pan, caracul wig $850.00
   1953 – 1954, as groom . . . . $650.00 up
   1953 – 1954, as bride . . . . $700.00 up
   1953 – 1954, girl with wig . . . . $650.00 up
   1953, girl without wig, in romper suit $575.00
Rachel/Rachael — 8", 1989 (see Belks & Leggett under Special Events/Exclusives)
Radiant Ruby — 10", #33360, red and gold gown, ruby jewelry $140.00
Raining Cats and Dogs — 8", #38850, 2004, includes dog and cat $100.00
Randolph, Martha — 1976 – 1978, first set Presidents' Ladies/First Ladies Series (Louisa) $125.00
Rapunzel — 10", #M31, 1989 – 1992 only, Portrette, gold velvet (Cissette) $100.00
   14", #1539, 1993 – 1994, Doll Classics, limited to 3,000, comes with 8" Mother Gothel . . . . $250.00 set
   14", #87005, 1996, purple gown (Louisa) $125.00
   8", #14542, 1995, Brothers Grimm Series, pink gown with gold

Rebecca, 14" (Mary Ann) 1970 – 1985.

                     scallops, pink cone hat, #13980, 1997 – 2003 . . . . $75.00
                     5", #36300, 2004, vinyl, petite, pink gown, cone hat $25.00
                     14", #25460, 2000 – 2001, lavender dress, cone hat with tulle
                        (Margaret) $130.00
                     8", #13980, 2004, pink dress $85.00
Really Ugly Stepsister — 8" h.p., #13450, 1997 – 1998, Cinderella
                     Series $85.00
Rebecca — 14" – 17", 21" compo., 1940 – 1941
                     (Wendy Ann) . . . . $600.00 – 1,000.00
                     14" h.p., 1948 – 1949 (Margaret) . . . . $850.00 up
                     14" plastic/vinyl, #1485, 1968 – 1969, Classic Series, two-tiered skirt in pink
                        (Mary Ann) $175.00
                     #1485, #1515, #1585, 1970 – 1985, one-piece skirt, pink pindot or
                        checked dress $70.00
                     #1586, 1986 – 1987, blue dress with striped pinafore $75.00
                     8", #14647, 1996 . . . . $65.00
Record Album — "Madame Alexander Collector's Album," 1978,
                     children's stories told by Madame, cover is like Alexander box . .$35.00
Red Boy — 8" h.p., BK, #740, 1972 (Wendy) $125.00
                     #0740, 1973 – 1975, marked "Alex" $75.00
                     #440, 1976 – 1988, marked "Alexander" $65.00

Red Cherries — 8", 33050, 2002, red dress, smocked with cherries $80.00
Red Cross Nurse — 18", #16002, Rag Doll Series . . . . .not available for sale
Red Riding Hood — 7" compo., 1936 – 1942 (Tiny Betty) $325.00
    9" compo., 1939 – 1940 (Little Betty) $375.00
    8" h.p., SLW, #608, 1955, cape sewn under arms (Wendy Ann) $650.00
    8" h.p., BKW, #382, 1962 – 1965, Storybook Series (Wendy Ann) $275.00
    8" h.p., BK, #782, 1965 – 1972 . . . .$125.00
    8" h.p., straight leg, #0782, #482, 1973 – 1975, marked "Alex" $75.00
    8" h.p., straight leg, #482, 1976 – 1986 (1985 – 1987 white face), marked "Alexander" $60.00
    8", #485, #463, 1987 – 1991 (Maggie), 1992 – 1993 (Wendy Ann), #140463, 1994, #13970, 1998 – 1999 . . . . .$60.00
    14", #24617, 1995, patchwork dress with red cape (Mary Ann) $100.00
    14", #87004, plaid dress with red cape (Mary Ann) $75.00
    8", #25970, 2000 – 2002 print dress, red cape, braided hair $85.00
    14", #28620, 2001 (Margaret), print dress, red cape $140.00
    8", #33390, 2002 – 2004, red check dress, 7½" plush wolf, basket $100.00
    5", #36290, 2004, vinyl, petite, print dress, red cape $25.00
Red Queen — 8", h.p., 1997 – 1999, #13010, red and gold gown $110.00
Red Queen and White King Set — 8" pair, #13030, 1997 . . . .$225.00
Red Sequin — 10", #19974, 1998 (Cissette), long red velvet gown $125.00
Red Shoes — 8", #14533, 1995, ballerina with same head as Spain $75.00
    8", #35635, 2003, white lace and tulle tutu, red shoes $75.00
Refreshing Coca-Cola — 8", #33000, 2002, with tin box $90.00
Renaissance Bride — 10", #25000, 2000 (Cissette) $140.00
Renoir — 21" compo., 1945 – 1946, extra make-up, must be excellent condition (Wendy Ann) . . . .$2,200.00 up
    14" h.p., 1950 only (Margaret) . . . .$875.00 up
    21" h.p./vinyl arms, 1961 only (Cissy) . . . .$900.00 up
    18" h.p./vinyl arms, vinyl head, 1963 only (Elise) . . . .$575.00 up
    21" h.p./vinyl arms, #2154, 1965, pink gown (Jacqueline) $700.00
    14", #28620, 2001 (Margaret), print dress, red cape $150.00
    21", #2062, 1966, blue gown with black trim (Coco) . . . .$2,200.00 up
    21", #2175, 1967, navy blue gown, red hat $800.00
    21", #2194, #2184, 1969 – 1970, blue gown, full lace over dress $625.00
    21", #2163, 1971, all yellow gown $600.00
    21", #2190, 1972, pink gown with black jacket and trim $575.00

Refreshing Coca-Cola, 8", 2002, (Wendy), with tin Coca-Cola box.

Renoir, 10", 1968 (Cissette). Navy blue taffeta dress and red hat.

Renoir, 10", 1969 (Cissette). All original.

Renoir

21", #2190, 1973, yellow gold gown, black ribbon $450.00
10" h.p., #1175, 1968, all navy with red hat (Cissette) $450.00
10", #1175, 1969, pale blue gown, short jacket, striped or dotted skirt $475.00
10", #1180, 1970, all aqua satin $400.00
Renoir Child — 12" plastic/vinyl, #1274, 1967 only, Portrait Children Series (Nancy Drew) $175.00
14", #1474, 1968 only (Mary Ann) $150.00
Renoir Girl — 14" plastic/vinyl, #1469, #1475, 1967 – 1968, Portrait Children Series, white dress with red
    ribbon trim (Mary Ann) $175.00
#1477, 1969 – 1971, pink dress, white pinafore $75.00
#1477, #1478, #1578, 1972 – 1986 (14-year production), pink multi-tiered lace gown $75.00
#1572, 1986 only, pink pleated nylon dress $70.00
Renoir Girl with Hoop — #1574, 1986 – 1987, Classic and Fine Arts Series $85.00
Renoir Girl with Watering Can — #1577, 1985 – 1987, Classic and Fine Arts Series $85.00
8" h.p., #22150, 1997, navy taffeta dress $75.00
Renoir's on the Terrace — 8", 1999 (Wendy), blue dress with white overdress $80.00
Rhett — 12", #1380, 1981 – 1985, Portrait Children Series, black jacket/gray pants (Nancy Drew) $75.00
8", #401, 1989 only, Jubilee II (Wendy Ann) $100.00
8", #638, #642, 1991 – 1992 only, Scarlett Series, all white/blue vest $85.00
8", #642, 1993, #160642, 1994, tan pants/vest/tie with white jacket $75.00
10" h.p., #15050, 1997, Gone with the Wind Series $80.00
Ribbon Celebration — 10", #36135, 2003, pink ballgown with ribbon and flowers $150.00
Riding Habit — 8", 1990 only, Americana Series (Wendy Ann) $65.00
#571, 1956 . . . . $500.00
#373G, 1957 . . . . $475.00
#541, 1958 . . . . $550.00
#355, 1962 . . . . $350.00
#623, 1965 . . . . $350.00
Riley's Little Annie — 14" plastic/vinyl, #1481, 1967 only, Literature Series (Mary Ann) $200.00
Ring Around the Rosey — 8", #12813, Nursery Rhymes Series $60.00
8", #13520, 1998 – 2000, pink and white lacy dress $80.00
Ringbearer — 14" h.p., 1951 only, must be near mint (Lovey Dove) . . . . $550.00 up
8", #28655, 2001 – 2002, white jacket, black pants $80.00

Renoir, 21", #2184, 1969 – 1970, (Jacqueline).

Renoir, 14" (Mary Ann), 1972 – 1986, all original.

Rhett (right & left) 12" (Nancy Drew), were made from 1981 to 1985.

Ringmaster — 8" (see Collectors United under Special Events/Exclusives)

Riverboat Queen (Lena) — (see M.A.D.C. under Special Events/Exclusives)

Riviera Night — 16", print dress, matching hat $170.00

Roaring 20's Bride — 10", #22630, 1999, white lace, pink roses, limited to 2,500 ....$175.00

Roaring 20's Catherine — 16" porcelain, blue satin fringed costume $200.00

Robin Hood — 8", #446, 1988 – 1990, Storybook Series (Wendy Ann) $60.00

Rock and Roll Group — #22110, 1997, four 8" dolls, mod costumes $350.00

Rocking Bear Doll — 8", #36910, 2003, lavender checked dress, bear $90.00

Rococo Bride — 10", pink satin and lace gown, #22460, 1999 – 2000 ....$150.00

Rococo Catherine — 16" porcelain, elaborate pink satin gown $225.00

Rodeo — 8" h.p., #483, 1955 only (Wendy Ann) ....$850.00 up

Rodeo Rosie — 14", #87012, 1996, red checked western costume $100.00

Rogers, Ginger — 14" – 21" compo., 1940 – 1945 (Wendy Ann) ....$2,500.00 up

Roller Blades — 8" "Throughly Modern Wendy" (see Disney under Special Events/Exclusives)

Roller Skating — 8" h.p., SL, SLW, BKW, #556, 1953 – 1956 (Wendy Ann) ....$675.00 up

Romance — 21" compo., 1945 – 1946, extra make-up, must be mint (Wendy Ann) ....$2,100.00 up

Romeo — 18" compo., 1949 (Wendy Ann) ....$1,300.00 up

    8" h.p., #474, 1955 only (Wendy Ann) ....$950.00 up

    12" plastic/vinyl, #1370, 1978 – 1987, Portrait Children Series (Nancy Drew) $60.00

    12", reintroduced 1991 – 1992 only, Romance Collection (Nancy Drew) $70.00

    8", 1994, mid-year introduction (see M.A.D.C. under Special Events/Exclusives)

Ronald McDonald — 8", 2000 – 2001, red and yellow outfit $65.00

Ron Weasley — 8", #38425, Harry Potter Series, with Scabbers $85.00

    10", #36635, vinyl black robe, 2004 ....$35.00

Roosevelt, Edith — 1988, fifth set Presidents' Ladies/First Ladies Series (Louisa) $100.00

Roosevelt, Eleanor — 14", 1989 – 1990, sixth set Presidents' Ladies/First Ladies Series (Louisa) $100.00

Rosamund Bridesmaid — 15" h.p., 1951 only (Margaret, Maggie) ....$600.00 up

    17" – 18" h.p., 1951 only (Margaret, Maggie) ....$750.00 up

Rose — 9" early vinyl toddler, 1953 only, pink organdy dress and bonnet $125.00

Rose Blossom — 8", #38405, 2004, red ballet costume $80.00

Rose Bouquet — 10", #28880, 2001, white and red dress with red roses $100.00

Rosebud — 16" – 19" cloth/vinyl, 1952 – 1953 ....$150.00

    13", 1953 only $175.00

    23" – 25", 1953 only $175.00

Robin Hood, 8", 1988 – 1990 (Wendy).

Rosette, 10", #1115, 1987 – 1989 (Cissette).

Rosebud (Pussy Cat)

Rosebud (Pussy Cat) — 14" – 20", 1986 only, white . . . .$50.00 – 125.00

    14", black $75.00

Rose Fairy — 8" h.p., #622, 1956 only (Wendy Ann) . . . .$1,500.00 up

    8", #22640, 1999, yellow and rose costume with wings, limited to 1,500 . . . .$80.00

Rose Garden Ball Gown — 10", #34170, 2002, pink satin gown, limited to 1,000 . . . .$130.00

Rosette — 10", #1115, 1987 – 1989, Portrette, pink/rose gown (Cissette) $75.00

Rosette Dreams — 8", #36275, blonde, pink satin dress $85.00

    8", #36276, brunette, pink satin dress $85.00

    8", #36277, African-American, 2004 . . . .$85.00

Rosey Posey — 14" cloth/vinyl, 1976 only $75.00

    21" cloth/vinyl, 1976 only $100.00

Rosie the Riveter — 8", #17530, 1999, overalls, lunch bucket $80.00

Ross, Betsy — 8" h.p., Americana Series, 1967 – 1972 (Wendy Ann), bent knees, #731 . . . .$125.00

      Straight legs, #0731, #431, 1973 – 1975, Storybook Series, marked "Alex" $75.00

      Straight legs, #431, 1976 – 1987 (1985 – 1987 white face) $65.00

    8", #312, reintroduced 1991 – 1992 only, Americana Series $60.00

      #312, 1976 Bicentennial gown (star print) $125.00

    8", #35705, 2003 – 2004, with flag $85.00

Rosy — 14", #1562, 1988 – 1990, Classic Series, all pink dress with cream lace trim (Mary Ann) $80.00

Round Up Cowgirl — 8" (see Disney under Special Events/Exclusives)

Row, Row, Row Your Boat — 8", #13510, 1998 – 1999, comes with boat $100.00

Roxanne — 8" h.p., #140504, 1994 only, Storyland Series $75.00

Royal Bouquet — 8", #28895, 2001, white dress, pink sash $100.00

Royal Evening — 18" h.p., 1953 only, cream/royal blue gown (Margaret) . . . .$2,400.00 up

Royal Wedding — 21" compo., 1947, full circles trimmed in lace on lower skirt (Wendy Ann) . . . .$3,200.00 up

Rozy — 12" plastic/vinyl, #1130, 1969 only (Janie) $325.00

Ruby (July) — 10", #1151, 1992 only, Birthstone Collection, all red/gold (Cissette) $125.00

Ruffles Clown — 21", 1954 only $425.00

Rumania — 8" h.p., BK, #786, 1968 – 1972 (Wendy) $100.00

    8" straight leg, #0786, #586, 1973 – 1975, marked "Alex" $65.00

    8" straight leg, #586, #538, 1976 – 1987, marked "Alexander" $60.00

    8", #538, 1986 – 1987 . . . .$55.00

Running Away to Grandma's, 8", 2003 – 2004 (Wendy), with bear and suitcase.

Russian, 9", composition, 1935 – 1938. All original, tagged "Madame Alexander, N. J., U.S.A."

Rumbera/Rumbero — 7" compo., 1938 – 1943 (Tiny Betty) ....$350.00 ea.

   9" compo., 1939 – 1941 (Little Betty) ....$375.00 ea.

Rumpelstiltskin & Miller's Daughter — 8" and 14", #1569, 1992 only, limited to 3,000 sets ....$275.00 set

   8" and 5" porcelain, #27750, 2001 ....$200.00 set

Running Away to Grandma's — 8", #34035, 2002 – 2004, with bear and suitcase, #34036, African-American ..$110.00

Russia — 8" h.p., BK, #774, 1968 – 1972 (Wendy Ann) $100.00

   8" straight leg, #0774, 1973 – 1975, marked "Alex" $65.00

   8" straight leg, #574, #548, 1976 – 1988 (1985 – 1987 white face), marked "Alexander" $60.00

   8", #548, 1985 – 1987, white face $60.00

   8", #581, 1991 – 1992 only $60.00

   8", #110540, 1994 only, long blue gown with gold trim $60.00

   8", #24150, 1999 – 2001, comes with painted stacking doll and miniature doll $125.00

Russian — 7" compo., 1935 – 1938 (Tiny Betty) $300.00

   9" compo., 1938 – 1942 (Little Betty) $325.00

Russian Ballerina — 8" h.p., #36770, 2003 – 2004, white tutu, bouquet $85.00

Rusty — 20" cloth/vinyl, 1967 – 1968 only $300.00

Sagittarius — 8", #21410, 1998 (Maggie), horse costume $90.00

Sailor — 14" compo., 1942 – 1945 (Wendy Ann) $750.00

   17" compo., 1943 – 1944 ....$875.00

   8" boy, 1990 (see U.F.D.C. under Special Events/Exclusives)

   8" boy, 1991 (see FAO Schwarz under Special Events/Exclusives)

Sailor, Columbian — (see U.F.D.C. under Special Events/Exclusives)

Sailorette — 10" h.p., #1119, 1988 only, Portrette Series, red, white, and blue outfit (Cissette) $65.00

Sally — 10", #26430, 2001 – 2002, Peanuts Gang, red dress $35.00

   10", #35900, 2003, Trick or Treat, blue dot dress, bag, candy $60.00

Sally Bride — 14" compo., 1938 – 1939 (Wendy Ann) ....$475.00 up

   18" – 21" compo., 1938 – 1939 ....$500.00 – 725.00

Salome — 14", #1412, 1984 – 1986, Opera Series (Mary Ann) $85.00

Salute to the Century — 8", #17630, 1999, white chiffon long gown, limited to 4,000 ....$100.00

Samantha — 14" 1989 (see FAO Schwarz under Special Events/Exclusives)

   14", #1561, 1991 – 1992 only, Classic Series, gold ruffled gown (Mary Ann) $150.00

   10", h.p., #15300, from the *Bewitched* TV series $125.00

Samson — 8", #14582, 1995 only, Bible Series $125.00

Sandy McHare — cloth/felt, 1930s $675.00

San Genero Festival — 8", #38140, 2004, red check outfit $90.00

Santa and Mrs. Claus — 8", mid-year issue (see Madame Alexander Doll Co. under Special Events/Exclusives)

Santa Claus — 14", #24608, 1995, Christmas Series $125.00

Santa's Little Helper — 8", #19660, 1998 – 1999, elf with candy cane trim $90.00

Santa's World — 8", #38545, 2004, Santa, reindeer, 5" elf, toys $130.00

Sapphire (September) — 10", 1992 only, Birthstone Collection $125.00

Sarah — 5", #27415, 2001 – 2003, petite, kite dress $20.00

Sardinia — 8", #509, 1989 – 1991 only (Wendy Ann) $60.00

Sargent — 14", #1576, 1984 – 1985, Fine Arts Series, dressed in lavender (Mary Ann) $80.00

Sargent's Girl — 14", #1579, 1986 only, Fine Arts Series, dressed in pink (Mary Ann) $80.00

Saturday's Child — 8", #27795, 2001, watering can $100.00

Scarecrow — 8", #430, 1993, #140430, 1994 – 1996, Wizard of Oz Series, #13230, 1997 – 2004 ....$70.00

   5", #28690, 2002, porcelain $85.00

Scarlett, Miss —14" (see Belks & Leggett under Special Events/Exclusives)

Scarlett O'Hara — (Before movie, 1937 – 1938)

   7" compo., 1937 – 1942 (Tiny Betty) $475.00

   9" compo., 1938 – 1941 (Little Betty) $550.00

   11", 1937 – 1942 (Wendy Ann) $700.00

   14" – 15" compo., 1941 – 1943 (Wendy Ann) $750.00

   18" compo., 1939 – 1946 (Wendy Ann) $1,200.00

   21" compo., 1945, 1947 (Wendy Ann) $1,500.00

   14" – 16" h.p., 1950s (Margaret) $1,700.00

Scarlett O'Hara

14" – 16" h.p., 1950s (Maggie) $1,750.00

20" h.p., 1950s (Margaret) . . . .$1,800.00 up

21", 1955, blue taffeta gown w/black looped braid trim, short jacket (Cissy) . . . .$1,600.00 up

    1958, jointed arms, green velvet jacket and bonnet trimmed in light green net, rare . . . .$2,000.00 up

    1961 – 1962, straight arms, white organdy, green ribbon inserted into tiers of lace on skirt,
        white picture hat, rare . . . .$2,000.00 up

18" h.p./vinyl arms, 1963 only, pale blue organdy with rosebuds, straw hat (Elise) . . . .$950.00 up

12" h.p., 1963 only, green taffeta gown and bonnet (Lissy) $1,500.00

7½" – 8", 1953 – 1954, white gown with red rosebuds, white lace hat (Wendy Ann) . . . .$1,400.00 up

7½" – 8" h.p., #485, 1955, two layer gown, white, yellow, and green trim (Wendy Ann) . . . .$1,500.00 up

8" h.p., BKW, 1956, pink, blue, or yellow floral gown . . . .$1,500.00 up

8" h.p., BKW, #431, 1957, white lace and ribbon trim (dress must be mint) . . . .$1,600.00 up

8" h.p., BK, #760, 1963 . . . .$650.00 up

8" BK, 1965, in white or cream gown (Wendy Ann) . . . .$750.00 up

8" BK, 1971 only, bright pink floral print $650.00

8" BK, #725, 1966 – 1972, Americana and Storybook Series, floral gown $350.00

8", #0725, #425, 1973 – 1991 (18-year production), white gown (Wendy Ann) $100.00

    Straight legs, #425, #426, 1976 – 1986, marked "Alexander" $75.00

    #426, 1987, white face, blue dot gown $150.00

    Straight legs, #426, 1988 – 1989, floral gown $100.00

    1986 (see M.A.D.C. under Special Events/Exclusives)

    1989, #400, Jubilee II, green velvet/gold trim $125.00

    Straight legs, #626, 1990 only, tiny floral print $100.00

    #631, 1991 only, three-tier white gown, curly hair $90.00

    #627, 1992 only, rose floral print, oversized bonnet $100.00

    #641, 1993, white gown with green stripes and trim $100.00

    #643, 1993, #160643, 1994 (Honeymoon in New Orleans), trunk with wardrobe $275.00

    #160644, 1994 only, Scarlett Bride $100.00

    #160647, 1994 only, Scarlett Picnic, green/red floral on white, large ruffle at hem $100.00

    #16648, 1995 – 1996, white, four-tier organdy gown with red trim $85.00

    #16652, 1995 only, floral print picnic outfit with organdy overskirt $100.00

    #16553, green drapery gown, 100th Anniversary $100.00

    #16653, 1996, Ashley's Farewell, maroon taffeta skirt $80.00

    #17025, 1996, Tomorrow Is Another Day, floral gown $80.00

    #86004, 1996, Ashley's Birthday, red velvet gown $100.00

    #15030, 1997 – 1998, Shadow, rose picnic dress $80.00

    #14970, 1998 – 1999, Poor Scarlett, floral calico, straw hat $80.00

    #15180, 1999 – 2000, Sweet Sixteen, white dress, red ribbons . . .$80.00

    #26860, 2000, Picnic, print dress, straw hat $80.00

    #27825, 2001 – 2002, green drapery gown and hat $90.00

    #28750, 2001, Honeymoon Scarlett, white dress, hat,
        black trim $100.00

    #27825, 2002 . . . .$85.00

    #35955, 2003, Scarlett's Sash for Ashley, red and white dress $85.00

    #38820, 2004, Matron of the Mansion, long red and white gown .$100.00

8" h.p., 1990, M.A.D.C. Symposium (see M.A.D.C. under
    Special Events/Exclusives)

8", 1993, mid-year issue (see Madame Alexander Doll Co. under
    Special Events/Exclusives)

21" h.p./vinyl arms, #2153, 1963 – 1964 (became "Godey" in 1965
    with blonde hair) . . . .$1,500.00 up

21" h.p./vinyl arms, 1965, #2152, green satin gown
    (Jacqueline) . . . .$1,900.00 up

#2061, 1966, all white gown, red sash, and roses (also with plain
    wide lace hem; inverted "V" scalloped lace hem –   allow more for this
    gown) (Coco) . . . .$2,800.00 up

Scarlett, 21" (Jacqueline), 1975 – 1977.
Beautiful deep green satin dress.

#2174, 1967, green satin gown with black trim $675.00

#2180, 1968, floral print gown with wide white hem . . . .$850.00 up

#2190, 1969, red gown with white lace $675.00

#2180, 1970, green satin, white trim on jacket $550.00

#2292, #2295, #2296, 1975 – 1977, all green satin, white lace at cuffs $400.00

#2110, 1978, silk floral gown, green parasol, white lace $400.00

#2240, 1979 – 1985, green velvet $350.00

#2255, 1986 only, floral gown, green parasol, white lace $375.00

#2247, 1987 – 1988, layered all over white gown $350.00

#2253, 1989, full bangs, all red gown (Birthday Party gown) $400.00

#2258, 1990 – 1993 only, Scarlett Bride, Scarlett Series $375.00

#2259, 1991 – 1992 only, green on white, three ruffles around skirt $350.00

21", #162276, 1994 (Jacqueline), tight green gown, three-layered bustle $300.00

#009, porcelain, 1991 only, green velvet, gold trim $375.00

#50001, Scarlett Picnic (Jacqueline), floral gown $325.00

#15020, 1997, rose picnic dress, carries garden basket $325.00

#15170, Black Mourning Scarlett, 1999 . . . .$450.00

#25765, 2000, Atlanta Stroll Scarlett, striped bodice $400.00

#28760, 2001, Peachtree Promenade, limited to 500, blue dress, black trim $500.00

#33475, 2002, Matron of the Mansion Scarlett, red velvet, limited to 250 . . . .$500.00

#35950, 2003, Scarlett at the Mill, green plaid skirt, copper overdress, limited to 350 . . . .$475.00

10" h.p., #1174, 1968 only, lace in bonnet, green satin gown with black braid trim (Cissette) $475.00

#1174, 1969, green satin gown with white and gold braid $450.00

#1181, #1180, 1970 – 1973, green satin gown with gold braid trim $375.00

#1100, 1989 only, Jubilee II, burgundy and white $125.00

#1102, 1990 – 1991 only, Scarlett Series, floral print gown $125.00

#1105, 1992 only, Scarlett at Ball, all in black $125.00

#161105, 1993, 1994, green velvet drapes/gold trim $125.00

1994 – 1995, Scarlett in red dress with red boa $125.00

#16107, 1995 only, white sheath with dark blue jacket $125.00

#16654, 1996, mourning dress $100.00

#16656, 1996, Scarlett and Rhett, limited set $200.00

#15000, 1997 – 1998, Hoop-Petti outfit $100.00

#15040, 1997, mourning outfit $100.00

#14980, 1998 – 2000, blue satin gown, lace shawl (Cissette),
Portrait Scarlett $125.00

#25770, 2000, Sewing Circle Scarlett, white top, lavender skirt . .$100.00

#28755, 2001, Atlanta Stroll Scarlett, red, white striped dress . . .$125.00

#33470, 2002, Scarlett dressing gown and vanity set, limited to
500 . . . .$350.00

#36160, 2003, Sweet Sixteen Scarlett, white ruffle dress,
red ribbon $450.00

#38815, 2004, Shanty Town Scarlett O'Hara, black trimmed
gown $150.00

12", 1981 – 1985, green gown with braid trim (Nancy Drew) $125.00

14" plastic/vinyl, #1495, 1968 only, floral gown (Mary Ann) $400.00

#1490, #7590, 1969 – 1986 (18-year production), white gown,
tagged "Gone with the Wind" (Mary Ann) $100.00

#1590, #1591, 1987 – 1989, blue or green floral print on beige . . .$125.00

#1590, 1990, Scarlett Series, tiny floral print gown $150.00

#1595, 1991 – 1992 only, Scarlett Series, white ruffles, green
ribbon (Louisa, Jennifer) $125.00

#16551, 1995 (see Peachtree Lane)

#1500, 14", 1986 only, Jubilee #1, all green velvet (Mary Ann) . . .$150.00

#1300, 14", 1989 only, Jubilee #2, green floral print gown (Mary Ann) .$125.00

Scarlett, 8", 1986 (Wendy), floral print dress, straw hat.

School Girl

School Girl — 7" compo., 1936 – 1943 (Tiny Betty) $300.00

Scorpio — 8", #21400, 1998, scorpion costume, golden spear $90.00

Scotch — 7" compo., 1936 – 1939 (Tiny Betty) $300.00

    9" compo., 1939 – 1940 (Little Betty) $350.00

    10" h.p., 1962 – 1963 (Cissette) . . . .$900.00 up

Scots Lass — 8" h.p., BKW, #396, 1963 only (Maggie Mixup, Wendy Ann) . . . .$225.00 up

Scottish (Scotland) — 8" h.p., BKW, #796, 1964 – 1965 (Wendy Ann) $150.00

    8" h.p., BK, #796, 1966 – 1972 . . . .$100.00

    8" straight leg, #0796 – 596, 1973 – 1975, marked "ALEX" $75.00

    8" straight leg, #596, #529, 1976 – 1993 (1985 – 1987 white face), marked "Alexander" $65.00

    8" re-dressed, Scot outfit with English guard hat, 1994 . . . .$60.00

    8", #28550, 2001 – 2002, Scot costume, blue plaid, bagpipes $80.00

Scouting — 8", #317, 1991 – 1992 only, Americana Series $125.00

Scrooge — 14", #18401, 1996, Dickens (Mary Ann) $100.00

Sears Roebuck — (see Special Events/Exclusives)

Season's Greetings Maggie — 8", #26840, 2001, green smocked dress $90.00

Season's Greetings Wendy — 8", #26845, 2001, red smocked dress $80.00

Secret Garden, My — 8" (see FAO Schwarz under Special Events/Exclusives)

    14", #24616, 1995, has trunk and wardrobe (Louisa) $225.00

Sense and Sensibility — 10", #25340, 2000, long white gown with embroidery $100.00

September — 14", #1527, 1989 only, Classic Series (Mary Ann) $85.00

    10", #1152, 1992, Portrette, royal blue/gold flapper $100.00

Serenade — 10", #36170, 2003, long ballgown with triangle black sequin design on skirt $150.00

Sesame Street, 1,2,3 — Trunk Set, 2004, #39082, African-American $260.00

Sesame Street, 1,2,3 — Trunk Set, 2004, #39080, 8", Big Bird, etc. $260.00

Setting Sail — 8", #37960, Asian, #37961, Caucasian, 2004, dress with stars $85.00

Seven Dwarfs — Compo., 1937 only, must be mint . . . .$550.00 ea.

Seventies Strut Shadow Cissette — 10", #38760, Caucasian, 2004, #38761, African-American,

    black outfit . . . .$250.00 ea.

Seventy-Fifth Anniversary Wendy — 8", #22420, 1998, pink outfit $100.00

Shadow of Madame — (see Doll & Teddy Bear Expo under Special Events/Exclusives)

Shadow Stepmother — 8", #14638, 1996 . . . .$125.00

Shaharazad — 10", #1144, 1992 – 1993 only, Portrette (Cissette) $90.00

    8", #33520, 2002, navy blue suit, dimsum $85.00

Shanghai — 8", #33520, 2003, navy blue silk outfit, dim sum $85.00

Shea Elf — 8" (see Collectors United under Special Events/Exclusives)

Shepherd and Drummer Boy Set — 8", #19490, 1997 – 2000, Nativity Set $200.00

Shepherdess with Lamb — 8", #20010, 1999 – 2000, red robe, headdress $85.00

She Sells Seashells — 8", #14629, 1996, Nursery Rhymes Series (Maggie) $70.00

Shimmering Dance — 8", #30645, 2001 – 2003, ballerina, blonde $70.00

Shimmering 1930s Catherine — 16", porcelain, long white gown $175.00

Shirley's Doll House — (see Special Events/Exclusives)

Shoemaker's Elf — 8", #33665, 2002 – 2003, purple costume, 8" shoe $130.00

Shoemaker's Elf Boy — 8", #14637, 1996 . . . .$65.00

Shoemaker's Elf Girl — 8", #14636, 1996 . . . .$65.00

Sicily — 8", #513, 1989 – 1990 (Wendy Ann) $65.00

Signature Wendy — 8", #38865, 2004, pink print dress, stationery $90.00

Silver Star — 8", #28875, 2001, silver satin and tulle $80.00

Simone — 21" h.p./vinyl arms, 1968 only, in trunk (Jacqueline) . . . .$2,150.00 up

Simply Sweet Flower Girl — 8", #32985, pink dress, rose bouquet, 2002 . . . .$80.00

Sir Lapin Hare — cloth/felt, 1930s $700.00

Sister Brenda — (see FAO Schwarz under Special Events/Exclusives)

Sitting Pretty — 18" foam body, 1965 only, rare $375.00

Skater's Waltz — 15" – 18", 1955 – 1956 (Cissy) . . . .$650.00 up

Skating Doll — 16", 1947 – 1950 (untagged "Sonja Henie" after contract expired) $700.00

Sledding Wendy — 8", #36015, 2003 – 2004, pink jacket, blue pants, sled $80.00

Sleeping Beauty — 7" – 9" compo., 1941 – 1944 (Tiny Betty and Little Betty) ....$325.00 – 450.00

    15" – 16" compo., 1938 – 1940 (Princess Elizabeth) $475.00

    18" – 21" compo., 1941 – 1944 (Wendy Ann) ....$650.00 – 950.00

    10", #1141, 1991 – 1992 only, Portrette, blue/white gown $90.00

    21", #2195, 1959 only year this head used, authorized by Disney, blue satin brocade, net cape, gold tiara .....$850.00 up

    16" #1895, same head as 21" on Elise body, authorized by Disney $650.00

    10" h.p., 1959 only, authorized by Disney, blue gown (Cissette) $350.00

    14" plastic/vinyl, #1495, #1595, 1971 – 1985 (14-year production), Classic Series, gold gown (Mary Ann) $85.00

    14", #1596, 1986 – 1990, Classic Series, blue gown (Mary Ann) $100.00

    14", #87010, 1996, pink and gold ballgown (Mary Ann) $100.00

    8", #14543, 1995, Brothers Grimm Series, blue with silver crown $65.00

    8", #13600, 1997 – 2000, blue satin gown, spinning wheel $65.00

    16", #25325, 2000, gold and lilac long ballet costume $175.00

    8", #30680, 2001 – 2004, blue gown, lace and rose trim $80.00

    16", #25325, 2001, lilac ballerina costume $165.00

    10", #36570, 2004, pink satin ballgown, three 2" fairy figures $160.00

Sleeping Beauty's Prince — 8", #13650, 1999 – 2000 (Wendy), bent knees, purple costume $85.00

Sleigh Riding Wendy — 8", #35650, 2003 – 2004, plaid vintage costume, sleigh, and plush horse $160.00

Slumbermate — 11" – 12" cloth/compo., 1940s ....$250.00 up

    21" compo./cloth, 1940s ....$475.00 up

    13" vinyl/cloth, 1951 only ....$250.00 up

Slumber Party Chloe — 14", #30065, 2001, pajamas, sleeping bag $60.00

Smarty — 12" plastic/vinyl, #1160, #1136, 1962 – 1963 ....$325.00

    1963 only, "Smarty & Baby" $375.00

    1963 only, with boy "Artie" in case with wardrobe $950.00

Smee — 8", #442, 1993, #140442, 1994, Storybook Series (Peter Pan), wears glasses $60.00

Smiley — 20" cloth/vinyl, 1971 only (Happy) $250.00

Smokey Tail — cloth/felt, 1930s $650.00

Snap, Crackle & Pop Set — 8", #12120, 1998 – 1999, Rice Krispies Dolls set $225.00

Snips and Snails — 8", #31330, 2000 – 2002, sweater, jeans, dog $70.00

Snoopy Beagle Scout — 8" dog, #38810, 2004, with Woodstock $70.00

Snowflake — 10", #1167, 1993 only, Portrette, ballerina dressed in white/gold outfit (Cissette) $90.00

Snowflake Symposium — (see M.A.D.C. under Special Events/Exclusives)

Snow Queen — 10", #1130, 1991 – 1992 only, Portrette, silver/white gown (Cisette) $100.00

    8", #14548, Hans Christian Andersen Series, white with gold trim ...$70.00

    8", #32150, 2000 – 2002, white gown, fur-trimmed robe $100.00

Snow White — 13" compo., 1937 – 1939, painted eyes

    (Princess Elizabeth) $475.00

    12" compo., 1939 – 1940 (Princess Elizabeth) $450.00

    13" compo., 1939 – 1940, sleep eyes (Princess Elizabeth) $475.00

    16" compo., 1939 – 1942 (Princess Elizabeth) $550.00

    18" compo., 1939 – 1940 (Princess Elizabeth) $750.00

    14" – 15" h.p., 1952 only (Margaret) $750.00

    18" – 23", 1952 only ....$800.00 – 1,200.00

    21" h.p., rare (Margaret) ....$1,200.00 up

    14", #1455, 1967 – 1977, Disney crest colors (Mary Ann) $300.00

    8" h.p., 1972 – 1977, Disney crest colors (Wendy) $350.00

    8", #495, 1990 – 1992 only, Storyland Series (Wendy) $85.00

    8", #14545, 1995, Brothers Grimm Series, crest colors but

    with red bodice, #13800, 1997 – 2004 ....$80.00

    12", 1990 (see Disney under Special Events/Exclusives)

    14" plastic/vinyl, #1455, #1555, 1970 – 1985 (15-year production),

    Classic Series, white gown (Mary Ann) $125.00

    #1556, #1557, 1986 – 1992, ecru & gold gown, red cape

    (Mary Ann, Louisa) $100.00

Sleeping Beauty, 14", #1596, 1986 – 1988
(Mary Ann).

Snow White

14", #14300, 1995, crest colors but red bodice (Louisa) $125.00
14", #87013, 1996, Snow White's trunk set (Mary Ann) $125.00
10", Disney crest colors (see Disney under Special Events/Exclusives)
14", #28615, 2001, white gown, red cape $150.00
10", #35520, 2002 – 2004 (Cissette), Disney colors, gift set with 5" vinyl (7) dwarfs $300.00
10", #37815, 2004, vinyl, Disney colors $35.00
Snow White's Prince — 8", #14639, 1996 . . . . $65.00
Snow White Wedding — 8", #30460, 2001 – 2002, white gown, red cape, flower coat $90.00
So Big — 22" cloth/vinyl, 1968 – 1975, painted eyes $225.00
18", #30310, 2001, cloth, Mary Engelbreit $45.00
Soccer Boy — 8", #16350, sports outfit with soccer ball, 1997 . . . . $60.00
Soccer Girl — 8", #16341, sports outfit with soccer ball, 1997 – 1998 . . . . $60.00
Sock Hop 1950 — 8", #17780, 1999, poodle skirt $85.00
Soda Shop Coca-Cola — 8", #38695, 2004, with glass and chair $90.00
Soldier — 14" compo., 1943 – 1944 (Wendy Ann) $375.00
17" compo., 1942 – 1945 (Wendy Ann) $850.00
So Lite Baby or Toddler — 20" cloth, 1930 – 1940s . . . . $375.00 up
Sophie — 10", #28301, 2002 – 2003, green check dress, sweater $40.00
10", #35815, 2003, Fun Loving, blue sweater $40.00
Sound of Music —
Large set, 1965 – 1970
14", #1404, Louisa (Mary Ann) $275.00
12", #1107 Friedrich (Janie or Smarty) $275.00
14", #1403 Brigitta (Mary Ann) $225.00
14", #1405 Liesl (Mary Ann) $275.00
12" Marta, 12" Gretl (Smarty or Janie) $225.00
17", #1706 Maria (Elise or Polly) $325.00
Full set of seven dolls $1,100.00
Small set, 1971 – 1973
12" Maria (Nancy Drew) $325.00
8", #801 Gretl (Wendy Ann) $175.00
8", #802 Marta, #807 Friedrich (Wendy Ann) $225.00

Friedrich, 12" (Janie), 1965 – 1970, large set Sound Of Music.

Gretl, 12", 1965 – 1970 (Janie), large set Sound of Music.

Liesl, 14", large set Sound of Music (Mary Ann). 1965 – 1970, all original.

10" Brigitta (Cissette) $200.00
10" Liesl (Cissette) $250.00
10" Louisa (Cissette) $300.00
Set of seven dolls $1,200.00
Dressed in sailor suits and tagged, dates unknown
    17" Maria (Elise or Polly) $500.00
    14" Louisa (Mary Ann) $500.00
    10" Friedrich (Smarty) $375.00
    14" Brigitta (Mary Ann) $375.00
    14" Liesl (Mary Ann) $375.00
    10" Gretl (Smarty) $350.00
    10" Marta (Smarty) $375.00
    Set of seven dolls . . . .$2,700.00 up
    12", 1965, in sailor suit (Lissy) . . . .$800.00 up
    12", 1965, in Alpine outfit (Lissy) $650.00
All in same oufits: red skirt, white attached blouse, black vest that ties in
    front with gold cord, very rare . . . .$500.00 – 800.00 ea.
Reintroduced 1992 – 1993
    8", #390, #391, 1992 – 1993 only, Gretl and Kurt (boy in sailor suit) $125.00
    8", #390, #392, 1992 – 1994, Brigitta $100.00
    8", #394, 1993 only, Friedrich dressed in green/white playsuit $125.00
    8", #393, 1993 only, Marta in sailor dress $200.00
    10", 1992 – 1993 only, Maria (Cissette) $125.00
    10", 1993 only, Liesl $125.00
    12", 1992 only, Maria Bride (Nancy Drew) $125.00
    10", Maria at Abbey, dressed in nun's outfit (Cissette), 1993 only $125.00
Reintroduced 1998
    8", #14060, Gretl Von Trapp (Wendy), green, gray sailor suit $100.00
    8", #14050, Marta Von Trapp (Maggie), sailor suit $100.00
    9", #14040, Brigitta Von Trapp (Wendy), sailor outfit $100.00
    10", #14030, Captain Von Trapp (Cissette), gray Tyrolean suit $125.00
    10", #13890, Maria at the Abbey (Cissette), navy dress, guitar $125.00

Louisa, 14" (Mary Ann), large set Sound of Music, 1965 – 1970. All 10", original.

Marta, 12" (Janie), 1965 – 1970, large set Sound of Music.

Southern Belle, 10", 1970 (Cissette). All original and mint.

Sound of Music

#13870, Mother Superior (Cissette), black and white nun habit $130.00
10", #13880, Maria Travel Ensemble (Cissette), pleated skirt, bolero $125.00
9", #14020, Friedrich Von Trapp (Maggie), blue and gray sailor suit $100.00
10", #14160, Louisa Von Trapp (Wendy), blue, gray pleated sailor suit $100.00
10", #14090, Kurt Von Trapp (Wendy), sailor uniform $100.00
10", #14170, Liesl Von Trapp (Cissette), blue and gray sailor outfit $100.00

South American — 7" compo., 1938 – 1943 (Tiny Betty) $300.00
9" compo., 1939 – 1941 (Little Betty) $300.00

Southern Belle — 10", #25985, 2000, long white gown with lace, limited to 2,000 . . . .$150.00

Southern Belle or Girl — 8" h.p., SLNW, 1953, white dress, straw hat with pink silk roses . . . .$850.00 up
8" h.p., #370, 1954 (Wendy Ann) . . . .$1,000.00 up
8" h.p., #437, #410, 1956, pink or blue/white striped gown (Wendy Ann) . . . .$1,100.00 up
8" h.p., #385, 1963 only (Wendy Ann) $650.00
12" h.p., 1963 only (Lissy) . . . .$1,600.00 up
21" h.p./vinyl arms, #2155, 1965, blue gown with wide pleated hem (Jacqueline) $1,600.00
21", #2170, 1967, white gown with green ribbon trim $450.00
10" h.p., #1170, 1968, white gown with green ribbon through three rows of lace (Cissette) $450.00
1969, white gown with four rows of lace, pink sash (Cissette) $475.00
#1185, 1970, white gown with red ribbon sash (Cissette) $400.00
#1185 (#1184 in 1973), 1971 – 1973, white gown with green ribbon sash $350.00
10" (see My Doll House under Special Events/Exclusives)

Southern Flower Girl — 8", #25980, 2000, long pink gown, basket, limited to 2,800 . . . .$100.00

Southern Girl — 11" – 14" compo., 1940 – 1943 (Wendy Ann) . . . .$350.00 – 650.00
17" – 21" compo., 1940 – 1943 (Wendy Ann) . . . .$700.00 – 950.00

Southern Symposium — (see M.A.D.C. under Special Events/Exclusives)

Spanish — 7" – 8" compo., 1935 – 1939 (Tiny Betty) $275.00
9" compo., 1936 – 1940 (Litte Betty) $300.00

Spanish Boy — 8" h.p., BK & BKW, #779, 1964 – 1968 (Wendy Ann) $300.00

Spanish Girl — 8" h.p., BKW, #795, #395, 1962 – 1965, three-tiered skirt (Wendy Ann) $125.00
8" h.p., BK, #795, 1966 – 1972, three-tiered skirt $100.00
8" straight leg, #0795, #595, 1973 – 1975, three-tiered skirt, marked "ALEX" $65.00
8" straight leg, #595, 1976 – 1982, three-tiered skirt, marked "Alexander" $60.00
8" straight leg, #595, 1983 – 1985, two-tiered skirt $60.00
8" straight leg, #541, 1986 – 1990, white with red polka dots (1986 – 1987 white face) $60.00
8" straight leg, #541, 1990 – 1992, all red tiered skirt $60.00
8" h.p., #110545, 1994 – 1995, red, two-tiered polka dot gown $60.00
8" h.p., #24160, 1999 – 2000, red rose and black gown $85.00
8", #35605, 2003 – 2004, red satin outfit, plush ball $90.00

Spanish Matador — 8", #530, 1992 – 1993 only (Wendy) $65.00

Sparkle Fairy — 8", #38615, 2004, pink dress with wings $90.00

Sparkling Sapphire — 10", #32080, 2000 – 2002, red and blue long gown $175.00

Special Girl — 23" – 24" cloth/comp., 1942 – 1946 . . . .$500.00

Spiegel's — (see Spiegel's under Special Events/Exclusives)

Spring — 14", 1993, Changing Seasons, doll and four outfits $125.00
5", #25850, 2000, porcelain, pink dress, straw hat $65.00

Spring Angel — 10", #28370, 2001 – 2002, long gown, feather wings $120.00

Spring Bouquet — 8", #30890, 2001 – 2003, white ballet outfit, green top, blonde $70.00

Spring Break — (see Metroplex Doll Club under Special Events/Exclusives)

Spring Garden Flower Girl — 8", #34390, 2002 – 2003, flower trimmed dress $90.00

Spring Promenade — 10", #27810, 2001, long white dress, straw hat $125.00

Springtime — 8" (see M.A.D.C. under Special Events/Exclusives)

Starlight Angel — 10", #10790, 1999 – 2000 (Cissette), star-accented gown $125.00

Stars and Stripes — 10", #33740, 2002, red stripe overskirt $125.00

Stepmother — 8", 1997, #13820, velvet cape, satin dress $80.00

Stick Piggy — 12", 1997, #10030, sailor outfit $95.00

Stilts — 8", #320, 1992 – 1993 only, clown on stilts $85.00

Story Princess — 15 – 18" h.p., 1954 – 1956 (Margaret, Cissy, Binnie) ....$600.00 – 950.00

    8" h.p., #892, 1956 only (Wendy Ann) ....$1,300.00 up

Straw Piggy — 12", 1997, #10020, plaid pants, straw hat $95.00

Stuffy (Boy) — h.p., 1952 – 1953 (Margaret) ....$850.00 up

Suellen — 14" – 17" compo., 1937 – 1938 (Wendy Ann) ....$975.00 up

    12", 1990 only, yellow multi-tiered skirt, Scarlett Series (Nancy Drew) $85.00

    8" pink bodice, floral skirt, apron, #160645, 1994 – 1995 ....$80.00

    Special for Jean's Doll Shop (see Special Events/Exclusives)

Suellen O'Hara — 8", #15200, 1999 ....$100.00

Suffragette 1910 — 10", #17730, 1999 ....$100.00

Sugar and Spice — 8", #13530, 1998 – 1999, pink and white lace dress $90.00

    8", #32145, 2000 – 2002, three rows of ribbon on skirt, lollipop $60.00

Sugar Darlin' — 14" – 18" cloth/vinyl, 1964 only ....$65.00 – 125.00

    24", 1964 only $150.00

    Lively, 14", 18", 24", 1964 only, knob makes head and limbs move ....$125.00 – 225.00

Sugar Plum Fairy — 10", #1147, 1992 – 1993 only, Portrette, lavender ballerina $85.00

    8" (Wendy), 1999 – 2000, #12640, pink satin and tulle $75.00

    16", #80780, 2000, long ballet costume from *The Nutcracker* $150.00

Sugar Tears — 12" vinyl baby, 1964 only (Honeybea) $100.00

Sulky Sue — 8", #445, 1988 – 1990, marked "Alexander" (Wendy Ann) $60.00

Summer — 14", 1993, Changing Seasons, doll and four outfits $100.00

    5", #25855, 2000, porcelain, blue dress, straw hat $65.00

Summer Angel — 8", #27640, 2001 – 2002, multicolored tulle, blonde $100.00

Summer Garden Vintage — 8", #28915, 2002 – 2003, with basket of flowers, blue striped pinafore $75.00

Sunbeam — 11", 16", 19", 1951 only, newborn infant, clean and in fair condition ....$100.00 – 200.00

    16", 20", 24" cloth/vinyl, 1950, Divine-a-Lite Series (reg #573, #313), scowling expression $125.00

Sunbonnet Sue — 9" compo., 1937 – 1940 (Little Betty) $300.00

Sunday Best — 8", #38845, 2004, dress with flowers, hat $90.00

Sunday's Child — 8", #27800, 2001, angel costume $100.00

Sunflower Clown — 40" all cloth, 1951 only, flower eyes ....$850.00 up

Sun-Maid Raisin Girl — 8", #26190, 2000, red costume $65.00

Sunny — 8" (see C.U. under Special Events/Exclusives)

Susannah Clogger — 8" (see Dolly Dears under Special Events/Exclusives)

Susie Q — cloth, 1940 – 1942 ....$700.00

    8", #14590, 1995, Toy Shelf Series, has yarn braids and pink polka dot dress with green jacket $65.00

Suzy — 12" plastic/vinyl, 1970 only (Janie) $325.00

Swan Lake — 16", #22040, 1998, Odette in white tutu $200.00

    10", #35870, 2003, white tutu, feathers $140.00

Swan Princess — 10", #14106, 1995 only, Fairy Tales Series $85.00

    8", #33690, 2002, white dress, crown, limited to 1,000 ..... $125.00

Sweden (Swedish) — 8" h.p., BKW, #392, #792, 1961 – 1965

    (Wendy Ann) $125.00

    8" h.p., BK, #792, 1966 – 1972 ....$100.00

    8" straight leg, #0792, #592, 1973 – 1975, marked "Alex" $75.00

    8" straight leg, #592, #539, #521, 1976 – 1989, marked

      "Alexander" $65.00

    8", 1986 ....$60.00

    8", #580, reintroduced 1991 only $60.00

    BKW with Maggie $150.00

    8", #35980, 2003 – 2004, print dress, red hat, wooden horse ..$80.00

Swedish — 7" compo., 1936 – 1940 (Tiny Betty) $300.00

    9" compo., 1937 – 1941 (Little Betty) $325.00

Sweet Baby — 18½" – 20" cloth/latex, 1948 only ...$75.00 – 150.00

    14", 1983 – 1984 (Sweet Tears) $75.00

    14", reissued 1987, 1987 – 1993 (1991 has no bottle)

    (Sweet Tears) $85.00

Sweet Tears. Left, 14"; right, 9", vinyl, rooted hair. All original with poodle.

Sweet Baby

14", 1990 – 1992 only (1991 has bottle), in carry case $125.00

14", reintroduced 1993 only, pink striped jumper or dress $65.00

Sweetie Baby — 22", 1962 only $125.00

Sweetie Walker — 23", 1962 only .... $275.00 up

Sweet Irish Dancer — 8", #36495, red hair, green decorated dress, 2003 – 2004 .... $65.00

Sweet Kisses for Grandma — 8", #36155, 2003 – 2004, white dress, red trim $65.00

Sweet Sixteen — 14", #1554, 1991 – 1992 only, Classic Series (Louisa) $100.00

10", #21060, 1997, pink silk dress, lace stole $90.00

8", #35985, 2004, black velvet top, tulle skirt $90.00

Sweet Tears — 9" vinyl, 1965 – 1974 .... $85.00

9" with layette in box, 1965 – 1973 .... $175.00

14", 1967 – 1974, in trunk/trousseau $175.00

14", 1965 – 1974, in window box $175.00

14", 1979, with layette $150.00

14", 1965 – 1982 .... $75.00

16", 1965 – 1971 .... $85.00

Sweet Violet — 18" h.p., 1951 – 1954 (Cissy) .... $875.00 up

Swiss — 7" compo., 1936 (Tiny Betty) $300.00

9" compo., 1935 – 1938 (Little Betty) $325.00

10" h.p., 1962 – 1963 (Cissette) $825.00

Switzerland — 8" h.p., BKW, #394, #794, 1961 – 1965 .... $125.00

8" h.p., BK, #794, 1966 – 1972 .... $100.00

8" h.p., straight leg, #0794, #594, 1973 – 1975, marked "Alex" $75.00

8" h.p., straight leg, #594, #540, #518, 1976 – 1989, marked "Alexander" $60.00

8", #546, 1986 .... $60.00

#518, 1988 – 1990, costume change $60.00

8" BKW, Maggie smile face $150.00

8", #25795, 2000, pink and white costume with watch $65.00

Symposium — (see M.A.D.C. under Special Events/Exclusives)

Taft, Helen — 1988, fifth set Presidents' Ladies/First Ladies Series (Louisa) $100.00

Tara — #14990, 1998, two-sided home of Scarlett $125.00

Taurus — 8", #21340, 1998 – brown and white bull costume $90.00

Team Canada — 8", #24130, 1998 – 1999, hockey skater $80.00

Swiss, 9" composition, 1930s,
tagged "Swiss."

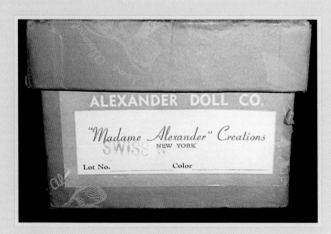

Original box for 9", 1930s composition Swiss.

Team Mates — 8", #38885, 2004, with dog, baseball, and bat $85.00

Tea Rose Cissette — 10", #22370 – 1998, floral silk cocktail dress $125.00

Teeny Twinkle — 1946 only, cloth with flirty eyes $525.00

Tennis — 8" h.p., BKW, #415, #632 (Wendy Ann) $450.00

Tennis Boy — 8", #16331, 1997 . . . .$60.00

Tennis Girl — 8", #16320, 1997 . . . .$60.00

Tess — 10", #28405, 2001, green, pink vintage gown $125.00

Texas — 8", #313, 1991 only, Americana $75.00

Texas Shriner — (see Shriner's under Special Events/Exclusives)

Thailand — 8" h.p., BK, #767, 1966 – 1972 (Wendy) $100.00

   8" straight leg, #0767, #567, 1973 – 1975, marked "Alex" $75.00

   8" straight leg, #567, 1976 – 1989, marked "Alexander" $65.00

Thanksgiving — 8", #35680, 2003, sweater, pumpkin print skirt, turkey $65.00

Thank You — 8", #21110, 1997 – 1998, comes with a thank-you card $60.00

That Girl — 10", #26345, 2000 (Cissette), navy blue suit $90.00

"There's No Place Like Home" Doll House — trunk set, #13260, 1997 – 1999 . . . .$150.00

There Was a Little Girl — 14", #24611, 1995, Nursery Rhymes Series (Mary Ann) $90.00

Thinking of You — 8", #21500, 1998 – 1999, print dress, straw hat $70.00

Thomas, Marlo — 17" plastic/vinyl, 1967 only (Polly) . . . .$650.00 up

Three Little Kittens — 8", #26970, 2000 – 2001, blue plaid dress, three kittens $90.00

Three Little Pigs & Wolf — Compo., 1938 – 1939, must be mint . . . .$675.00 up ea.

Three Little Pigs Set — 12", #10000, 1997, brick, straw, and stick Piggy $300.00

   8", #33656, 2003, three pigs, each with house bank $150.00

Three Wise Men Set — 8", #19480, 1997 – 1999, Nativity Set $400.00

Thumbelina & Her Lady — 8" and 21" porcelain, 1992 –1993, limited to 2,500 sets $475.00

Thursday's Child — 8", #27785, 2001, comes with suitcase $100.00

Tibet — 8" h.p., #534, 1993 only $60.00

Tierney, Gene — 14" – 17" compo., 1945, must be mint (Wendy Ann) . . . .$3,300.00 up

Tiger Lily — 8", #469, 1992 – 1993 only, Storybook Series (Peter Pan) (Wendy Ann) $95.00

Time Out for Coca-Cola Sock Hop — 10", #26225, 2000 . . . .$125.00

Timmy Toddler — 23" plastic/vinyl, 1960 – 1961 . . . .$150.00

   30", 1960 only $250.00

Tinker Bell — 11" h.p., #1110, 1969 only, Peter Pan Series (Cissette) . . . .$500.00 up

   Magic wand and wings, #13960 in 1998 – 2000 . . . .$75.00

   14", #87009, 1996 (Mary Ann) $100.00

   8", #30675, 2001, pink, blue costume, lace wings, limited to

     2,500 pieces $75.00

   8", #34100, 2004, pink outfit, wand $80.00

   8", #34100, 2002 – 2003, white costume, silver wand $80.00

   5", #30455, 2002, porcelain, pink and blue costume $85.00

   10", #31750, 2003, green costume, shoes, gold wand $125.00

   5", #38325, 2004, vinyl, petite, with wand $25.00

Tinkles — 8", #10400, 1995, Christmas Series $60.00

Tin Man — 8", #13210, 1998 – 2004, Wizard of Oz Series, silver

   face and costume $70.00

   5", #28685, 2001 – 2003, porcelain $85.00

Tin Woodsman — 8", #432 in 1993, #140432 in 1994 – 1995 . . . .$100.00

Tiny Betty — 7" compo., 1935 – 1942 . . . .$300.00 up

Tiny Tim — 7" compo., 1934 – 1937 (Tiny Betty) . . . .$325.00 up

   14" compo., 1938 – 1940 (Wendy Ann) $625.00

   cloth, early 1930s . . . .$700.00 up

   8", #18001, 1996, Dickens (Wendy Ann) $65.00

Tippi Ballerina — 8" (see Collectors United under Special Events/Exclusives)

Tippy Toe — 16" cloth, 1940s $600.00

Toast to Madame Alexander — 8", #36145, pink long dress with

   fur at neck and hem, champagne bottle, 2003 . . . .$90.00

Tinker Bell, 10" (Cissette), 1969 only,
Peter Pan Series. All hard plastic.

91

Today I Feel Excited and Sad

Today I Feel Excited and Sad — 8", #33685, 2002, cloth $35.00

Today I Feel Silly — 14", #80710, 2000 – 2004, dressed cloth doll with four interchangeable faces $50.00

Today I Feel Silly and Angry — 8", #33680, cloth, includes cat $35.00

To Market, To Market — 8", #38775, 2004, with pig $50.00

Tommy — 12" h.p., 1962 only (Lissy) $800.00

Tommy Bangs — h.p., 1952 only, Little Men Series (Maggie, Margaret) $875.00

Tommy Snooks — 8", #447, 1988 – 1991, Storybook Series $60.00

Tommy Tittlemouse — 8", #444, 1988 – 1991, Storybook Series (Maggie) $60.00

Tom Sawyer — 8" h.p., #491, 1989 – 1990, Storybook Series (Maggie Mixup) $60.00

Tony Sarg Marionettes — (see Marionettes)

Tooth Fairy — 10" Portrette, 1994 only $90.00

    8", #10389 – 10391, 1995 only, Special Occasions Series, three hair colors $65.00

    8", #21550, 1999 – 2000, pink sparkling outfit, satin pillow $70.00

    8", #30660, 2001 – 2002, lavender costume, silver bag, and crown, white wing $85.00

To Oz Bear Set — #33634, 2002, four 3" bears ....$120.00 set

To Oz Cowardly Lion — 8", #33632, 2002, with 3" bear $95.00

To Oz Dorothy — 8", #33630, 2002, with 3" plush bear $100.00

To Oz Scarecrow — 8", #33633, 2002, with 3" plush bear $95.00

To Oz Tin Man — 8", #33631, 2002, with 3" plush bear $95.00

Topsy-Turvy — Compo. with Tiny Betty heads, 1935 only ....$300.00 up

    With Dionne Quint head, 1936 only $350.00

    Cinderella — #14587, 1995 only, two headed, one side gown; other side dress with apron $125.00

    Red Riding Hood — 8", #14555 (three-way) Red Riding Hood, Grandma, Wolf $125.00

    Wicked Stepmother — 8", #14640, 1996, evil witch, stepmother $150.00

Toulouse-Lautrec — 21", #2250, 1986 – 1987 only, black/pink outfit $300.00

Toy Box Wendy — 8", #36270, 2003 – 2004, print dress, toy box with toys and books $120.00

Toy Soldier — 8", #481, 1993, #140481, 1994, #13210 – 1998, white face, red dots on cheeks $70.00

Train Journey — 8" h.p., #486, 1955, white wool jacket, hat, red plaid dress $550.00

Trapeze Artist — 10", #1133, 1990 – 1991, Portrette (Cissette) $90.00

Treena Ballerina — 15" h.p., 1952 only, must be near mint (Margaret) ....$750.00 up

    18" – 21", 1952 only ....$650.00 – 875.00

Tree Topper — 8" (half doll only), #850, 1992 only, red/gold dress $100.00

    8" (half doll only), #852, 1992 – 1994, Angel Lace with multi-tiered ivory lace skirt (Wendy) $100.00

    8" (half doll only), #853, 1993 – 1994, red velvet/gold and green (Wendy) $100.00

    10" (half doll only), #854, 1993 – 1994; #54854, 1995, pink Victorian (Cissette) $125.00

    8" (half doll only), #540855, 1994; #540855 – 1995, all antique white (Wendy) $100.00

    8", #84857, 1995 – 1996, Yuletide Angel dressed in red and gold (Wendy), #19600, 1997 ......$100.00

    8", #84859, 1995 – 1996, Christmas Angel dressed in white and gold (Wendy) $100.00

    10", #54860, Glorious Angel dressed in red and white, gold crown, #19590, 1997 – 1998 (Cissette) $100.00

    10", #19610, 1997 – 1998, Heavenly Angel, gold and ivory costume (Wendy) $100.00

    10", Glistening Angel, 1998 – 1999, #19700 (Wendy), silver brocade $100.00

    10", Winter Lights — #20000, 1999 – 2000 (Wendy), AC illuminated $100.00

    10", Holiday Trimmings, 2000 – 2001, #2704 (Wendy), red plaid gown $100.00

    10", Golden Dream, 2000, #27055, gold and white gown $100.00

    10", Caroler Tree Topper, 2000, #27045, red jacket, fur muff $100.00

    10", Star Tree Topper, 2000, #26100, gold star, tassels $75.00

    8", Shining Bright Angel Fiber Optic Tree Topper, #28265, 2001 – 2002, white, gold (Wendy), fur wings ...$150.00

    10", Starburst Angel Tree Topper, #28535, 2001, red, gold gown (Wendy) $100.00

    10", Peace on Earth, #33445, 2002 – 2003, red gown, feather wings $135.00

    8", Lighting the Christmas Tree Topper, #35920, 2003, gold wings, white dress $135.00

Trellis Rose Flower Girl — 8", #28650, 2001 – 2002, long white dress $85.00

Trick and Treat — (see Child at Heart under Special Events/Exclusives)

Triumphant Topaz — 10", #32165, 2000 – 2002, black and gold ballgown $150.00

Truman, Bess — 14", 1989 – 1990, sixth set Presidents' Ladies/First Ladies Series (Mary Ann) $100.00

Tuesday's Child — 8", #27775, 2001, white dress, blue ribbon $100.00

Tunisia — 8", #514, 1989 only, marked "Alexander" (Wendy) $65.00

92

Turkey — 8" h.p., BK, #787, 1968 – 1972 (Wendy) $100.00
   8" straight leg, #0787, #587, 1973 – 1975, marked "Alex" $75.00
   8" straight leg, #587, 1976 – 1986, marked "Alexander" $65.00
'Twas the Night Before Christmas — 8", #27305, 2001, long white gown $85.00
Tweedledee & Tweedledum — 14" cloth, 1930 – 1931 . . . .$750.00 ea.
   8" h.p., #13080, 1998 – 1999, checked pants, red jackets, propeller caps $150.00
      (see Disney under Special Events/Exclusives)
Twelve Days of Christmas — 8", #35555, 2002 – 2004, with tree and ornaments, plaid dress, red pinafore $110.00
   5", #31745, 2003 – 2004, set of 12 dolls, display box $300.00
20's Bride — #14103, 1995, Nostalgia Series $125.00
20's Traveler — 10", #1139, 1991 – 1992 only, Portrette, M.A. signature logo on box (Cissette) $150.00
25th Anniversary — 1982 (see Enchanted Doll House under Special Events/Exclusives)
Twilight Angel — 8", #10780 (Wendy), 1999 – 2000, white organza gown $100.00
Twinkle Toes — 8", #36905, 2003 – 2004, ballerina, bear with tutu $85.00
Twinkle, Twinkle Little Star — 8", #11630, 1997 . . . .$65.00
Twirling Confetti — 8", 2003, #35075, pink tutu, flower trimmed $50.00
Twirling Rose — 8", #33145, 2002 – 2003, long blue ballet costume $70.00
Tyler, Julia — 1979 – 1981, second set Presidents' Ladies/First Ladies Series (Martha) $100.00
Tyrolean Boy & Girl* — 8" h.p., BKW (girl – #398, #798; boy – #399, #799), 1962 – 1965 (Wendy Ann) . . .$150.00 ea.
   8" h.p., BK (girl – #798; boy – #799), 1966 – 1972 . . . .$100.00 ea.
   8" straight leg (girl – #0798; boy – #0799), 1973, marked "ALEX" . . . .$75.00 ea.
   8" BKW (Maggie Mixup) . . . .$150.00 ea.
U.F.D.C. Sailor Boy — 1990 (see Special Events/Exclusives)
Ugly Stepsister — 10" h.p., #13340, 1997 – 1998, Cinderella Series $85.00
Ukraine — 8", #34325, 2002 – 2003, cultural costume, with decorated egg, flower hat $75.00
Ultimate Angel — 21", #10770, 1999, blue silk and lace gown $550.00
Uncle Sam — 8", #10353, 1995 only (Wendy) $70.00
   8" h.p., #24170, 1999 – 2000, astronaut costume, United States of America $90.00
Union Officer — 12", #634, 1990 – 1991, Scarlett Series (Nancy Drew) $85.00
   Soldier, 8", #634, 1991 only, Scarlett Series $125.00
United States — 8" h.p., #559, straight leg, 1974 – 1975, marked "Alex" $75.00
   8", #559 Alex. mold, misspelled "Untied States" $100.00
      straight leg, #559, 1976 – 1987, marked "Alexander" $65.00
      #559, #516, 1988 – 1992 (Maggie) $60.00
   8", #11562, 1996, Statue of Liberty costume, #24000, 1997 – 1998 . . . .$80.00
United States Air Force — 8", #12000, 1998 (Wendy), uniform and flag $80.00
United States Armed Forces Set — four dolls, five flags, and flag stand $350.00
United States Army — 8", #12010, 1998 (Wendy) $80.00
United States Marines — 8", #12030, 1998 (Wendy) $80.00
United States Navy — 8", #12020, 1998 (Wendy) $80.00
U.S.A. — 8" h.p., #536, 1993 – 1994 (#110536) (also see Neiman-Marcus trunk set, 1994) $75.00
   Las Vegas, 8", #28565, 2001, silver costume $90.00
   Sacajawea, 8", #28575, 2001 – 2002, includes papoose $85.00
Valentine — (see Lady Valentine & Lord Valentine)
Valentine Kisses — 8", #27050, 2000 – 2001, red and silver outfit $65.00
Van Buren, Angelica — 1979 – 1981, second set Presidents' Ladies/First Ladies Series (Louisa) $100.00
Velvet Party Dress — 8" h.p., #389, 1957 only, very rare (Wendy Ann) . . . .$2,000.00 up
Vermont Maid — 8" (see Enchanted Doll House under Special Events/Exclusives)
Victoria — 21" compo., 1939, 1941, 1945 – 1946 (also see Flavia) (Wendy Ann) . . . .$2,000.00 up
   20" h.p., 1954 only, Me & My Shadow Series (Cissy) . . . .$2,000.00 up
   14" h.p., 1950 – 1951 (Margaret) $900.00
   18" h.p., 1954 only, Me & My Shadow Series, slate blue gown (Maggie) . . . .$2,000.00 up
   8" h.p., #0030C, 1954 only, matches 18" doll (Wendy Ann) . . . .$1,300.00 up
   14" baby, 1975 – 1988, 1990 – 1997 . . . .$90.00
   18" baby, 1966 only $75.00

* Became Austrian in 1974.

Victoria

18", reintroduced, 1991 – 1993, 1997 ....$65.00 – 125.00
20" baby, 1967 – 1989 ....$100.00
20" 1986 only, in dress/jacket/bonnet $100.00
18" vinyl, 1998, velour romper, #29420 white, #29423 African-American $100.00
14", "Mozart Music" Concertina, #26915, 2000, plays Mozart music $90.00
18", "Mozart Music" Symphony, #26900, 2000, plays Mozart music $125.00
14" – 18", 2002 – 2004, variety of outfits ....$90.00 – 130.00

Victorian — 18" h.p., 1953 only, pink taffeta/black velvet gown, Glamour Girl Series (Margaret) ....$1,500.00 up

Victorian Bride — 10", #1148, 1992 only, Portrette $100.00
10", blue satin and lace gown $100.00

Victorian Bride — (see Debra)

Victorian Catherine — 16", #90010, porcelain, elaborate gown $225.00

Victorian Christmas — 8", #19970, red velvet and lace $100.00

Victorian Coca-Cola — 8", #36020, 2003 – 2004, red vintage dress and hat, Coke glass $85.00

Victorian Countess — 10", #28885, 2001, long white dress with lace $150.00

Victorian Girl 1954 — 10" h.p., 2000 (Cissette), remake of 1954 Victoria $100.00

Victorian Skater — 10", #1155, 1993 – 1994, Portrette, red/gold/black outfit (Cissette) $150.00

Victorians — 8" Adorable silk, #26875, 2000, flower adorned dress $100.00
8" Charming silk, #25035, 2000 – 2001, white silk dress $100.00
8" Innocent silk, #25045, 2000 – 2001, white lace trimmed silk dress $100.00
8" Sophisticated silk, #26780, 2000 – 2001, lilac silk costume $100.00
8" Sweet silk, #25040, 2000 – 2001, pink silk dress $100.00
8" Marigold, #27805, 2001, short yellow dress, hat with lace $100.00
8" Sailorette, #33555, 2002 – 2003, pleated vintage costume $85.00

Victorian Valentine — 8", #30615, 2000 – 2003, pink pleated dress, hat, trimmed with lace, valentine $80.00

Vietnam — 8" h.p., #788, 1968 – 1969 (Wendy Ann) $250.00
#788, 1968 – 1969 (Maggie Mixup) $275.00
8", #505, reintroduced in 1990 – 1991 (Maggie) $65.00

Vintage Violet Silk Victorian — 8", #30405, 2001 – 2002, pink dress $100.00

Violet — (see Sweet Violet)

Violet — (Nutcracker Ballerina) 10" Portrette, 1994 only $70.00

Violetta — 10", #1116, 1987 – 1988, all deep blue (Cissette) $65.00

Virgo — 8", #21380, pink pleated outfit, gold helmet $90.00

Visions of Sugarplums — 8", #37805, 2003 – 2004, red and green dress, sunglasses, lollipop ...$90.00

Wendy Ann, 21" composition (Wendy Ann), 1939 – 1940. All original.

W.A.A.C. (Army) — 14" compo., 1943 – 1944 (Wendy Ann) .....$750.00 up

W.A.A.F. (Air Force) — 14" compo., 1943 – 1944 (Wendy Ann) ....$750.00 up

Waiting for Santa Boy — 8", #37090, 2003 – 2004, red p.j.'s, plush bear, cookies, milk $80.00

Waiting for Santa Girl — 8", #37085, 2003 – 2004, red p.j.'s, plush bear, cookies, milk $80.00

Waltz — 16", 1999, pink gown trimmed in marabou $150.00
8" h.p., #476, 1955 only (Wendy Ann) ....$700.00 up

Want — 8", #18406, 1996, Dickens (see Ghost of Christmas Present) (sold as set)

Washington, Martha — 1976 – 1978, first set Presidents' Ladies/First Ladies Series (Martha) $225.00

Watchful Guardian Angel — 10", #10740, 1998 – 1999, blue, white outfit $175.00

Watchful Guardian Angel Set — three dolls, bridge, gift card $325.00

W.A.V.E. (Navy) — 14" compo., 1943 – 1944 (Wendy Ann) .....$750.00 up

Wedding Rings Ring Bearer — 8", #36280, 2003, blonde, green and white costume $75.00

Wedding Wishes — 16", #28455, 2001, white gown with lace around hem, bouquet with red roses $200.00

Weeping Princess — 8", #11104, 1995 only, International Folk Tales (Maggie) $65.00

Welcome Home — Desert Storm, 8", 1991 only, mid-year introduction, boy or girl soldier, black or white $50.00

    8", #38145, 2004, blue stripe dress with "Welcome Home" banner $85.00

Wendy — 8", 1989, first doll offered to club members only (see M.A.D.C. under Special Events/Exclusives)

    5", #30350, 2001 – 2003, petite, pink check dress $20.00

Wendy And Muffy — 8" doll, bag with tiny bear, #33635, 2004 . . . .$150.00

Wendy And The Yellow Brick Road — 8", #38720, 2004 (Wendy) $85.00

Wendy Angel — 8" h.p., #404, 1954 (Wendy Ann) . . . .$850.00 up

Wendy Ann — 11" – 15" compo., 1935 – 1948 . . . .$325.00 – 575.00

    9" compo., 1936 – 1940, painted eyes $350.00

    14", 1938 – 1939, in riding habit, molded hair or wig $425.00

    14", any year, swivel waist, molded hair or wig $450.00

    17" – 21" compo., 1938 – 1944 . . . .$600.00 – 1,100.00

    14½" – 17" h.p., 1948 – 1949 . . . .$600.00 – 850.00

    16" – 22" h.p., 1948 – 1950 . . . .$675.00 – 975.00

    23" – 25" h.p., 1949 . . . .$850.00 up

    8", #79516, 1995, 100th anniversary, wearing dress, coat, and bonnet, limited production $125.00

Wendy Ann Felt — 12", #37945, 2004, molded felt doll, linen dress $300.00

Wendy Ballerina — 8" (Wendy), 1999, pink trim on white lace tutu $75.00

(Wendy) Being Just Like Mommy — 8", #801, 1993, has baby carriage, #120801, 1994 . . . .$125.00

(Wendy) Being Prom Queen — #120808, 1994 . . . .$65.00

Wendy Bride — 14" – 22" compo., 1944 – 1945 (Wendy Ann) . . . .$325.00 – 575.00

    15" – 18" h.p., 1951 (Margaret) . . . .$650.00 – 900.00

    20" h.p., 1956 (Cissy) . . . .$950.00 up

    8" h.p., SLW, #475, 1955 (Wendy Ann) $650.00

Wendy Cheerleader — 8", #16500, 1998, pleated skirt, red sweater $65.00

Wendy Elf — 8", #12818, 1995, Christmas Series $65.00

Wendy (from Peter Pan) — 15" h.p., 1953 only (Margaret) . . . .$550.00 up

    14" plastic/vinyl, #1415, 1969 only (Mary Ann) $275.00

    8", #466 in 1991 – 1993; #140466 in 1994; Storyland Series, pom-pons on slippers (Peter Pan) $70.00

Wendy Go Bragh! — 8", #35435, 2002 – 2003, white dress, green shamrocks $65.00

(Wendy) Goes to the Circus — 8", #12819, 1996 (Wendy Ann) $60.00

(Wendy) Her First Day at School — 8", #120806, 1994 – 1995 . . . .$70.00

(Wendy) Her Sunday Best — 8", #120807, 1994 – 1995 . . . .$75.00

(Wendy) Her Sundress — #120804, 1994 . . . .$60.00

Wendy Kin Baby — 8", one-piece vinyl body with hard plastic Little Genius head, 1954 . . . .$375.00

(Wendy) Learning to Sew — 8", #120809, 1994, in wicker case $110.00

Wendy Learns Her ABC's — (see ABC Unlimited Productions under Special Events/Exclusives)

Wendy Loves Being Loved — 8", 1992 – 1993 only, doll and wardrobe $150.00

Wendy Loves Donald and Daisy — 8", 2004, cloth Donald, Daisy $95.00

Wendy Loves Goofy and Pluto — 8", #39565 . . . .$95.00

Wendy Loves Clifford The Big Red Dog — 8", #38730, 2004, 3" dog $80.00

Wendy Loves Mickey and Minnie — 8", #39555, red dress $95.00

Wendy Makes It Special — 8", #31050, 1997 – 1998, pink satin dress $80.00

Wendy Salutes the Olympics — 8", #86005, 1996, Olympic Medal $125.00

Wendy's Anniversary Trunk Set — 8", #36130, 2003, trunk, clothes, shoes, accessories $200.00

Wendy's Doll House Trunk Set — 8", #12820, 1996 . . . .$275.00

Wendy's Fabulous Fifties Trunk Set — 8", #37925, 2003 – 2004, hat box trunk, three sets of clothes $290.00

Wendy's Favorite Fairy Tales — 8", #35655, 2003 – 2004, pink dress with pinafore, rabbit, cape, book, etc. $100.00

Wendy Shops FAO — (see FAO Schwarz under Special Events/Exclusives)

Wendy's Puppet Show — 8", #33780, 2002 –2003, four puppets and theaters $180.00

Wendy's Special Cheer — 8", #16500, 1998 – 1999, cheerleading outfit $70.00

(Wendy) Summer Box Set — #805, 1993; #120805, 1994 . . . .$100.00

Wendy Tap Dancer — 8" h.p., #13930, 1998, white jacket, gold tap pants $85.00

(Wendy) The Country Fair — 8", #802, 1993, has cow, #120802, 1994 . . . .$75.00

Wendy the Gardener — 8", #31400, 1998 – 1999, sunflower outfit, watering can, sunflowers $85.00

Wendy Visits World's Fair — (see Shirley's Doll House under Special Events/Exclusives)

(Wendy) Winter Box Set

(Wendy) Winter Box Set — #120810, 1994, boxed doll and wardrobe $100.00
Wendy Woodkin — 8", #37910, 2004, jointed wooden doll with tiny wooden doll $250.00
Wendy Works Construction — 8", #31420, 1998 – 1999, includes tools and toolbox $85.00
Wheels on the Bus, The — 8", #34135, 2002 – 2003, yellow check dress, bus on skirt $50.00
Where Oh Where Has My Little Dog Gone — 8", #35675, 2003 – 2004, with blanket and dog $80.00
White Christmas — 10", #10105, 1995 only, Christmas Series $80.00
White Christmas Pair — 10", #15380, Betty and Bob from the movie $175.00
White Hat Doll — 8", #25315, 2000, Maud Humphrey design $75.00
White Iris — 10", #22540, 1999 – 2000 (Cissette), white lace and roses $100.00
White King — 8" h.p., #13020, 1997 – 1998, white suit, cape $100.00
White Rabbit — 14" – 17" cloth/felt, 1940s ....$500.00 – 750.00
    8", #14509, 1995, Alice in Wonderland Series $125.00
    8", #14616, 1996, White Rabbit in court $100.00
Wicked Stepmother — 21", #50002, 1996, limited edition $325.00
Wicked Witch of the West — 10", #13270, 1997 – 2004 (Cissette), black witch costume, broom $135.00
    21", #27760, 2000, long black costume with Dorothy globe $425.00
Wilson, Edith — 1988, fifth set Presidents' Ladies/First Ladies Series (Mary Ann) $100.00
Wilson, Ellen — 1988, fifth set Presidents' Ladies/First Ladies Series (Louisa) $100.00
Window Shopping — 8", #37920, 2004, with store front, mannequin $95.00
Winged Monkey — 8" h.p. (Maggie), #140501, 1994 only $150.00
    8" h.p. #25950, 2000 – 2002 (Wendy), blue jacket, hat, blue feather wings $75.00
Winnie The Pooh — 8", #38365, 2004, with plush Pooh, Tigger, Piglet, and Eeyore $100.00
Winnie Walker — 15" h.p., 1953 only (Cissy) ....$325.00 up
    18" – 25", #1836 ....$350.00 – 650.00
    1953 – 1954, in trunk/trousseau ....$850.00 up
Winter — 14", 1993, Changing Seasons, doll and four outfits $125.00
    5" porcelain, #25865, 2000, fur-trimmed white coat and hat $65.00
Winter Angel — 10", #28365, 2001 –2004, blue costume, white fur wings $100.00
Winter Fun Skater — 8", #10357, 1995, Christmas Series $65.00
Winter Sports — 1991 (see Shirley's Doll House under Special Events/Exclusives)
Wintertime — (see M.A.D.C. under Special Events/Exclusives)
Winter Wonderland — 10", #19990, 1999 – 2000, white satin, fur, jewels $125.00
Winter Wonderland (Nashville Skater #1) — 1991 – 1992 (see Collectors United under Special Events/Exclusives)
Wishes Come True — 8", #33315, 2002, ballerina outfit $80.00
Wishing Fairy — 8", #36035, 2003 – 2004, pink costume, crystal snowflake $85.00
Wisteria Flower Girl — 8", #30370, 2001 – 2002 (Maggie), lavender gown $90.00
        Witch — 8", #322, 1992 – 1993, Americana Series $75.00
        Witch/Halloween — (see Collectors United under Special Events/Exclusives)
        Withers, Jane — 12" – 13½" compo., 1937, has closed mouth ....$1,000.00 up
           15" – 17", 1937 – 1939 ....$850.00 – 1,300.00
           17" cloth body, 1939 ....$1,500.00
           18" – 19", 1937 – 1939 ....$1,500.00
           19" – 20", closed mouth ....$1,400.00 up
           20" – 21", 1937 ....$1,700.00 up
        With Love — 8", #17003, 1996, pink gown, comes with a heart $65.00
           8", #17001, 1996, same as above except African-American $75.00
        Wizard of Oz — 8", mid-year special (see Madame Alexander Doll Co. under
           Special Events/Exclusives)
           8", #13281, plaid pants, green tailcoat, 1998 – 2000 ....$100.00
           8", with state fair balloon, #13280, Wizard, 1998 – 2000 ....$150.00
           5", #38200, 2003 – 2004, set of four – Daisy, Lollipop, Coroner,
              and Town's Lady $100.00
           #38400, Wizard of Oz house trunk for 8" dolls $150.00
           5", Petite Set, Tin Man, Cowardly Lion, Scarecrow, Dorothy, 2004 ....$25.00 ea.
        Wooden Wendy — 8", #33820, 2003 – 2004, fully jointed wooden doll in pink

Jane Withers, 11", 1937, composition. Printed cotton dress. Gold script name pin.

           dress $275.00

Workin' Out with Wendy 1980 — 8", #17810, 1999, BK, striped bodysuit $70.00

1860s Women — 10" h.p., 1990 (see Spiegel's under Special Events/Exclusives) (Beth)

Wynkin — (see Dutch Lullaby)

Yankee Doodle — 8", #35945, 2003 – 2004, blonde, vintage patriotic costume $90.00

Yellow Butterfly Princess — 8", #25680, 2000 – 2001 (Maggie) $70.00

Yellow Daffodil — 10", #25620, 2000, long white and yellow gown $100.00

Yellow Hat Doll — 8", #25320, 2000, Maud Humphrey design $85.00

Yes, Virginia, There Is a Santa Claus — 8", #20200, 1999 – 2001, green dress with lace collar and trim $100.00

Yolanda — 12", 1965 only (Brenda Starr) ....$375.00 up

Yugoslavia — 8" h.p., BK, #789, 1968 – 1972 (Wendy) $90.00

    8" straight leg, #0789, #589, 1973 – 1975, marked "Alex" $65.00

    8" straight leg, #589, 1976 – 1986, marked "Alexander" $60.00

    8", 1987 (see Collectors United under Special Events/Exclusives)

Yukon — 8", #38610, 2004, with sled and three dogs $110.00

Yuletide Angel — (see Tree Toppers)

Zoe — 10", #35821, 2003 – 2004 (Hanna), African-American, yellow dress, blue trim $40.00

Zorina Ballerina — 17" compo., 1937 – 1938, extra make-up, must be mint condition (Wendy Ann) ....$1,900.00 up

Special Events/Exclusives

Shops and organizations are listed alphabetically.

ABC Unlimited Productions
    Wendy Learns Her ABC's — 8", 1993, wears blue jumper and beret, ABC blocks
    on skirt, wooden block stand, limited to 3,200 ....$125.00
Amanda Callahan's Susan's Dolls
    Amanda Sue — 8", #38120, 2004 (Maggie) limited to 250 ....$100.00
Ashton-Drake Galleries
    Apple of Grandma's Eye, The — 8", 2004, denim and red check outfit, basket of cherries $90.00
    Grandma's Little Honey — 8", 2004, yellow flower dress, straw hat $90.00
    Grandma's Little Sweetheart — 8", 2004, red print holiday outfit, gingerbread cookie $90.00
    Some Bunny Loves Me, Grandma — 8", 2004, print dress and hat, with bunny $90.00
    Jacqueline Kennedy Bride — porcelain, 2004, taffeta wedding gown with rosettes of lace $150.00
Bay Area Alexander Doll Club
    Now I Am Ten — 8", #33855, 2002, white dress, pink trim $110.00
Belk & Leggett Department Stores
    Miss Scarlett — 14", 1988 ....$150.00
    Rachel/Rachael — 8", 1989, lavender gown $75.00
    Nancy Jean — 8", 1990, yellow/brown outfit $65.00
    Fannie Elizabeth — 8", 1991, limited to 3,000, floral dress with pinafore $100.00
    Annabelle at Christmas — 8", 1992, limited to 3,000, plaid dress, holds Christmas cards $125.00
    Caroline — 8", 1993, limited to 3,600 ....$115.00
    Holly — 8", 1994, green eyes, freckles, wears red top with white skirt $90.00
    Elizabeth Belk Angel — 8", #79648, 1996, red velvet $175.00
Bloomingdale's Department Store
    10", 1997, coral and leopard Cissette with Bloomie's big brown bag $125.00
    Golden Holiday Tree Topper — 1999, limited to 1,000 pieces, gilded gold and silver embroidery on satin $150.00
    Millennium Angel Tree Topper — 10", #27955, 2000, gold lamé dress with jewels $150.00
    8", Angelic Tree Topper, #32035, 2001, limited to 300, burgundy velvet $150.00
    Snowflake Skater Sarah, #32030 ....$100.00
Boscov's
    Bubbles — 8", #33815, 2003 (Wendy) limited to 500, pink outfit $95.00
    Frosted Dreams — 8", #35455, 2003, white outfit with fur $100.00
Celebrations Fantastic
    Let's Hop — 8", #33810, 2003, poodle skirt $100.00

Sizzling Cissy, 21", #39195, 2004.
C.U. Gathering, Atlanta.

Sizzling Cissy, African-American, 21", 2004. C.U.
Atlanta.

98

Celia's Dolls
   David, The Little Rabbi — 8", 1991 – 1992, 3,600 made, three hair colors $75.00

Child at Heart
   Easter Bunny — 8", 1991, limited to 3,000 (1,500 blondes, 750 brunettes, 750 redheads) $225.00
   My Little Sweetheart — 8", 1992, limited to 4,500 (1,000 blondes, 1,000 brunettes with
      blue eyes, 1,000 brunettes with green eyes, 1,000 redheads with green eyes, 500 blacks) $65.00
   Trick and Treat — 8", 1993, sold in sets only (400 sets with red-haired/green-eyed "Trick" and black
      "Treat"; 1,200 sets with red-haired/green-eyed "Trick" and brunette/brown-eyed "Treat"; 1,400
      blonde/blue-eyed "Trick" and red-haired/brown-eyed "Treat") ....$200.00 set

Christmas Shoppe
   Boy and Girl, Alpine — 8" twins, 1992, in Alpine Christmas outfits, limited to 2,000 sets ....$225.00 pr.

Collectors United (C.U.)

C. U. Gathering (Georgia)
   Yugoslavia — 8", F.A.D., limited to 625 ....$80.00
   Tippi Ballerina — 8", 1988, limited to 800 ....$325.00
   Miss Leigh — 8", 1989, limited to 800 ....$100.00
   Shea Elf — 8", 1990, limited to 1,000 ....$125.00
   Ringmaster — 8", 1991, limited to 800 ....$90.00
   Faith — 8", 1992, limited to 800 ....$225.00
   Hope — 8", 1993, limited to 900, blue dress (1910 style) $175.00
   Love — 8", 1994, limited to 2,400, has gold necklace and pearls on cap $100.00
   Diane — 8", 1995, limited to 800, Back to the Fifties $75.00
   C.U. Varsity Sweater — white sweater, 1995, special event souvenir $40.00
   Olympia — 8", 1996, pants costume, with flag, limited to 800 ....$100.00
   Olympic Bag — 1996, special Alexander event souvenir $40.00
   C.U. Salutes Broadway — 8", 1997, burgundy theater outfit $150.00
   Black Fur Stole — 1997, special Alexander event souvenir $30.00
   Polynesian Princess — 8", 1998, print skirt and top $175.00
   Grass Skirt — 1998, special Alexander event souvenir $30.00
   Fortune Teller — 1999, 8", red print costume trimmed in gold $150.00
   Fortune Teller — 1999, 21", red print costume trimmed in gold $950.00
   Fortune Teller Accessories — scarves and bangle bracelets, 1999, special event $35.00
   Carnival Queen — limited to 24, 1999, 16", pink or blue gown $350.00

April, C.U. Nashville 2004, 8" (Wendy), BK, white dress with pansy trim, straw hat with lavender ribbon.

Irish Cissy, 21", 2000 C.U. Nashville, limited to 200. Gorgeous long green dress with silver cape.

Special Events/Exclusives

Majestic Midway — 21", 1999, gold costume ....one-of-a-kind
Bonnie Blue Returns to Atlanta — 8", #31485, 2001, blue dress, limited to 500 ....$125.00
Return to Tara — Scarlett, #32105, 2001, with Tara, limited to 100 ....$250.00
Scarlett — 21", #31540, 2001, white dress, green sash $350.00
Greta — 16", #35530, 2002, orange check dress, white straw bag, limited to 150 ....$175.00
Georgia Peach — 8", 2002, blonde or brunette, peach taffeta dress, straw hat $75.00
Coca-Cola Cissy — #35160, 2002, red check blouse, Coke bottle, straw hat $375.00
Coca-Cola Cissy — #35161, 2002, African-American, limited to 40 ....$475.00
Sizzling Cissy — 21", #39195, 2004, limited to 150 ....$395.00
Sizzling Cissy — 21", 2004, African-American $450.00
Candi Corn — 8", #40035, 2004, with kitty and game $100.00
April — 8", #31705, 2004 (Wendy), white dress, pansy trim, hat $95.00

C.U. Nashville Winter Wonderland
Nashville Skater — 8", 1991, F.A.D., limited to 200 (Black Forest) $125.00
Nashville Skier — 8", 1992, F.A.D., limited to 200 (Tommy Tittlemouse) $100.00
First Comes Love — 8", 1993, limited to 200, F.A.D. $250.00
Captain's Cruise — 1994, limited to 250, with trunk and wardrobe $225.00
Nashville Goes Country — 8", 1995, western outfit with guitar $125.00
Nashville Sunny — 8", 1996, yellow raincoat, hat $150.00
Miss Tennessee Waltz — 8", 1977, long ballgown, coat $150.00
C.U. Goes to Camp — 8", 1998 ....$110.00
Irish Cissy — 21", #27460, 2000, limited to 200, green gown, silver cape $500.00
Shannon — 8", #27255, 2000, green costume $75.00
Lindsey — 8", #28920, 2001, print dress, straw hat, limited to 100 ....$75.00
Wendy Learns Nursery Rhymes — 8", #34520, 2002, with cardboard wardrobe and extra clothes $150.00
Blue Danube — 21", #30685, 2001, blue gown $300.00
    21", African-American, limited to 36 ....$350.00
    8", #28211, blue gown, 2001 ....$100.00
    8", African-American, 2001, limited to 100 ....$135.00

C.U. Greenville Show
Bride — 8", 1990, F.A.D. of Tommy Snooks, limited to 250 (Betsy Brooks) $125.00
Witch/Halloween — 8", 1990, F.A.D., limited to 250 (Little Jumping Joan) $100.00
Oktoberfest — 8", 1992, F.A.D., limited to 200 ....$125.00
C.U. Columbia, S.C. Camelot — 8", 1991, F.A.D. (Maid Marian), limited to 400 ....$125.00
C.U. Columbia S.C. Homecoming Queen — 21", #28205, 2000, white gown, limited to 200 ....$350.00
C.U. Columbia S.C. Homecoming Queen — 21", 2000, African-American, limited to 24 ....$600.00
C.U. Jacksonville — 8" Greta, 1996, black doll, blue sundress $200.00

C.U. Doll Shop Exclusives
Cameo Lady — 10", 1991, limited to 1,000, white dress, black trim $125.00
Le Petit Boudoir — 10", 1993, F.A.D., limited to 700 ....$175.00
America's Junior Miss — 8", 1994, white gown, medallion, limited to 1,200 ....$75.00
Fitness — 8", 1995, tennis outfit $60.00
Judge's Interview — 8", 1996, limited to 500 ....$75.00
Talent — 8", 1996, gold tuxedo jacket, black shorts $70.00
Easter of Yesteryear — 8", 1995, comes with rabbit $75.00
Sailing with Sally — 8", 1998, white dress, wooden boat $100.00
Gary Green — 8", 1998 ....$75.00
Christmas Morn — 8", 1999, #80130, nightgown, teddy bear, limited to 411 pieces $75.00
Sterling Light, Sterling Bright — 8", #30721, 2000, Silver Angel lighted tree topper $150.00
Katy — 8", #28925, 2000, printed dress, straw hat, limited to 100 ....$95.00

Colonial Southwest
Tanya — 8", 1999, limited to 550, honors M.A.D.C. former president Tanya McWhorter $225.00

Colonial Williamsburg
Charlotte — 10", #26985, 2000, pink taffeta, eighteenth century dress $150.00
Colleen — 10", #31535, 2001, vintage cotton dress with panniers $150.00

Caroline — 8", #35230, 2002, eighteenth century cape, green costume $100.00
Catherine — 8", #33890, 2003, long satin dress, cape $100.00

Disney Annual Showcase of Dolls

Cinderella — 10", 1989, #1, blue satin gown, limited to 250 . . . .$700.00
Snow White — 12", 1990, #2, limited to 750 (Nancy Drew) $150.00
Alice in Wonderland/White Rabbit — 10", 1991, #3, limited to 750 . . . .$375.00
Queen of Hearts — 10", 1992, #4, limited to 500 . . . .$400.00
Alice in Wonderland/Jabberwocky — 11" – 12" (Lissy), 1993, #5, limited to 500 . . . .$325.00
Tweedledee & Tweedledum — 8", 1994, #6, wear beany hats with propellers, names on collar, limited to 750 .$300.00 pr.
Morgan LeFay — 10", #797537, 1995, #7, limited to 500 . . . .$375.00
Bobby (Bobbie) Soxer — 8", 1990 – 1991 . . . .$175.00
Mouseketeer — 8", 1991, blue skirt, white top $175.00
Roller Blades — 8", 1992, "Thoroughly Modern Wendy" $125.00
Round Up Cowgirl — 8", 1992, blue/white outfit $165.00
Annette (Funicello) — 14" porcelain portrait sculpted by Robert Tonner, 1993, limited to 400 . . . .$475.00
Monique — 8", 1993, made for Disney, limited to 250, lavender with lace trim $500.00
Snow White — 10", 1993, Disney crest colors $200.00
Belle — 8" h.p., gold gown, 1994 . . . .$125.00
Cinderella — 14", 1994, Disney catalog, has two outfits, limited to 900 . . . .$200.00
  14", 1995, different gown, no extra outfits $175.00
Wendy's Favorite Pastime — 8", 1994, comes with hula hoop $85.00
Sleeping Beauty — 14", 1995, waist-length hair, blue gown from movie and two other outfits $200.00
Blue Fairy Tree Topper — 10", #79545, 1995 catalog exclusive (Cissette) $175.00
Snow White — 14", 1995 . . . .$175.00
Mary Poppins — 10", 1996, #79403 . . . .$125.00
Alice — 14", 1996, limited to 1,500, catalog exclusive $175.00
Knave — 8", 1996, #8, limited to 500, wears two of Spades card $175.00
Toto — 8", 1997, #9, limited to 750, comes with wooden basket $150.00
Goldilocks and Baby Bear — 8", 1998, #10, purple print costume with Raikes Bear $275.00
Mouseketeers — 8", 1999, Alex and Wendy as Mouseketeers, #11 . . . .$250.00
My Little Buttercup — 8", 2000, #12, yellow dress and hat trimmed in flowers and ribbons, #30320, limited to 200 .$150.00
Sleeping Beauty — 8", 1999, pink satin gown, limited to 1,000 . . . .$150.00
Snow White — 8", 1999, Disney crest colors, limited to 1,000 . . . .$150.00
Ariel — 8", 1999, #25085, long red hair, green mermaid costume $100.00
Belle — 8", 1999, #25075, yellow ballgown with gold trim $125.00
Cinderella — 8", 1999, #25080, blue satin gown, limited to 1,000 . . . .$125.00
Michael and Jane Banks — 8", 1999, #80450, 8" girl, boy limited to 200 . . . .$150.00
Jasmine — 8", 1999, #25095, lavender chiffon harem outfit $125.00
Belle Tree Topper — #31770, 2001 . . . .$175.00
Wendy's Wardrobe — 8", #31780, 2001, three dresses, cardboard wardrobe, limited to 170 . . . .$150.00

Disney, Walt

Disney World Auction — 21", one-of-a-kind dolls, therefore no prices shown.
Sleeping Beauty — #1 in Series, 1989, 21", long blonde hair, in pink with rhinestones and pearls
Christine (Phantom of the Opera) — #2, 1990, blue/white outfit with white mask (Jacqueline)
Queen Isabella — #3, 1991, green/gold gown, long red hair (Jacqueline)
It's a Girl — #4, 1992, comes with 8" baby in carriage (Cissy, Baby Genius)
Emperor and Nightingale — #4, 1992, 8" winged Wendy Ann (23" Emperor bear by Gund)
Women in the Garden — #5, 1993, four dolls (Cissette) dressed like 1867 Monet painting
Cissy Bride — 1923 and 8" Flower Girl and Ring Bearer, #5, 1993
Romeo & Juliet — #6, 21" h.p., 1994, using 1950s bald nude "Maggie" dolls, rewigged, dressed in blue,
  burgundy, and gold
Sir Lancelot duLac — #7, 1995, 1950s doll dressed in burgundy and gold
Queen Guinevere — #7, 1995, 1950s doll dressed in burgundy and gold
Chess Set — 35 dolls from 8" to 21" on a satin chess board
Mary Poppins and Children — 1999, 21" Mary Poppins, 14" Jane and Michael

Special Events/Exclusives

Doll & Teddy Bear Expo

Madame (Alexander) or Shadow of Madame — 8", 1994, in blue, limited to 500 first year $200.00

Madame with Love — 8", #79536, 1995, has hat with "100" on top, limited to 750 ....$85.00

Maggie's First Doll — 8", 1996, pink cotton dress, carries cloth Alice doll $250.00

Miss Eliza Doolittle — 21", 1996, white lace dress, auction piece ....one-of-a-kind

Josephine Baker — 21", black Cissy, 1996, banana costume, auction piece ....one-of-a-kind

Gingerbread — outfit only, for 8" doll $65.00

Love Is in the Air — 8", Bride, 1999, limited to 100 ....$125.00

Holiday Magic — 8", 1999, limited to 100, red and gold metallic gown $150.00

American as Apple Pie — 8", #27490, 2000, 100 pieces (Maggie) $150.00

America the Beautiful Outfit — 2000, with boots $75.00

Wild, Wild West — 8", #27495, 2000, limited to 100 ....$225.00

Wendy Visits the World's Fair — 8", #28905, 2002, red check, limited to 100 ....$100.00

Happy Birthday — 8", #35885, 2002, purple print party dress $90.00

Doll Finders

Fantasy — 8", 1990, limited to 350 ....$200.00

Dolls and Ducks

Ice Princess — 8", 1999, silver gown and tiara $150.00

Dolls 'n Bearland

Pandora — 8", 1991, limited to 3,600 (950 brunette, 950 redheads, 1,700 blondes) $150.00

Dolly Dears

Bo Peep — 1987, holds staff, black sheep wears man's hat, white sheep
wears woman's hat (sheep made exclusively by Dakin) $225.00

Susannah Clogger — 8", 1992, has freckles, limited to 400 (Maggie) $250.00

Jack Be Nimble — 8", 1993, F.A.D., limited to 288 ....$100.00

Princess and the Pea — 8", 1993, limited to 1,000 ....$125.00

Elegant Doll Shop

Elegant Easter — 8", 1999, pink check with bunny $125.00

Heart of Dixie — 8", 1999, red and lace outfit $100.00

Enchanted Doll House

Rick-Rack on Pinafore — 8", 1980, limited to 3,000 ....$275.00

Eyelet Pinafore — 8", 1981, limited to 3,423 ....$275.00

Blue or Pink Ballerina — 8", 1983 – 1985, F.A.D., blonde or brunette doll in trunk with extra clothes $175.00

Cinderella and Trunk — 14", has glass slipper, 1985 ....$275.00

Holiday Magic, 8", 1999 (Wendy),
Doll & Teddy Bear Expo.

Twilight Tango Cissy, 21",
#35210, 2003, FAO Schwarz
exclusive. Limited to 100.

25th Anniversary (The Enchanted Doll) — 10", 1988, long gown, limited to 5,000 ....$150.00

Ballerina — 8", 1989, blue tutu, limited to 360 ....$150.00

Vermont Maiden — 8", 1990 – 1992, official Vermont Bicentennial doll,
   limited to 3,600 (800 blondes, 2,800 brunettes) $75.00

Farmer's Daughter — 8", 1991, limited to 4,000 (1,000 blondes, 1,500 redheads, 1,500 brunettes) $100.00

Farmer's Daughter — 8", 1992, "Goes To Town" (cape and basket added), limited to 1,600 ....$125.00

FAO Schwarz

Pussy Cat — 18", 1987, pale blue dress and bonnet $100.00

Brooke — 14", 1988, blonde or brunette (Mary Ann), with Steiff Bear $125.00

David and Diana — 8", 1989, in red, white, and denim, with wooden wagon ....$225.00 set

Samantha — 14", 1989, white with black dots (Mary Ann) $125.00

Me & My Scassi — 21", 1990, dressed in all red, Arnold Scassi original (Cissy) $400.00

Sailor — 8", 1991 ....$125.00

Carnavale Doll — 14", 1991 – 1992 (Samantha) $150.00

Beddy-Bye Brooke — 14", 1991 – 1992 (Mary Ann) $125.00

Beddy-Bye Brenda (Brooke's sister) — 8", 1992, sold only as set with 14" doll ....$225.00 set

Wendy Shops FAO — 8", 1993, red/white outfit, carries FAO Schwarz shopping bag $125.00

My Secret Garden — 8", trunk with wardrobe, 1994 ....$325.00

Little Huggums — 12", red dress, bib and headband, has FAO logo horse, 1994 ....$65.00

Little Women — 8", 1994, dressed in outfits from movie, limited to 500 sets (five dolls) and 700 of
   each girl ....$125.00 ea., $750.00 set

Princess trunk set — 8", #79526, 1995 ....$300.00

Fun with Dick & Jane — 8", #70509, 1995, limited to 1,200 pieces ....$325.00 set

Lucy Ricardo — 8", limited to 1,200 ....$250.00

I Love Lucy — 8" Fred, Ethel, Lucy, and Ricky, sold as set only, limited to 1,200 ....$750.00 set

Twilight Tango Cissy — 21", #35210, 2003, limited to 100, black and white gown $350.00

Wendy Loves Patrick — 8", #37200, 2003, with dog Patrick $125.00

Chinoiserie Cissy — 21", #33335, 2003, long sheath gown $325.00

The Little Rascals — 8" Alfalfa, Darla, Spanky, Buckwheat, and dog, Petey, 1996, limited to 2,000 sets ....$550.00 set

Singing in the Rain — 8" Gene Kelly, Debbie Reynolds, with lamppost, 1996, 1952 film ....$300.00 set

I Dream of Jeannie — 8", harem outfit, military uniform $275.00

Lucy and Ethel — 8", 1997, candy factory episode $200.00

The Honeymooners — 8", 1997, Ralph and Alice Norton and Trixie, limited to 2,000 sets $500.00

Grease — 1998, 10" Danny and Sandy in leather outfits $175.00

Fay Wray with Steiff King Kong — 1998, 10" doll $500.00

Silver Sensation — 16" Alex fashion doll, limited to 100 ....$275.00

Gallery Opening Alex — 16", limited to 500 ....$350.00

Publisher's Meeting Alex — 16", limited to 200 ....$175.00

Magnificent Mile Alex — 16", 2000, limited to 40 pieces $650.00

Wendy Loves FAO — 8", #34580, 2003, with FAO Bear $175.00

Star Wars — 8" Luke Skywalker, Han Solo, Leia, #35515, 2003, limited to 1,000 ....$400.00

Pinocchio and Blue Fairy — 8", #34035, 2003, limited to 160 ....$175.00

80th Anniversary Wendy Trunk Set — 8", #35215, 2003 ....$250.00

First Modern Doll Club (N.Y. Doll Club)

Autumn in N.Y. — 10", 1991, F.A.D., red skirt, fur trim cape, hat, muff, and skates, limited to 260 ....$175.00

GoCollect.Com

Morning Ritual Cissy — 21", 2001, bath robe, Yardley soap $275.00

Afternoon Out — 16", #30315, 2001, red hair, sheath dress $225.00

Little Wendy Alexander — 8", #31920, 2001, pink gingham dress $85.00

Grant-a-Wish

Tour D'Jour — 16" Alex fashion doll, #34740, 2002, limited to 350, tweed coat, tan skirt $175.00

Show Stopper Alex — faux fur coat, 16", 2002, red dress ....one-of-a-kind

Home Shopping Network

Blue Angel — 8", 1997, #19972, dark blue and gold dress and halo, resin wings, limited to 3,000 ....$175.00

Special Events/Exclusives

Horchow

Pamela Plays Dress Up — 12", 1993, in trunk with wardrobe, limited to 1,250 (Lissy) $375.00
Pamela Trousseau — 12", 1994, trunk and trousseau, limited to 265 . . . .$400.00
14" trunk set, 1995 . . . .$250.00
Mary Ann Dances for Grandma Trunk Set — 14", 1996 . . . .$250.00

Imaginarium Shop (I. Magnin)

Little Huggums — 12", 1991, special outfits, bald or wigged, two wig colors $50.00

I. Magnin

Cheerleader — 8", 1990, F.A.D., "5" on sweater $80.00
Miss Magnin — 10", 1991 – 1993, limited to 2,500 (Cissette) $150.00
Little Huggums — 12" with cradle, 1992 . . . .$125.00
Little Miss Magnin — 8", 1992, with tea set and teddy bear, limited to 3,600 . . . .$225.00
Bon Voyage Miss Magnin — 10", 1993, navy/white gloves, has steamer trunk, limited to 2,500 . . . .$250.00
Bon Voyage Little Miss Magnin — 8", sailor dress, carries teddy bear/suitcase, limited to 3,500, 1993 . . . .$225.00
Little Miss Magnin Supports the Arts — 8", 1994, pink painter smock, wears red ribbon for AIDS Awareness .$175.00

Jacobsons

Wendy Starts Her Collection — 1994, has bear, limited to 2,400 . . . .$175.00
Little Huggums — 1995 . . . .$65.00

Jean's Doll Shop

Suellen — 12", 1992, F.A.D. $125.00
Wendy Walks Her Dog — 8", #79549, 1995, limited to 500 pieces $80.00

Lenox China Company

My Own Bell — 8", #27475, 2000, holiday dress with bell, limited to 1,000 . . . .$150.00
Little Miss American Pride — 8", #34540, 2003, long white gown $125.00
My Valentine — 8", #33725, 2003, red and white dress $125.00
Snowflake Elegance — 8", #34525, 2003 . . . .$125.00
Christmas Holly — 8", #34535, 2003 . . . .$85.00
Faith — 8", #31895, 2001, pink dress, basket $95.00
Easter Lily — 8", #33750, 2003, limited to 1,000, lavender dress $95.00
Lil' Sweetheart — 8", #36420, 2003, with heart ornament $100.00
Little Miss Firecracker — 8", #36425, 2003, long dress, red hair $100.00
Miss Butterfly — 8", #36430, 2003, with Halloween ornament $100.00
Christmas Candy — 8", #36435, 2003 (Wendy), with ornament $100.00
Winter Rose — 8", #36440, 2003, long rose gown, with ornament $100.00

Lillian Vernon

Christmas Doll — 8", #79630, 1996, green and gold holly print dress $100.00
Miss Millennium — 8", 1999, #80580, blue ballgown, watch $125.00
Christmas 2000 — 8", #27555, 2000, gown of white net with silver flecks,
  angel wings, silver crown, Christmas 2000 banner $80.00
St. Valentine's Day — 8", #26410, 2000, red and white outfit, limited to 2,000 . . . .$100.00
Easter — 8", #26150, 2000, white dress, plush bunny $90.00
Halloween Magic — 8", #27750, 2000, black velvet top $80.00
Nutcracker — 8", #27560, 2000, Nutcracker outfit $100.00
1940s Christmas — 8", #31740, 2001, red velvet coat $90.00
Autumn Fairy — 8", #32040, 2001, bronze and gold outfit $80.00
Halloween — 8", #31465, 2001, black and orange cat costume $80.00
4th of July — 8", #33615, 2003, white dresss $80.00
Peace Angel — 8", #35130, 2003, white gown $125.00
St. Patty's Day — 8", #31695, 2003, green costume $85.00
Trick or Treat Masquerade — 8", #33620, 2003, long black dress $125.00
Valentine's Day — 8", #33620, 2003, red velvet $90.00
Winter Wonderland — 8", #35120, 2003, red velvet, skates $90.00
Angel of Hope — 8", #37155, 2003, velvet costume $125.00
Easter Portrait — 8", #35205, 2003, lavender dress, rabbit $90.00
Happy Holidays to You — 8", #37150, 2003, red check dress $85.00

He Loves Me — 8", #35145, 2003, valentine outfit $75.00
Irish Eyes — 8", #35150, 2002, red hair, green outfit $75.00
Pumpkins For Sale — 8", #37165, 2003, with pumpkin cart $100.00
Spiderella — 8", #37160, 2003, Halloween outfit $85.00

Lord & Taylor
Victoria — 14", 1989 . . . .$80.00

Madame Alexander Doll Club (M.A.D.C.) Convention Dolls
Fairy Godmother Outfit — 1983, for 8" non-Alexander designed by Judy LaManna $350.00
Ballerina — 8", 1984, F.A.D., limited to 360 . . . .$225.00
Happy Birthday — 8", 1985, F.A.D., limited to 450 . . . .$275.00
Scarlett — 8", 1986, F.A.D., red instead of green ribbon, limited to 625 . . . .$250.00
Cowboy — 8", 1987, limited to 720 . . . .$400.00
Flapper — 10", 1988, F.A.D., black outfit instead of red, limited to 720 . . . .$175.00
Briar Rose — 8", 1989, uses Cissette head, limited to 804 . . . .$275.00
Riverboat Queen (Lena) — 8", 1990, limited to 925 . . . .$300.00
Queen Charlotte — 10", 1991, blue/gold outfit, limited to under 900 . . . .$400.00

Blue Bonnet Maiden, 8", Twenty Plus event souvenir, 2004.

Chisholm Trail Cowpoke, 8", All in A Row centerpiece, 2004 convention.

Chisholm Trail Cowgirl, 8", All in A Row souvenir, 2004 Convention.

Cinco de Mayo Cissette, 10", Cissette centerpiece, 2004 M.A.D.C. convention.

Hugs African-American Friendship Luncheon Helper doll, 8", 2003, white dress, with x's and o's for hugs and kisses.

Lone Star Wendy, 8", convention special in 2004.

Special Events/Exclusives

Prom Queen (Memories) — 8", 1992, limited to 1,100 . . . .$150.00
Drucilla — 14", 1992, limited to 268 . . . .$225.00
Diamond Lil (Days Gone By) — 10", 1993, black gown, limited to 876 . . . .$375.00
Anastasia — 14", 1993, F.A.D., available at convention, limited to 489 . . . .$225.00
Navajo Woman — 8", 1994, comes with rug, sheep, and Hopi Kachina, limited to 835 . . . .$350.00
Flower Girl — 8", companion to 1995 souvenir doll, could be purchased separately $200.00
Folsom, Frances — 10", 1995 convention doll, #79517 (married Grover Cleveland) $275.00
Showgirl — 10", 1996 convention doll, pink, blue, green, lavender, white feathers $275.00
    10", 1996 convention, black feather, limited to 20 pieces $500.00
A Little Bit of Country — 8", 1997, #79080, with guitar $250.00
Rose Festival Queen — 8", #79450, 1998, white gown, cape with roses $225.00
Margaret O'Brien — 1998 Convention Companion doll, 8", #79590 . . . .$225.00
Orange Blossom — 10", 1999, long peach dress and gold straw hat $150.00
Electra — 8", 1999, Convention Companion doll, silver costume $85.00
Lilly Pulitzer — 21", 1999, Cissy Luncheon centerpiece doll, limited to 25 . . . .$1,400.00
Cissy Accessories — 1999, no doll, accessories for 21" doll $60.00
Little Miss Bea — 2000, #26410, 8", honors Madame Bea Alexander, limited to 500 . . . .$225.00
Going to M.A.D.C.C. — 8", #26415, 2000 convention doll, black bodice, ecru tulle, limited to 700 . . . .$250.00
Seaside Serenade Gala 2000 — 16" (Alex), long blue gown with rhinestones $350.00
Abigail Adams — 10", #31510, 2001 convention doll, blue and lavender dress (Cissette) $200.00
Louisa May Alcott — 8", #31511, 2001, limited to 325, vintage blue and white gown $125.00
Aviatrix — 8",#31512, 2001, leather bomber jacket, khaki pants $125.00
Aviatrix centerpiece — 8", 2001, African-American, limited to 52 . . . .$175.00
Evening at the Pops Cissy — 21", #31735, 2001, luncheon doll, lavender dress, hat $300.00
Seaside Serenade Gala 2000 Centerpiece — 16", #27510, pink dressing gown (Alex) $450.00
Charles River Regatta Alex — 16", limited to 310, 2001, navy linen pants, white top $300.00
Alex Regatta Ball — 16", #31650, 2001, limited to 52 . . . .$425.00
Cissy Gala — 21", 2000 luncheon doll, long blue and silver gown, limited to 300 . . . .$450.00
Cissy Gala 2000 Centerpiece — 21", #27265, 2000, lavender dress, blonde $800.00
Skating Into Your Heart — 8", #26250, 2000, Travel Party $175.00
Little Miss USA — 8", 2001, short patriotic costume $85.00
Cissy Diva — #31730, 2001 centerpiece doll, fitted satin gown, faux fur, limited to 45 . . . .$700.00
San Antonio Rose — 8", #34485, 2002, travel doll $175.00

Quanah Parker, 8", historically accurate costume. 2004 M.A.D.C. convention centerpiece.

Silver Spurs, 21", Cissy centerpiece M.A.D.C. convention, 2004. Denim jacket, pants, leather chaps.

Special Kisses Friendship Luncheon Helper doll, 8" (Maggie), 2003.

Princess Fairy — 8", #34455, 2002, All in a Row souvenir doll, gold star wand with hearts, limited to 230 . . . . .$150.00

Navajo Boy — 8", #34480, 2002, travel doll centerpiece doll, limited to 45 . . . .$350.00

Alice in Wonderland — 10", #35415, 2002, Welcome Breakfast centerpiece doll, comes
 with 8" plush bunny, limited to 65 . . . .$275.00

Cissy Bridesmaid — 21", #34960, 2002, Cissy Luncheon centerpiece doll, pink lace over satin, limited to 40 . . .$650.00

Cissy Bride — 21", 2002, Cissy Luncheon doll, white lace over satin, #34955, June Bride $375.00

Sketchbook Cissy — 21", #34460, 2002, Banquet centerpiece doll, long pale pink gown, limited to 70 . . . .$550.00

Sketchbook Cissette — 10", #34445, 2002, Kansas City Convention doll, limited to 450, matches 21" doll $250.00

Masquerade Alex — 16", #34470, 2002, Alex souvenir, limited to 285, long sleek lavender gown $175.00

Viva LaParis — 16", #34490, 2002 centerpiece, limited to 40, African-American,
 lavender feather showgirl costume $275.00

Madame Sketchbook II — 8", #34465, 2002 companion, light pink dress $75.00

White Rabbit — 10", plush, limited to 450, 2002 souvenir, blue dress $20.00

M.A.D.C.C. Flapper — 21", red taffeta with beading, raffle (Cissy) .one-of-a-kind

Georgia — 10", #37005, 2003 companion, limited to 200, white Victorian dress, lavender sash $200.00

Savannah — 8", #36995, 2003 convention doll, limited to 525, trunk, basket $200.00

Savannah Slumber Party — 8", #32456, gown, blue robe, panties, shoes in black stripe hat box, outfit only $50.00

Wendy Visits Tybee Island — 8", #37040, 2003, travel doll, shorts, lavender top, pink bag, limited to 300 . . . .$100.00

Billy Visits Tybee Island — 8", #37245, 2003, travel centerpiece, red top, shorts $200.00

Taylor Debutante Alexandra Fairchild Ford — 16", #37765, 2003, Alex centerpiece, limited to 35,
 white long dress, red curly wig $350.00

Sweater Set — #32459, 2003, Savannah 20+ souvenir outfit, only for 8", pink knit sweater and hat in black
 stripe box, limited to 60 . . . .$45.00

Midnight Cissy — 21", #37015, 2003, Cissy event souvenir, black and white suit, hat, limited to 259, olive skintone .$475.00

Mademoiselle Cissy — 21", 37010, 2003, Cissy event centerpiece, suit, hat, limited to 40 . . . .$600.00

Southern Belle Cissy — 21", 31105, 2003, Banquet centerpiece, blue raw silk and lace antebellum dress,
 limited to 65 . . . .$550.00

Yellow Rose of Texas — 8", #39180, 2004 souvenir doll, yellow and white bustle gown, silver boots and spurs,
 hat $225.00

Cinco de Mayo Cissette — 10", Cissette Event centerpiece, #34180, red satin dress limited to 50 . . . .$200.00

Mariachi Cissette — 10", #34220, souvenir doll, 2004, black jacket, skirt $125.00

Quanah Parker — 8", Breakfast centerpiece, #33930, 2004, Indian outfit, blanket, long feather headdress $400.00

Blue Bonnet Maiden — 8", #34125, 2004, 20+ Event, Indian outfit, limited to 65 . . . .$350.00

Lone Star Wendy — 8", #34410, 2004, Convention Special, black check shirt $200.00

Billy Bob's Bronco Rider — 8", #33905, 2004, Travel Doll, red shirt, chaps $125.00

Chisholm Trail Cowgirl — 8", #34156, 2004, All in a Row, blue check shirt $175.00

Chisholm Trail Cowpoke — 8", #34255, 2004, AIR centerpiece, chaps $225.00

Texas Ranger Companion Doll — 8", #33900, 2004, brown suit, long black coat $100.00

Western Matinee Lissy Outfit — blue and white cowgirl outfit, blue boots $95.00

1950s Lissy Cowgirl Centerpiece Outfit — red and brown outfit, brown boots $200.00

Dance Hall Cissy — 21", 2004, 77 each of green, red, purple, and turquoise costumes $375.00

Silver Spurs — Cissy centerpiece, 21", #33970, 2004, denim pants, jacket, leather chaps $650.00

Cattle Baron — Banquet centerpiece, 21", #33975, 2004, black suit, hat $600.00

M.A.D.C. Dolls, Exclusives (available to club members only)

Wendy — 8", 1989, in pink and blue, limited to 4,878 . . . .$150.00

Polly Pigtails — 8", 1990 (Maggie Mixup), limited to 4,896 . . . .$125.00

Miss Liberty — 10", 1991 – 1992, red, white, and blue gown (Cissette) $125.00

Little Miss Godey — 8", 1992 – 1993 . . . .$100.00

Wendy's Best Friend Maggie — 8", 1994 . . . .$75.00

Wendy Loves Being Best Friends — 8", name embroidered on apron, 1994 . . . .$75.00

Wendy Loves the Dionnes — 8", one-of-a-kind set of five dolls, made for 1994 convention . . . . .not available

Ultimate Cissy — 21", one-of-a-kind for 1996 convention . . . . .not available

Wendy Joins M.A.D.C. — 8", #79552, 1995 . . . .$275.00

Wendy Honors Margaret Winson — 8", 1996 postmistress outfit, honoring first M.A.D.C. president $75.00

From the Madame's Sketchbook — 8", 1997, replica of 1930s Tiny Betty $125.00

Special Events/Exclusives

Skate with Wendy — 8", 1998, plaid skating outfit, silver key $75.00
M.A.D.C. Boutique — 8", 1998 – 2002, frilly panties, white top $40.00
Electro — 8", 1999 (Maggie), silver space costume, boy $80.00
M.A.D.C. Angel — 8", 2000, pink gown, limited to 800 . . . .$175.00
M.A.D.C. Ballerina — 8", 2001, blue ballerina $125.00
Springtime Darling — 8", 1999, blue dress, pink trim $75.00
Summer Blossom — 8", 1999, bikini, skirt, sandals $75.00
M.A.D.C. Story Princess — 8", #79550, 2002, rose gown, silver crown $175.00
Recipe for Contentment — 8", #37185, 2003, pink outfit $80.00
Glamour Girl — 8", 2004, #35020, red print dress $85.00

M.A.D.C. Symposium/Premiere

Pre-Doll Specials (M.A.D.C. Symposium)
    Disneyworld — 1984 – 1985 (1984 paper doll) $60.00
    Wendy Goes to Disneyworld — #1 Sunshine Symposium, 1986, navy dress with
      polka dots, Mickey Mouse hat, pennant (costume by Dorothy Starling), limited to 100 . . . .$125.00

M.A.D.C. Snowflake Symposium

1st Illinois, 1986, tagged orange taffeta/lace dress, metal pail, and orange, limited to 200 . . . .$85.00
2nd Illinois, 1987, tagged, little girl cotton print dress (costume by Mary Voigt) $85.00
3rd Illinois, 1988, tagged, gold/white print dress, gold bodice (created by Pamela Martenec) $85.00
4th Illinois, 1989, tagged, red velvet ice skating costume (created by Joan Dixon) $100.00
5th Illinois, 1990, bride by Linda's Bridal Shop (also Michelau Scarlett could be purchased) $95.00
    Scarlett — 8", 1990, #6, F.A.D. (white medallion – Snowflake Symposium; red medallion –
    Premiere Southern Symposium), limited to 800 . . . .$175.00
Springtime — 8", 1991, #7, floral dress, scalloped pinafore, straw hat, limited to 1,600 . . . .$125.00
Wintertime — 8", 1992, #8, all white, fur trim and hat (six locations), limited to 1,650 . . . .$175.00
Homecoming — 8", 1993, #9 car coat with color trim (eight different colors – one for each location),
    limited to 2,000 . . . .$225.00
Setting Sail for Summer — 8" 1994, #10 (eight locations), limited to 1,800 . . . .$150.00
Snowflake — 8", #79404, #11, 1995 (six locations), gold skater, limited to 1,200 . . . .$150.00
Wendy Starts Her Travels — 8", 1996, #12 (three locations), trunk set, different color checked coat each location . .$200.00
Bobby Takes a Picture — 8", 1996, limited to 215 pieces, California companion doll $225.00
Cheshire Cat — 8", 1996, limited to 215 pieces, Texas companion doll $200.00
    Wendy Tours the Factory — 8", 1996, New Jersey companion doll $175.00
    Wendy's Tea Party — 8", #13, 1997 (four locations), pink organdy dress, tea set $175.00
    Boo — 8", 1996, 150 pieces, ghost costume over Mother's Day doll, Illinois event $125.00

Premiere Flower Girl, 5", petite, 2004, #34369. Premiere favor.

    Diamond Pixie — 8", 1998, #14 (three locations), red Pixie costume $225.00
    Starlett Glamour — 10", 1999, #15, black evening gown $250.00
    Millennium Wendy — 8", 2000, #25155, blue dress, straw hat, watch $175.00
    On the Town Alex — 16", 2001, gold dress and coat $225.00
    Evening on the Town Alex — 16", 2001, centerpiece doll,
      long black gown, stole $350.00
    Spring Garden Party — 8", #34495, 2002 (Maggie), yellow dress $150.00
    Spring Garden Party Centerpiece — 10", 2002, #34510 (Cissette),
      yellow outfit $325.00
    M.A D.C. March Winds, travel party outfit, red stripe skirt $50.00
    Wendy Turns 50 — 8", #36220, souvenir doll, 2003, lavender satin dress,
      limited to 400 . . . .$100.00
    Wendy Turns 50 Centerpiece — 8", #36621, 2003, mint green satin dress,
      limited to 45 . . . .$150.00
    Wendy Turns 50 Travel Outfit — 2003, red straw hat, red dot
      bathing suit $40.00
    Premiere Going Away Wendy — 8", #35801, 2004, white satin dress
      and hat $125.00
    Premiere Bride and Groom Centerpiece — 8", #36595, 2004,
      limited to 60 . . . .$250.00

Premiere Bridesmaid Wendy Blue Companion — 8", #34920, 2004, limited to 110 . . . .$150.00

Premiere Bridesmaid Wendy Violet Companion — 8", #34605, 2004, limited to 110 . . . .$150.00

Premiere Flower Girl — 5", #34369, 2004, pink satin dress $60.00

M.A.D.C. Friendship Luncheon (outfit only)

Friends Around the Country — print dress and pinafore outfit, 1997 . . . .$50.00

Wendy Plays Masquerade — 1998, pink butterfly costume $50.00

Wendy, Out and About with Friends — 1999, brown felt coat, leopard tam and purse $50.00

Wendy Emcees Her School Play — 2000, pinafore, print dress, pink tam, standing microphone, limited to 700 . .$50.00

Wendy Starts Holiday Shopping — #31815, 2001, red and black dress and hat $50.00

Thanksgiving at Grandma's — 2002, silk plaid dress $50.00

Thanksgiving at Grandma's Centerpiece — 8", braids, plaid dress $125.00

Hugs Wendy — 8", #36230, 2003, souvenir doll, black velvet top, white skirt with x's and o's, limited to 700 . . . .$75.00

Kisses — luncheon centerpiece, #36231, 2003 (Maggie), pink shirt with x's and o's $100.00

Special Kisses — Helper doll — 8", #36234, 2003 (Maggie), pink skirt, limited to 25 . . . .$125.00

Special Hugs — Helper doll, #36232, 2003, Wendy, special hairdo, limited to 20 . . . .$150.00

Hugs African-American — Helper doll, 8", #36233, 2003, white skirt, limited to 30 . . . .$200.00

Madame Alexander Doll Company

Melody & Friends — 25", 1992, limited to 1,000, designed and made by Hilegard Gunzel,
   first anniversary dolls . . . .$700.00 up set

Courtney & Friends — 25" and 8" boy and girl, 1993, second anniversary, limited to 1,200, by Gunzel . . .$725.00 up set

Rumpelstiltskin & Miller's Daughter — 8" and 14", #1569, 1992 only, limited to 3,000 . . . .$275.00

Special Event Doll — 8", 1994, organza and lace in pink with special event
   banner, ribbon across body, front of hair pulled back in curls $80.00

Wendy Makes it Special — 8", 1998, #31050, pink and white dress, hat box $90.00

Wendy Salutes the Olympics — 8", #86005, 1996, Olympic medal $125.00

Maggie Mixup — 8", 1998, #31000, Post Office commemorative, blue gingham $50.00

75th Anniversary Wendy — 8", #22420, 1998, pink outfit $80.00

Wendy's Special Cheer — 8", #16510, cheerleader, 1999 . . . .$70.00

George and Martha Washington — 8", 1999, limited . . . .$200.00 set

Mary McFadden Cissy* — 21", 1999, black and gold gown . . . . .one-of-a-kind

Isaac Mizrahi Cissy* — 21", 1999, gray skirt, red sweater . . . . .one-of-a-kind

Carmen Marc Valvo Cissy* — 21", 1999, long evening gown . . . . .one-of-a-kind

Nicole Miller — 21", 1999, dress and fur coat . . . . .one-of-a-kind

Diane Von Furstenberg Cissy* — 21", 1999, black dress, fur coat . . . . .one-of-a-kind

Yeohlee Cissy* — 21", 1999, black skirt, long black coat . . . . .one-of-a-kind

Betsy Johnson Cissy* — 21", 1999, black short dress trimmed in pink . . . . .one-of-a-kind

Scaasi Cissy* — 21", 1999, white lace gown, red coat with feather $450.00

Jessica McClintock Cissy* † — 21", 1999, #22780, long gold ballgown $475.00

Fernando Sanchez Cissy* † — 21", 1999, #22720, long white gown $425.00

Josie Natori Cissy* † — 21", 1999, #22730 . . . .$450.00

Anna Sui Cissy* † — 21", 1999, #22590, has braids, brown dress, coat $450.00

Linda Allard for Ellen Tracy Cissy* † — 21", 1999, brown skirt, long black coat $475.00

Dana Buchman Cissy* † — 21", 1999, green dress, coat $475.00

Donna Karan Cissy* † — 21", 1999, long black dress . . . . .one-of-a-kind

James Purcell Cissy* † — 21", 1999, long white gown with black circles $450.00

Madame Alexander Celebrates American Design Cissy* † — 21", 1999, #22560 . . . .$250.00

Badgley Mischka Cissy* † — 21", 1999, #22740, long evening gown $450.00

Marc Bouwer Cissy* † — 21", 1999, #26125, African-American doll, long gown $550.00

Carolina Herrera Cissy* † — 21", 1999, #26121, red and white ballgown $475.00

"An American Legend" book and doll in display box $225.00

Mid-Year Specials for Madame Alexander Doll Company

Welcome Home — 8", 1991, black or white, boy or girl, Desert Storm Soldier $50.00

Wendy Loves Being Loved — 8", 1992, doll and wardrobe $125.00

* Cissy dolls made in limited editions for 1999.

† 1999 designer Cissy dolls were designed to be auctioned for Fashion Targets Breast Cancer.

Special Events/Exclusives

Queen Elizabeth II — 8", 1992, 40th anniversary of coronation $150.00
Christopher Columbus — 8", 1992, #328, burgundy and brown costume $125.00
Queen Isabella — 8", 1992, #329, green velvet and gold gown $125.00
Santa or Mrs. Claus — 8", 1993 ....$125.00 ea.
Scarlett O'Hara — 8", 1993, yellow dress, straw hat $175.00
Wendy Ann — 8", 1995, 100th anniversary, pink coat and hat $150.00
Sir Lancelot DuLac — 8", 1995, burgundy and gold knight's costume $125.00
Queen Guinevere — 8", 1995, burgundy and gold gown $125.00
Wizard of Oz — 8", 1994, green metallic costume, black hat $150.00
Dorothy — 8", 1994, emerald green checked dress $225.00
Wicked Witch — 8", 1994, green face, black costume $250.00
Little Miss USA — 8", 2002, red skirt, blue jacket, hat, baton, charity for 9-11 ....$75.00

Marshall Fields
Avril, Jane — 10", 1989, red/black can-can outfit (tribute to T. Lautrec) (Cissette) $125.00
Madame Butterfly — 10", 1990, blue brocade kimono, gold obi $150.00

Matilda Company
Sweet Parfait Blonde — 8", #33590, 2003, silk outfit $90.00
Sweet Parfait Red — 8", #33591, 2003, silk outfit $90.00
Sweet Parfait African-American — 8", #33592, 2003, silk outfit $90.00

Metroplex Doll Club
Spring Break — 8", 1992, two-piece halter/wrap skirt outfit, limited to 400, beach bag $175.00
Victorian Tea — 8", #34000, 2002, blue pleated skirt, UFDC Luncheon $100.00

Meyers 80th Year
8", "Special Event" doll with banner, 1994 ....$75.00

Modern Doll Convention
Modern Romance Alex — 16", 2000, long strapless dress, limited to 200 ....$350.00
Modern Romance Alex centerpiece — 16", 2000, long strapless henna dress, limited to 20 ....$700.00
Up-to-the-Minute "Mod" Alex — 16", 2002, #35710, limited to 30, black gown $200.00
Up-to-the-Minute "Mod" Cissette — 10", 2002, #35711, limited to 55, centerpiece doll, black gown $175.00

M. Pancner's House of Collectibles
1920s Golden Girl — 10", #17740, 1999, limited to 25 ....$125.00
1950s Sock Hop — 8", #17780, 1999, limited to 50 ....$75.00

My Doll House
Southern Belle — 10", 1989, F.A.D., all pink gown with parasol and picture hat, limited to 2,300 ....$150.00
Queen Elizabeth I — 10", 1990, limited to 2,400 ....$125.00
Empress Elizabeth of Austria — 10", 1991, white/gold trim, limited to 3,600 (Cissette) $150.00

Neiman-Marcus
Doll with four outfits in trunk — 8", 1990, called "party trunk," limited to 1,044 ....$300.00
Caroline Loves Storyland — 8", 1993, trunk and wardrobe $275.00
Caroline's Adventures — 8", 1994, trunk and costumes for USA, China, Germany, Kenya (Maggie) $250.00
Anne Series — 8", 1994, trunk set, character from Lucy M. Montgomery books $275.00
ABC Huggums — limited to 650 pieces $70.00
Miss St. John — 21", 1998, limited to 750 ....$550.00
Crayola sets — 1999, dolls from regular line in ethnic sets $70.00
Holly Day — 8", #28195, #28196, #28197, 2000, red velvet dress $100.00
Alex Zenra — 16", #31860, 2001, limited to 250, maroon dress $130.00
Morning Dew Victoria — #28636, 2001, African-American $95.00
Pink Bunny Huggums— #28961, 2001, African-American $70.00
Shopping For Mommy — 8", #40089, 2004, limited to 75, pink dress, shopping bag $150.00

New England Collector Society
Noel — 12", 1989 – 1991, porcelain Christmas doll, limited to 5,000 ....$250.00
Joy — 12", 1991, porcelain Christmas doll, limited to 5,000 ....$225.00

Shopping For Mommy, 8", 2004, Wendy, #40089, pink dress, shopping bag, present, and necklace. Neiman Marcus.

Special Events/Exclusives

New York Doll Club
Autumn in New York — 10", F.A.D., limited to 260 . . . . $175.00

Oma's Doll Shop
Victorian Seaside Wendy — 8", #35475, 2003, limited to 1,000, vintage bathing
suit $100.00

Paris Fashion Doll Convention
City Lights Alex — 16", 2001, long white gown, limited to 200 . . . . $700.00
City Lights centerpiece — 16", 2001, limited to 20 . . . . $1,500.00
Festival Paris — 16", 2002, #34545, limited to 50, white dress, black velvet coat $700.00
Festival Alex — 16", 2002, #34550, lavender 20s dress, limited to 50 . . . . $700.00
Alex — 16", #37690, 2003, Paris Festival souvenir, blue gown $425.00

Penney, J.C.
At the Hop — 8", #27860, 2000, skirt with hoops $85.00

QVC
Summer Cherry Picking — 8", #79760, 1998 (Wendy), cherry print dress, limited to 500 . . . . $250.00
Betsy Ross — 8", #79990, 1998 (Wendy), red striped dress, limited to 500 . . . . $100.00
Pilgrim Girl — 8", #79980, 1998 (Wendy), long blue dress, limited to 500 . . . . $100.00
Home for the Holidays — 10", #79800, 1998 (Cissette), limited to 400 . . . . $125.00
A Rose for You — 8", 1999 (Wendy), lace-trimmed white dress with rose $85.00
Lavender Rose — 10", 1999, lavender ballgown $125.00
Pollyana — 8", 1999 (Maggie), blue check dress, straw hat, limited to 500 . . . . $90.00
Blossom — 8", 1999, pink print dress (Wendy), limited to 500 . . . . $90.00
Little Bo Peep — 8", 1999, pink gown trimmed in lace, limited to 700 . . . . $90.00
Investigator Wendy — 8", 1999 (checked coat and hat), limited to 500 . . . . $100.00
Autumn Breeze — 8", 1999 . . . . $80.00
Alice — 8", 1999 . . . . $80.00
Kiss Me, I'm Irish — 8", 1999 (Maggie), limited to 500, green skirt $80.00
Ladybug Garden — 8", 1999 . . . . $75.00
Fun at Halloween — 8", 1999, limited to 500 pieces (Maggie), yellow and black costume $80.00
Golden Light Tree Topper — 8", 1999, yellow and black costume, limited to 400 . . . . $125.00
Spring Flowers — 8", 1999, print dresss, basket of flowers (Maggie) $70.00
Fourth of July — 8", 1999 . . . . $75.00
Springtime Bride — 10", 1999, white slender dress, limited to 400 . . . . $125.00

Robert Moore and Company
Azalea Trail Maid — 8", #34555, 2003, long peach silk gown $150.00
Azalea Trail Green — 8", #35590, Tosca, #33591, brunette $150.00

Saks Fifth Avenue
Christmas Carol — 8", 1993, tartan plaid taffeta dress with velvet bodice $150.00
Joy of Christmas — 1994, second in series, forest green taffeta dress $125.00
Book Tour Alex with Saks Bag — 16", #31207, 2001 . . . . $125.00

Savannah Doll Club
Georgia State Day — 8", 2002, limited to 160, white dress with black rim $125.00

Sears-Roebuck
Little Women — 1989 – 1990, set of six 12" dolls (Nancy Drew) . . . . $600.00 set

Shirley's Doll House
Angel Face — 8", 1990 (Maggie Mixup), blue gown, white wings, limited to 3,500 . . . . $100.00
Winter Sports — 8", 1991, F.A.D. (Tommy Snooks), skates, tagged hat, limited to 975 . . . . $75.00
Wendy Visits World's Fair — 1993, 100th anniversary Chicago World's Fair, limited to 3,600 . . . . $100.00
Winter Angel — 1993, has cape with hood, wings, and holds golden horn, exclusive limited to 1,000 . . . . $100.00
Maypole Dance — 8", 1994, shop's 20th anniversary doll, pink organdy dress and
blue pinafore, limited to 3,000 (Wendy Ann) $75.00
Grandma's Darling — 8", 1996, #79617, yellow dress, white blanket $75.00
Little Collector — 8", 1999, #79820, navy dress, straw hat, basket $85.00
Grandma's Girl — 8", #31545, 2001, limited to 300, brown dress with book $80.00
Once Upon a Time — 8", #31550, 2001, pink dress, crown $85.00

Special Events/Exclusives

Shriner's 1st Ladies Luncheon
8" boy, 1993, wears fez, jeans, shirt, vest/Texas star on back, limited to 1,800 . . . . $425.00

South Carolina Chimney Sweep Guild
Lucky Dale — 8", #31975, 2001, top hat, tail, ladder $125.00

Spiegel's
Beth — 10", 1990, 125th anniversary special, 1860s women, pink brocade gown $125.00
Christmas Tree Topper (also called Merry Angel) — 8", 1991, gold and red velvet angel costume $150.00
Joy Noel — 8", 1992, tree topper angel, white satin/net with gold dots, gold lace,
   halo and skirt, limited to 3,000 . . . .$125.00
Mardi Gras — 10", 1992, elaborate costume of purple/gold/royal blue, limited to 3,000 . . . .$150.00

Two Daydreamers
Whitney — 8", #34106, 2001, ribbon and jewel crown, limited to 120 . . . .$125.00

U.F.D.C. – United Federation of Doll Clubs
Sailor Boy — 8", 1990, gray gabardine outfit, limited to 260 . . . .$700.00
Miss Unity — 10", 1991, cotton eyelet dress, limited to 310 . . . .$375.00
Little Emperor — 8", 1992, elaborate silk and gold costume, limited to 400 . . . .$450.00
Turn of the Century Bathing Beauty — 10", 1992, U.F.D.C. Region Nine Conference, F.A.D.
   (Gibson Girl), old-fashioned bathing suit, beach bag, and umbrella, limited to 300 . . . .$225.00
Columbian 1893 Sailor — 12", 1993 (Lissy) $175.00
Gabrielle — 10", 1998 (Cissette), limited to 400, black suit, dressmaker's stand $275.00
One Enchanted Evening — 16", 1999, #80260, limited to 310 . . . .$400.00
Windy City Chic — 16", 2000, pink and black gown, limited to 350 . . . .$175.00
Susan — 8", #27465, 2000, doll, three outfits, case, limited to 400 . . . .$250.00
Yardley in Lavender — 21", 2001, sheath dress and jacket, with dog, limited to 150 . . . .$300.00
Me & My Shadow Annette — 10", 2001, plum silk dress, limited to 360 . . . .$175.00
Me & My Shadow Annie — 8", 2001, plum silk dress, limited to 250 . . . .$150.00
Eloise in Moscow centerpiece — 8", #27735, 2000, yellow coat, black hat $125.00
The Love of Dolls Club Cissette — 10", #31960, 2001, long burgundy gown trimmed in fur $150.00
Buccaneer Bobby — 8", 2002, Denver luncheon doll, pirate sitting on shoulder, limited to 275 . . . .$150.00
Halloween — 8", 2002, centerpiece doll, #31465, black outfit $200.00
King Midas — 8", #33045, limited to 25, gold velvet robe, 2003 centerpiece doll $250.00
Golden Jubilee Wendy — 8", #37130, 2003, limited to 210 . . . .$150.00